The *Ultimate* Puppy

Edited by
Terry Ryan and Theresa Shipp

RINGPRESS

Published by Ringpress Books Ltd,
PO Box 8, Lydney,
Gloucestershire GL15 4YN

Designed by Sara Howell

First Published 2001
© 2001 RINGPRESS BOOKS

ISBN 1 86054 173 9

Printed and bound in Singapore

10 9 8 7 6 5 4 3 2 1

ACKNOWLEDGMENTS

The publishers wish to acknowledge the following breeders who helped with the photography for *The Ultimate Puppy*.

- Yvonne Angear
  Ridgegrove Dachshunds

- Veronica Bradley and Ken Burgess
  Dufosee Beagles

- Margaret Greening
  Hamaja Chihuahuas

- Jean Griffiths
  Riversflight Flat Coated Retrievers

- Mrs Veronica Hamilton
  Whiteshadow Maltese

- Sheila Hawes
  Bluesire Australian Shepherds

- Mrs Husk
  Wenvor Chow Chows

- Captain Tony and Mrs Lorna Ireland
  The Gables Kennels
  Pyrenean Mountain Dogs

- Tim and Sally Lewis
  Axeford Great Danes

- Sue Llewellyn
  Courtllyn Pembrokeshire Corgis

- Bill O'Loughlin
  Bassbarr Basset Hounds

- Mrs S M Parker
  Boncoeur Boston Terriers

- Jackie Ransom
  Tresilva Bichon Frisé

- Gillian Roden and Graham Hill
  Keigame German Shorthaired Pointers

- Sonya Saxby
  Saxsonya Miniature Pinschers

- Pauline Skyrme
  Emryks Rough Collies

- Eileen Speich
  Glarus American Cocker Spaniels

- Avril Stewart
  Ebrill Dobermanns

- Jean Stone
  Bilijees Pomeranians

- Elizabeth Thompson
  Zilann Miniature Pinschers

- Sue Thompson
  Shomont Alaskan Malamutes

- June Walsh
  Millcroft Irish Setters

CONTENTS

CONTRIBUTORS

THE EDITORS

TERRY RYAN has been a community dog obedience class instructor since 1968. A busy international workshop presenter, Terry also hosts frequent camps and seminars taught by well-known dog experts from around the world.

She spends several months a year in Japan teaching various dog training and instructor programmes.
See Chapter 5.

THERESA SHIPP, who is a member of the Association of Pet Dog Trainers, has been involved in dog training for eight years. She has been running her own dog training school – Shippshape School for Dogs – for five years. She specialises in pet dog training (puppies and beginners), and gundog classes aimed at the bored pet gundog. She also holds occasional clicker training workshops.
See Chapters 1, 4, and 9.

CONTRIBUTORS

JULIA BARNES has kept dogs all her life and has been involved with them professionally for nearly 20 years. Her speciality is training and rearing puppies.
See Chapter 2.

EILEEN GEESON has been actively involved in dog grooming for more than 30 years. She has been involved in showing Poodles since 1964, and has bred English, Fin. Swed. and International Champions. A Championship Show judge, with a world record of Standard Poodle entries to her credit, Eileen's knowledge of other breeds extends well beyond the Poodle ring. She has specialist grooming knowledge of all breeds, particularly Collies, Golden Retrievers, Pyrenean Mountain Dogs, Alaskan Malamutes and German Spitz.
See Chapter 7.

ALISON HORNSBY has considerable experience of breeding, raising, showing, and training dogs. She started working for the Guide Dogs for the Blind Association in 1973, where she became puppywalking and broodstock supervisor at the Association's breeding centre, specialising in the education and training of puppies and their walkers. She then went on to develop the puppywalking staff training programme. In all, she worked for the Guide Dogs for the Blind Association for 23 years.

Her work also involved supervising the puppies in the early days of the Dogs for the Disabled socialising scheme. She is now a dog training consultant, taking both adult and puppy classes, and has written books on the Border Collie, on dog training, and on assistance (service) dogs.
See Chapter 8.

DEBORAH JONES, Ph.D is a psycholo-gist who specialises in the study of learning theories and human/animal relationships. She is on the Board of Directors of the Association of Pet Dog Trainers. Dr Jones has produced three clicker-training videos (Clicker Fun series) and has written three dog training books *The Clicker Workbook, Teaching Clicker Classes*, and *Clicker Fun: Teaching Tricks & Games Using Positive Reinforcement*. In addition, Dr Jones teaches a variety of college classes in psychology. *See Chapter 3.*

DICK LANE, BSc FRCVS FRAgS, is a respected veterinary surgeon who has been in small-animal practice for the last forty-five years.

Dick was awarded the Fellowship of the Royal College of Veterinary Surgeons in 1968, and the Fellowship of the Royal Agricultural Societies in 1993. Other successes include the British Small Animal Veterinary Association's Dunkin Award in 1977 and the Association's Melton Award in 1987, and the first-ever JA Wright Memorial Award, awarded by the charity the Blue Cross in 2000.

Dick is a Guide Dog specialist, and is currently the Chairman of the Trustees of the charity, Dogs for the Disabled.

His literary feats are also notable, and he has written, contributed to, and edited numerous books, articles, and journals. *See Chapters 6 and 10.*

The Ultimate Puppy

1 ROLE MODELS

There are many things which need to be carefully considered before making the decision to buy, or adopt, a new puppy – especially if you are a first-time dog owner. Firstly, ask yourself the question, "What is a dog?"

All dogs, whatever their size, shape or form, are descended from wolves, and were originally kept purely to help us hunt for food, guard our property and livestock, and keep us warm. Dogs were also eaten by our ancestors as, indeed, they still are today in some countries. Over the last 10,000 years or so, we have dramatically altered their appearance, but all dogs are still closely related to that wolf ancestor.

No one breed of dog is more closely related to the wolf than another, be it a Toy Poodle, German Shepherd Dog, Great Dane or mixed breed. Most, if left to their own devices, are quite capable of hunting, and indeed killing, small prey for food.

It may come as a bit of a shock to the first-time dog owner to find that their cute puppy is not all 'sweetness and light'. The new puppy growls, bites, fights (in play), chews, can be noisy, throws up, makes a mess, and can generally cause havoc! Dogs, after all, are dogs (remember their wolf ancestry), but, with lots of patience and careful, kind training, they can learn to fit in with our way of living. Without the correct guidance from an early age, they will not.

Puppies are irresistible – but they can also be bundles of trouble.

THE EVOLUTION OF DOG TYPES

Dogs, being the social, co-operative, intelligent animals that they are, spread rapidly throughout the world and, today, there are over 400 breeds, some of which have been developed recently, while others have been with us for many hundreds of years.

Fossil remains, dating from the Bronze Age, have identified five distinct types of dog.

- MASTIFFS Mastiff-type dogs were used as dogs of war and for sporting purposes such as dog-fighting.
- GREYHOUNDS This type of dog was used for hunting purposes.
- SHEEPDOGS These dogs were used to protect and herd livestock.
- WOLF-LIKE OR SPITZ-TYPE DOGS They were developed as hunters, herders and as draught dogs.
- POINTERS This type of dog was used to hunt small game.

HUNTING DOGS

Sighthounds such as Greyhounds, Whippets and Afghan Hounds, are real canine athletes. They were developed for speed, and for their exceptional vision, which enables them to chase and catch their prey.

Scenthounds, such as Bloodhounds, rely on their brilliant sense of smell to track their prey. Some breeds of hound are still used today for sport; for example Greyhounds are used in racing, and Foxhounds and Beagles are part of hunting.

Gundogs, or sporting dogs – retrievers, pointers, spaniels and setters – were developed to find, flush and retrieve shot or wounded game, or were used by falconers to flush game for birds of prey.

Pointers and setters were used to find and 'point' or 'set' game, initially to be driven forward into nets. Later on, with the introduction of the gun, the 'pointers' or 'setters' would find game, hold on 'point' or 'drop' in the case of setters, until the hunter went forward to shoot the game, flushing it himself. These dogs are still used today and are ideal for open grouse moor.

Spaniels were developed to hunt game ahead of the hunter, while keeping close enough to him to allow him to hit his quarry. Instead of pointing, a spaniel would flush, instantly, any game it found, and would 'drop' or 'sit'. This enabled the hunter to fire his gun and, if the shot was successful, the spaniel would be sent to retrieve the game.

Spaniels are still used in this way today and are capable of tackling the thickest brambles and undergrowth in their quest for small game. Some are used purely for flushing game, working their way forward

The athletic Greyhound was developed to chase and hunt prey.

Dogs such as the Labrador Retriever were bred to retrieve shot game.

in the 'beating' lines on shoots, driving the pheasants towards the guns.

The most popular working spaniels nowadays are the English Springer Spaniel and the Cocker Spaniel, which were developed to hunt woodcock.

RETRIEVING DOGS
The retrieving breeds, such as the Flat Coated Retriever and Golden Retriever were developed to carry gently back to the hunter any game that was shot, especially waterfowl. They were often used alongside spaniels, who would flush the game, with the retrievers staying with the guns and then going out to do their job. The most popular working gundog today is the Labrador Retriever.

MULTI-PURPOSE DOGS
Many breeds have been developed that can hunt, point and retrieve. They are known as the HPR breeds and include the Weimaraner, the Hungarian Vizsla, the Munsterlander and the German Pointer (short-haired, wire-haired and long-haired varieties).

Then there are the dogs which were developed in the Arctic regions of the world, which we now call Spitz-type dogs. They were initially used to pull sleds, to hunt and to herd. Some of these breeds, such as the Malamute and the Siberian Husky, are very similar in appearance to the wolf.

TERRIERS
Most of the terrier breeds originated in Great Britain and were developed, relatively recently when you think of how long dogs have been domesticated, to be tenacious, feisty little dogs, fearless when confronted by a rat, fox or badger. They are tough, working dogs, used to accompanying fox-hunts.

The name terrier comes from the word 'terra' which means 'earth' in Latin. Some of the smaller terriers were used to 'go to

Terriers were developed
to hunt small mammals
and rodents.
Pictured: Cairn Terrier.

Sheepdogs have been used
to herd and guard livestock
for thousands of years.

ground' and hunt tunnel-dwelling mammals, but were mainly of use above ground, killing rats for a living, in and around the farmyard. The 'bull-type' terriers were originally bred for bull-baiting and dog-fighting, but were used as 'ratters' too.

WORKING DOGS

Our ancestors realised that dogs could be of use as guardians and drovers of livestock, and many countries have their own specialist breeds. The UK has the Old English Sheepdog, the Border Collie and the Corgi. Germany has the Rottweiler and Giant Schnauzer. The Komondor is found in Hungary and the Briard in France. Some breeds also doubled as guardians of property and are still used in this role today. The most commonly favoured is, of course, the German Shepherd.

TOY DOGS

The Toy breeds, such as the Pug, King Charles Spaniel, Maltese and Pekingese, were bred mainly as companion animals, often from working-type ancestors.

Not only did they make good hot-water bottles, keeping the feet warm in bed, but they were a great source of entertainment to their owners. They were highly popular in the Royal Courts of Europe and many young princes and princesses, enduring rather isolated upbringings, had no other playmates than these tiny dogs.

Toy breeds, many of whom possess an ancient history, are still as popular today as they were centuries ago. Do not be fooled by their size. They can be, and usually are, marvellous watchdogs!

THE MODERN DOG

Dogs today have an even wider range of uses. As well as their traditional roles as hunters, protectors, herders and companions, they can be trained to give assistance to deaf, blind and disabled people – and some are able to predict epileptic seizures!

They do an invaluable job with drug and explosive detection and are used by Customs and Excise, the Police and the Armed Forces. They are also used as therapy dogs, visiting the elderly, the sick and the

Even though many of their traditional roles are now obsolete, dogs still offer an invaluable contribution to society. This is Sweep, Dog for the Disabled for owner Sue Lee.

Taking on two pups can mean double the work and double the trouble.

terminally ill, giving a much-needed boost to those they meet.

Dogs enrich our lives in so many different ways that a life without them would be unimaginable.

COMMUNICATION

Dogs do not, of course, understand the spoken word, any more than we do as babies, and it is our job to teach them what certain words mean and how they are relevant.

Dogs and wolves communicate with each other, mainly, by the use of body language, which consists of a wide range of signals, such as tail-wagging, ear position, facial expressions, sniffing, scratching, and urinating, etc.

These highly visual, peace-keeping signals are necessary, in the case of wolves, to maintain harmony within the pack, and, in the case of pet dogs, to keep the peace with other dogs in the park and in the home. These signals are used by dogs to communicate with us, but very often they are not understood by us. A good trainer should be able to identify what, exactly, these signals are, and how they work.

Some dogs do, occasionally, get into fights (usually without any injuries occurring), and 'arguments' – just as we do. It is completely unreasonable to expect them to do otherwise. Just as we do not get along with everyone all the time, neither do dogs! A well-bred and well-socialised dog will mix quite happily and readily with its own kind, unless we interfere too much. Many doggy behavioural problems are caused by us, as owners. Maybe we have not socialised our dog properly, for instance, which leaves our dog lacking in all the necessary canine communication skills.

Remember: dogs are dogs. They are

genetically related to wolves, and should be treated with respect and understanding. They are not 'Hairy Human Beings!'

YOUR RESPONSIBILITIES

Your new puppy will depend on you for everything. Some dogs have a life-expectancy of 15 years, or even longer. Are you prepared for the cost of inoculations, veterinary care, kennelling fees, food, grooming etc., both now, and in the future?

If you are choosing to buy a pedigree puppy, it is important to research your chosen breed carefully. Talk to as many breeders and owners as possible. Find out about the breed's good, and bad, points. Is the breed suitable for your lifestyle? A highly active breed would not be ideal for someone who is inactive, and who wants a dog which would be content with a short walk around the block. This would be a recipe for disaster.

Is your house large enough to accommo-date a very large breed? It would not be fair to confine a giant-sized dog to a small flat or apartment.

All dogs are highly social animals. It would be very unfair to buy a puppy and leave him at home on his own, if you are out at work all day. It would be much wiser to wait until your circumstances change before getting a puppy, or, perhaps, you could take your puppy to work with you.

All dogs need to have off-lead exercise. Although walks will be short while the puppy is still young, when fully grown he may need more than you have time to give. Your puppy will also need to be mentally stimulated, through play and training. Do not buy a puppy which has been bred to work, with a high activity level, unless you are prepared for this commitment. A bored, frustrated puppy soon becomes branded as 'naughty', and 'destructive', through no fault of his own.

Some people consider acquiring two puppies from the same litter as company for one another. Unless you have a lot of time to spend training and playing with them individually, it is not such a good idea, as they become strongly bonded to each other, rather than to you. It is better to introduce a second puppy after your first puppy's training is established, and the relationship with you has been built.

All pups should be well socialised with children.

The mother not only passes on her genes, but also many aspects of her personality, through early interaction with the pups.

Same-sex puppies may be the best of friends when young, but might grow up rather intolerant of each other later on, as they reach maturity. This often leads to the heartbreaking decision of having to rehome one of them. Having littermates as pets *can* be successful, but, especially with first-time dog owners, is best avoided.

If you have children or grandchildren, nieces or nephews, they need to learn to treat the puppy with respect. Very young children tend to treat a puppy like a toy, and insist on trying to pick him up all the time, which puppies hate! Puppies can quickly become 'saturated' with too much attention, leading to the puppy becoming snappy, frightened, or just plain 'fed up'. If you do not have children, but are planning to start a family in the future, 'borrow' some, so that your puppy is used to them when the time comes.

Cleaning up after your dog, if he goes to the toilet when out for a walk, is your responsibility too! It is extremely antisocial not to do so. Many local authorities provide 'poo bins' in parks and public areas, and impose fines for failure to 'scoop the poop'!

Your puppy can be trained to use the garden as his toilet area, but accidents *do* happen. Always carry a plastic bag, just in case, to avoid embarrassment.

WHERE TO GET YOUR PUPPY

After much careful thought, and having made the decision to take on the responsibility of dog ownership, you will need to start looking for litters of puppies to view.

Always see the puppies with their mother, and beware of any breeder who makes excuses for you not being able to do so. If the mother cannot be seen, the puppies may have been bred on a 'puppy farm', or by people whose only interest is to make money from dog breeding by selling them on to 'puppy supermarkets' or pet shops. These shops or kennels often have many different breeds for sale, so, if in doubt, go elsewhere. Never feel sorry for these puppies and buy one anyway, as not only will you be encouraging this practice, but the puppies are often in poor health and sometimes die only hours after going to their new homes.

Ask breeders as many questions as possible about their dogs. A good breeder will ask you about your lifestyle, your family etc., as genuinely caring breeders will want to find the best possible homes for their puppies.

Assess the mother's temperament. Is she friendly and outgoing? A nervous, aggressive bitch is likely to pass on these traits to her offspring. Do the dogs look healthy? Have the parents had all the necessary health checks required for that particular breed, before being bred from?

Where have the puppies been kept? Puppies that have been kept in a kennel or outbuilding, should have been taken into the house for much-needed periods of play and socialisation. They should have well handled, by both adults and children, and been properly stimulated by play and toys. Just like children, puppies which are lacking in this area do not reach their full potential as adults. A puppy that is used to children, cats, rabbits, other dogs, visitors, washing machines, vacuum cleaners etc., and is used to family life in general, makes the best pet.

If considering getting a puppy from a rescue centre, they too should have taken care to socialise their puppies properly. The experiences that puppies have, while still with the mother, are of paramount importance. If you are in any way unsure about the litters that you see, never be afraid to say "No, thank you" and look elsewhere.

The following chapters in this book will help you to decide which breeds are suitable for your particular lifestyle, and how to prepare for your puppy's home-coming, your puppy's first lessons, and socialisation. They will also explain about your puppy's growth and development, with advice on correct feeding, exercise, neutering and health matters, grooming, and adolescence. Finally, but more importantly, this book will show you how to have fun with your puppy, through playing games and sports, which all lead to you having the perfect canine companion, and, hopefully, to you being the perfect human companion!

2 MAKING THE RIGHT MATCH

At last, the moment has come in your life when you are ready to take on the responsibility of owning a puppy. The next step is to choose the breed that is most likely to suit you, and which will fit in with your lifestyle. Do not let your heart rule your head: ignore all the appealing photos of puppies, and get down to some good, solid research. You have only one chance to get it right, and it is essential to find out as much as possible about the breeds you are attracted to before making a final decision. There are books and videos giving specialist breed information, or, better still, go to a dog show and take a look at the breeds being exhibited. When the classes are over, you can talk to the exhibitors, who will have extensive knowledge about the needs of their own breed.

Remember, looks are not everything. Temperament is of prime importance – you must be confident that you have the experience to train and control the breed of your choice, and, if you have children, you must make sure you choose a dog that will thrive on the hustle and bustle of family life. How much time do you have to give to your dog? Can you cope with a long-haired dog that needs daily grooming sessions, or would you be better off with one of the shortcoated, low-maintenance breeds. Finally, are you a keen walker who is prepared to go out in all weathers? Are you fit enough to go for long treks? Not all breeds need extensive exercise, so be realistic, and opt for a breed that you know you can cope with.

In the following guide, profiles are given of the most popular breeds, outlining their character, appearance, and their basic needs. This is just the starting point. If you see a breed you like, take the time to find out as much as you possibly can before making your final decision.

The profiles feature pure-bred dogs only. Crossbreeds (puppies with parents of different breeds, e.g. a Labrador Retriever crossed with a Golden Retriever) can be wonderful dogs to own, but there is less certainty when it comes to knowing how they will turn out. This uncertainty is increased tenfold if you choose a mongrel (a puppy whose parents are from completely mixed breeding) where size, coat, and temperament are a matter of pure speculation. Again, many mongrels make excellent pets, but you may prefer to have some idea about what you are going to end up with.

Generally, the most popular breeds have a worldwide following, but in some instances, a breed is particularly popular in one country. For this reason, our guide starts by featuring the breeds that are top of the pops in the US, and those that are firm favourites in the UK, before moving on to detail 50 of the most popular breeds worldwide.

American Cocker Spaniel

- **Good at...**
Looking glamorous, having a sunny outlook on life.

- **Needs...**
Specialised grooming care, close attention to keeping the ears clean.

- **Loves...**
Human companionship.

- **Hates...**
Being cold, wet and bedraggled.

- **Top tip...**
The breed has enjoyed immense popularity in the US, and, unfortunately, mass production of puppies has led to unsound temperament. This problem is now being addressed, and the merry, equable temperament is much in evidence again. Make sure you go to a responsible, conscientious breeder who produces only the very best from eye-tested stock of exemplary temperament.

- **Last word...**
Convenient in size, with spectacular good looks, the American Cocker is highly valued as a companion, but potential owners must have a real commitment to hair care.

- **Comes from...**
North America, developed from the English Cocker Spaniel to retrieve quail, but now one of the most popular show and companion dogs on this continent.

FACT FILE

Appearance: Well-balanced, compact and sturdy, the American Cocker has a strong back that slopes slightly towards the tail. The main difference is in the head, which is rounded, with the round-shaped eyes set to look straight ahead. The ears are long and fine.

Colours: The solid colours include black, buff, red, chocolate, black and tan; the particolours are black, red or chocolate with white, plus tricolours.

Coat/grooming: A silky coat that lies flat or can be slightly wavy. The hair is fine on the head, medium length on the body and well feathered on the ears, chest, abdomen and legs. Specialised grooming care, including trimming, is needed on a regular basis.

Size: UK: Dogs 14.25-15.25 ins (36.25-38.75 cms); bitches 13.25-14.25 ins (33.75-36.25 cms). US/FCI: 14.5-15.5 ins (37-39 cms); bitches 13.5-14.5 ins (34-37 cms).

Temperament, training and exercise: Equable in temperament, the American Cocker is easy to live with, sharing the same merry temperament as his English counterpart. Although bred to work, few do, and their exercise needs are moderate. A born showman, the American Cocker can be trained to a high standard in the show ring, and with the immaculate presentation that is almost the norm in the USA, the breed creates a most spectacular sight.

Health issues: Puppies and parents should be eye-tested for hereditary cataract (HC).

Boston Terrier

- **Comes from...**

The USA. This all-American dog was developed in the 1900s by crossing the Bulldog and the white English Terrier.

- **Good at...**

Adaptability and companionship – the Boston will also compete successfully in Obedience.

- **Needs...**

To be part of family activities.

- **Loves...**

Loads of attention.

- **Hates...**

Extremes of temperature.

- **Top tip...**

The short-nosed Boston cannot tolerate excessive activity in hot conditions. On the other side of the coin, he has a fine coat which means that he will appreciate a jacket and warm bedding when the weather gets very cold.

- **Last word...**

A good-tempered dog that will suit many different types of owners.

FACT FILE

Appearance: A smart, dapper dog, the Boston is compact and well balanced, with a short body, a deep chest, and a short or screw tail. The Boston is quick-stepping, and gives an impression of determination and activity. The head is flat on top with a short, square muzzle. The eyes are set wide apart and are large and round, and the ears are carried erect.

Colours: Brindle with white markings is the preferred colour, but the Boston may also be black or seal (black with a red cast when viewed in sunlight) with white markings.

Coat/grooming: A short, smooth coat that needs the minimum of grooming care.

Size: UK/US/FCI: *Lightweight:* under 15 lbs (6.8 kgs). *Middleweight:* 15-20 lbs (6.8-9.1 kgs). *Heavyweight:* 20-25 lbs (9.1-11.4 kgs).

Temperament, training and exercise: An easy dog to live with, the Boston has been dubbed the 'American gentleman' because of his well-mannered reputation. He is friendly and outgoing, with a degree of intelligence, which means that he is very responsive to training. His exercise needs are moderate, but he loves to be involved in everything that is going on.

Health issues: The prominent eyes are vulnerable to eye injuries. Patella luxation can be a problem.

Brittany

Brittany is a member of the versatile hunt, point, retrieve group of gundogs, and has gained tremendous popularity in the US.

• *Good at...*

Being a top-class shooting companion, who excels at Field Trials and Hunting Tests as well as Obedience.

• *Needs...*

A job of work to do.

• *Loves...*

Using his nose, pleasing his owner.

• *Hates...*

Inactivity.

• *Top tip...*

Valued as a superb bird dog, the Brittany lives to work. If he is not used as a shooting companion, an alternative occupation, such as competing in Obedience, should be found for him.

• *Last word...*

A happy, active dog that will thrive in a busy, stimulating environment.

• *Comes from...*

France. Although classed as a Spaniel, the

FACT FILE

Appearance: A workmanlike dog, the Brittany is leggier than the spaniel breeds, and is more setter-like in appearance. A breed characteristic is that the Brittany may be born without a tail. Docking is customary for those born with tails. The Brittany has an eager, alert expression, which is accentuated by the high-set ears. The eyes have the typical, soft expression of a bird dog.

Colours: Orange and white or liver and white (the white may be clear or roaned). Tricolours (liver, white and orange) are allowed, but not preferred.

Coat/grooming: The coat is dense, and may be flat or wavy, with some feathering. A relatively easy coat to care for, but regular combing is needed to keep the feathering free from tangles.

Size: UK/FCI: Dogs 19-20 ins (48-50 cms);

bitches 18-19 ins (47-49 cms). US: 17.5-20.5 ins (44.4-52 cms), both sexes.

Temperament, training and exercise: The Brittany is an affectionate dog that bonds closely with his owner. He gets on well with children, and is generally eager to please. Alert and intelligent, this is a sporting dog that needs mental stimulation, interaction with his owner, and plenty of exercise.

Health issues: Breeding stock should be hip-scored.

Chow Chow

• **Comes from...**

China, where he was used as a guard and as a hunting dog. In the 19th century, Queen Victoria was given a Chow Chow as a gift, and she was especially fond of her unusual pet. But it was when the Chow found his way to America at the end of the 19th century that he really took off as a popular companion – and he has been in the top ratings ever since.

• **Good at...**

Keeping a look-out and guarding the home and family.

• **Needs...**

His own space. Chows are not clingy dogs, and do not appreciate being overwhelmed with fuss and attention.

• **Loves...**

Being in the midst of his human family.

• **Hates...**

Excessive heat – Chows overheat very easily; water – no self-respecting Chow will fancy a walk in the rain.

• **Top tip...**

Establish a pattern of firm, kind leadership from the moment your Chow puppy arrives home. This will be the basis of a sound relationship of mutual respect.

• **Last word...**

This is not a breed for everyone, as the Chow's reserved nature must be understood and respected. He is not a playmate, but, as a devoted guardian of the family, he is second to none.

FACT FILE

Appearance: A compact, well-balanced dog of medium height. The Chow is famed for his noble, leonine appearance, his 'scowling' expression, and his blue-black tongue. The head is broad, with small ears set wide apart; the eyes are dark and oval-shaped. The Chow is strong and muscular in build with a deep chest and a short back. The tail is set on high and is carried well over the back.

Colours: Black, red, blue, fawn, cream.

Coat/grooming: There are two coat types: rough and smooth. The roughs have an abundant, harsh topcoat with a woolly undercoat. This requires daily grooming to keep in good condition. Smooths have a short, plush coat which is much easier to look after, although daily combing is needed when the coat is shedding.

Size: UK/FCI: Dogs 19-22 ins (48-56 cms); bitches 18-20 ins (46-51 cms). US: 17-20 ins (43.18-50.80 cms), both sexes.

Temperament, training and exercise: A reserved, aloof dog, the Chow shows tremendous loyalty towards his family, but is aloof with strangers. Firm discipline must be established, but harsh correction should never be implemented or it will be strongly resented. This is not a breed that responds to clockwork Obedience exercises, but he will respect the house rules, and will thrive on a regular daily routine. The Chow does not relish strenuous exercise, but interesting expeditions will add spice to his life.

Health issues: Entropion is a decreasing problem as breeders have been working hard to eradicate it from the breed.

Miniature Pinscher

• **Comes from...**

Germany. Thought to resemble the tiny, red deer that were found in German forests, he is not related to the larger Dobermann Pinscher – he is more likely to have been developed from Italian Greyhounds and Dachshunds.

• **Good at...**

Hunting, barking and playing.

• **Needs...**

Stimulation – much more than you would expect in a Toy breed.

• **Loves...**

Being given tricks to perform, and being rewarded with abundant praise.

• **Hates...**

Being confined indoors with nothing to do.

• **Top tip...**

Min. Pins. can move as fast as lightning, particularly when they see an open door. Many owners fit Min. Pin. gates in doorways to ward off escape bids.

• **Last word...**

Although small in size, the Min. Pin. is quite a demanding dog as he needs a lot of interaction with his owners. Most get on well with older children, but are not so good with toddlers.

FACT FILE

Appearance: A sturdy dog that is also elegant in appearance. The head is narrow with a strong muzzle, and is almost serpentine in shape. The ears may be carried erect or dropped. The body is square with a well-developed forechest and muscular hindquarters. The tail is customarily docked short. The Min. Pin. is at his best on the move, with his spectacular high-stepping hackney gait.

Colours: Solid red, black or chocolate with rust-red markings.

Coat/grooming: A smooth, short, hard coat that is very low-maintenance.

Size: UK/FCI: 10-12 ins (25.5-30 cms), both sexes.

US: 10-12.5 ins (25.5-31.75 cms), both sexes.

Temperament, training and exercise: A spirited, fun-loving dog, the Min. Pin. requires plenty of action to keep his inquisitive mind occupied. He is an enthusiastic guard, and his persistent barking will warn you if anyone is in the vicinity. He will respond well to training, but can be a little 'deaf' on the recall when in pursuit of something interesting. As a Toy breed, the Min. Pin. does not require a lot of exercise, but will enjoy hectic playtimes in the garden.

Health issues: Patella luxation can be a problem – but no more than in any other Toy breed.

Border Terrier

- **Comes from...**
The borders between England and Scotland. This is a relatively recent breed in historical terms. It was developed in the 19th century to work alongside hounds, going to ground after foxes and bolting them.

- **Good at...**
Adaptability, Mini-agility.

- **Needs...**
A busy, stimulating environment.

- **Loves...**
Long walks in the country, food (watch out – a Border can easily become overweight).

- **Hates...**
Being reprimanded.

- **Top tip...**
The Border Terrier has a sensitive side to his nature, and will take offence if he is shouted at. If needed, discipline should be administered quietly and firmly.

- **Last word...**
A deservedly popular breed to choose, but do remember the coat care that is required.

FACT FILE

Appearance: A rugged, good-looking dog who looks every ounce a worker. The forelegs are straight, the chest is fairly deep, and the hindquarters give an impression of speed. The tail is carrot-shaped. The Border Terrier's head resembles that of an otter, with a broad skull and a short muzzle. The eyes are dark and keen-looking; the ears are small and V-shaped.

Colours: Red, wheaten (pale yellow or fawn), grizzle and tan (a mixture of colours including bluish grey, red, and black), blue and tan.

Coat/grooming: A harsh, wiry topcoat with a thick undercoat. The coat is easy to maintain with regular brushing, but your Border will need to be hand-stripped twice a year. A professional groomer will do this for you, or you can learn to do it yourself, enlisting the help of an experienced Border breeder.

Size: UK/FCI: Dogs 13-15.5 lbs (5.9-7.1 kgs); bitches 11.5-14 lbs (5.1-6.4 kgs).

Temperament, training and exercise: The most adaptable of dogs, the Border Terrier takes life in his stride, and very little worries him. He loves children, lives happily with other dogs, and, with supervised introductions, accepts cats and other small animals as part of his family. The Border is eager to please, and so training poses few problems. Equally at home in the town or in the country, the Border Terrier enjoys long rambles with interesting smells, but will content himself with a brisk walk.

Health issues: No specific inherited conditions are associated with this breed.

Bull Terrier

- **Comes from...**

England. This 'gladiator of the canine race' was developed as a fighting dog in the 1800s. The breed is now held in high regard as a loyal companion.

- **Good at...**

Playing the clown, being a couch potato.

- **Needs...**

A loving home, ideally kept as a single pet.

- **Loves...**

Lazing on the sofa in the midst of his family.

- **Hates...**

Solitude.

- **Top tip...**

If this is your first Bull Terrier, it is advisable to choose a bitch, who will probably be less dominant and easier to train than a male.

- **Last word...**

A loving, fun companion, but this is a breed with a fighting history, and this element of his character should be considered.

FACT FILE

Appearance: The 'beautifully ugly' Bull Terrier has a truly unique appearance, which is the reason why he has such an enthusiastic following. A strongly-built, muscular animal, he gives an impression of fire and courage. The outstanding feature is the downfaced, egg-shaped head, with narrow eyes set obliquely. The ears are small and thin. They are set close together and pricked when alert.

Colours: The traditional colours are pure white, or white with a patch of colour, usually on the head. However, 'coloured' Bull Terriers are becoming increasingly popular, and these include black, brindle, red-fawn and tricolour.

Coat/grooming: A short, flat coat that is very easy to maintain – however, keeping a white dog clean in the winter poses some problems!

Size: This is an unusual breed in that no height or weight limits are stipulated. The Breed Standard (the written blueprint for the breed) states: "...there should be the impression of maximum substance for size of dog consistent with quality and sex".

Temperament, training and exercise: Amiable and even-tempered, the Bull Terrier is generally an easy-going companion who is very pro-people. Socialisation is essential in a breed that was bred to be a fearless fighter, and introductions to other dogs should be very carefully supervised. The Bull Terrier will learn to obey 'house rules' – but watch out for his stubborn streak, which can result in a battle of wills. The Bull Terrier adapts to the exercise he is given – but obesity can be a problem, so make sure you do shift him off the sofa and give him regular walks.

Health issues: Deafness is an inherited condition in the breed – puppies should have hearing tests before they are sold. Check for incidence of heart disease and kidney disease.

Cocker Spaniel

• Comes from...
England, although his roots (like all Spaniels) are in Spain. The smallest of the Spaniels, the Cocker was originally known as the 'cocking spaniel', as his principal function was to flush game birds, particularly woodcock.

• Good at...
Obedience and Agility. Cockers are still bred to flush and retrieve for the gun, but these lines tend to be smaller and lighter than those bred as show and companion dogs.

• Needs...
Regular grooming (which includes trimming), lots of walks.

• Loves...
To be busy – the Cocker is in his element foraging among fields and hedgerows – but he also loves the comforts and companionship of family life.

• Hates...
Being wet and cold after a walk – so make sure you always towel him dry. Being left alone for long periods.

• Top tip...
Seek the advice of an experienced Cocker breeder, or a groomer that is used to working with Cockers, when you need to get your Cocker trimmed.

• Last word...
The Cocker is a loving, affectionate dog, and will adapt well to living in a family with children, or with older people – as long as he gets sufficient exercise.

FACT FILE

Appearance: A sturdy, sporting dog with a balanced compact body. The Cocker's skull is slightly domed, and the muzzle is oblong in shape. The dark eyes are full and expressive. The ears are the outstanding feature. They are set on level with the eyes and should reach to the tip of the nose. The Cocker's tail is customarily docked.

Colours: The solid colours include black, golden, red, black and tan, and liver. The particolours range through black and white, orange and white, blue roans, orange roans, liver roans, and tricolours.

Coat/grooming: Flat and silky with feathering on the ears, forelegs, body and hindlegs. Regular grooming is essential to prevent tangles and knots forming in the feathers. Trimming is required.

Size: UK/FCI: Dogs 15.5-16 ins (39-41 cms); bitches 15-15.5 ins (38-39 cms). Weight 28-32 lbs (12.75-14.5 kgs), both sexes. US: Dogs 16-17 ins (40.6-43.2 cms); bitches 15-15.5 ins (38-39 cms). Weight: Dogs 28-34 lbs (12.7-15.4 kgs); bitches 26-32 lbs (11.8-14.5 kgs).

Temperament, training and exercise: A happy, merry, active dog, typified by his ever-wagging tail. Do not neglect the need for regular exercise, or your athletic little Cocker will quickly become obese, lethargic and unfit. Biddable and eager to please, the devoted Cocker likes working with his owner and training rarely presents a problem.

There has been a problem in recent years with some red and golden Cockers showing untypical aggressive behaviour. Responsible breeders have taken great care to eradicate this problem. If you are choosing a red or golden cocker, ensure that the puppy comes from parents of impeccable temperament.

Health issues: Breeding stock must be eye-tested. Buy only from a responsible breeder who specialises in the breed and has quality, healthy stock.

Staffordshire Bull Terrier

• **Comes from...**

England. The breed was developed by crossing a Bulldog and a native English Terrier to produce a smaller, faster animal for the sport of dog-fighting.

• **Good at...**

Being a fun-loving member of the family.

• **Needs...**

A comprehensive programme of socialisation to produce a well-balanced individual.

• **Loves...**

Children, playing games, armchairs, beds, and car rides.

• **Hates...**

Being ignored, cold weather.

• **Top tip...**

Start as you mean to go on. Establish control and authority over your Stafford and be entirely consistent in your training. Body language and tone of voice play a big part in establishing status, so make sure your Stafford always gets the right message.

• **Last word...**

Not the easiest dog to own, although Staffie enthusiasts would never dream of having any other breed. Better kept as a single dog.

FACT FILE

Appearance: A sturdy dog, with rugged good looks, the Stafford has great strength for his size. Broad-chested, with a short, straight back and muscular hindquarters, he should appear active and agile. The Stafford's head is broad with powerful jaws, and the ears are folded neatly at the side of the head. The eyes are round, set wide apart, and have a kind, honest expression.

Colours: The variety of colours is one of the attractions of the breed. They include red, fawn, white, black or blue, or any of these colours with white. Brindles come in a range of shades, plus brindle and white.

Coat/grooming: A smooth, short coat that is very easy to care for.

Size: UK/FCI: 14-16 ins (35.5-40.5 cms), both sexes. Weight: Dogs 28-38 lbs (12.7-17 kgs); bitches 24-34 lbs (11-15.4 kgs). US: No Standard available.

Temperament, training and exercise: Despite his historical links with fighting, the Staffie is a devoted companion dog, and the breed's kindness and gentleness with children is well known. However, this small, courageous dog can be a handful for the novice owner. He is highly intelligent, but needs to be motivated in his training. Regular exercise is important to avoid obesity, but mental stimulation is equally important, and time playing games with your Stafford is well spent.

Health issues: Parents and puppies should be eye-tested.

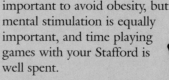

Akita

• Comes from…

Japan, where he has held an honoured place, both as hunter and guard, since earliest civilisations. He is now valued as a superb companion – and is ranked as one of Japan's great treasures.

• Good at…

Guarding, also successful as a sled dog.

• Needs…

A comprehensive programme of socialisation as a puppy, combined with firm, consistent training.

• Loves…

Keeping watch over his family.

• Hates…

Cats or any other fast-moving small animal (although he is fine if brought up with a cat); repetition (such as throw-and-catch games) which will bore him very quickly.

• Top tip…

The Akita rarely starts a fight with another dog, but he will certainly assert his authority if he feels his status is threatened. For this reason, it is better to keep a single dog, and be wary when you are liable to meet other dogs.

• Last word…

Make no mistake, this is a dominant dog. In the right hands, he makes a wonderful companion, but this is not a breed for the novice owner.

FACT FILE

Appearance: A fine, upstanding dog, with a proud, noble bearing. He gives an instant impression of power and strength, which comes from his size and substance – an adult male weighs around 110 lbs. The body is longer than it is high, with strong, straight front legs, and well-developed hindquarters. The tail is set high and carried over the back. The Akita has a large, broad head, a strong muzzle, and small, triangular ears. The eyes are relatively small, dark and almond-shaped.

Colours: They come in all colours including white, brindle and pinto (dark markings on a white background).

Coat/grooming: The outer coat is coarse and straight, and the undercoat is short and dense. The Akita's coat is easy to care for, but watch out for the twice-yearly 'blow' when the coat is shed in spectacular fashion.

Size: UK/US: Dogs 26-28 ins (66-71 cms); bitches 24-26 ins (61-66 cms). FCI: Dogs 25.25-27.5 ins (64-70 cms); bitches 23-25.25 ins (58-64 cms).

Training, temperament and exercise: Dignified and aloof with strangers, the Akita is a loving and loyal member of his own family 'pack'. He gets on well with older children, as long as mutual respect is established. Intelligent, and quick to learn, the Akita will never be slavishly obedient, but he will accept the rules you impose. Exercise should be limited during the vulnerable growing period but, thereafter, long walks, with plenty of variety, must be considered essential for this large, powerful dog.

Health issues: Parents and puppies should be eye-tested and hip-scored.

Alaskan Malamute

- **Good at...**

  Sledding, weight-pulling, carting, back-packing.

- **Needs...**

  A sense of leadership.

- **Loves...**

  Hard work.

- **Hates...**

  Being confined.

- **Top tip...**

  Do not make the mistake of thinking that an Alaskan Malamute will settle quietly into family life. He needs a sense of purpose, and this must be provided by training him in one of the canine disciplines that he is best suited to (see above).

- **Last word...**

  Not a dog for the apartment dweller, but a wonderful companion for those who are prepared to meet the needs of a powerful dog with a strong working instinct.

- **Comes from...**

  Western Alaska, and is one of the oldest Arctic sled dogs, named after the native Mahlemuts tribe.

FACT FILE

Appearance: A large, powerfully-built dog, with a strong, deep chest, a straight back, and well-muscled hindquarters. The tail is fairly high-set, and is carried over the back when the dog is working. The head is broad, wedge-shaped and powerful, with small, triangular ears, and dark almond-shaped eyes.

Colours: Range from light grey through all shades to black, or from gold through all shades to red or liver. The underbelly and the legs are white, and there are often masklike or caplike markings on the head. The only solid colour allowed is white.

Coat/grooming: A dense, oily undercoat, with a topcoat of coarse, thick guard hairs. Regular grooming is essential, particularly when the coat is shedding.

Size: UK: Dogs 25-28 ins (64-71 cms); bitches 23-26 ins (58-66 cms). Weight: 85-125 lbs (38-56 kgs), both sexes. US/FCI: Dogs 25 ins (64 cms); bitches 23 ins (58 cms). Weight: Dogs 85 lbs (38 kgs); bitches 75 lbs (34 kgs).

Temperament, training and exercise: The Alaskan Malamute is a friendly, affectionate dog and, although he is loyal to his family, he is not a 'one-man' dog. The pack instinct is very strong in him, and it is important to establish your own status – and his – at an early age. A tremendous workhorse, the Malamute responds well to training, and can become both vocal and destructive if he is bored. Regular and lengthy exercise is a must for this large, powerful dog.

Health issues: Breeding stock should be hip-scored. Dwarfism can occur in the breed.

Australian Shepherd

- **Comes from...**

Funnily enough, the breed did not originate in Australia. It is thought that the breed was developed in the Basque region of Spain, to guard and to herd sheep. Migrants went to Australia, and later to the United States, taking these versatile shepherd dogs with them.

- **Good at...**

Herding, Competitive Obedience, Agility, Flyball, Search and rescuc, Tracking.

- **Needs...**

To live in a stimulating environment.

- **Loves...**

Working.

- **Hates...**

Being bored.

- **Top tip...**

Many comparisons can be drawn between the Border Collie and the Australian Shepherd. Both have a strong herding instinct and a powerful work drive. However, the Aussie also has a strong protective and guarding instinct, and this trait should be taken into account.

- **Last word...**

Taking on a dog of any breed is a major commitment, but taking on an Aussie, with his strong working instincts, is an even greater undertaking. The rewards are enormous, but this is definitely not a breed for those with limited experience or sedentary tendencies.

FACT FILE

Appearance: A well-balanced, medium-sized dog, built on athletic lines. This is a breed that was bred for stamina and, as a result, his physique gives an impression of strength without exaggeration. The head is clean-cut and in proportion to the body, the ears are triangular in shape and set high on the head. The eyes may be brown, or more distinctively blue or amber, with flecks or marbling.

Colours: Blue merle, red merle, solid black and solid red – with or without white markings or tan points.

Coat/grooming: A medium-length, weather-resistant topcoat, plus an undercoat. There is some feathering, and dogs may have a more pronounced mane than bitches. Regular grooming is needed to keep the coat in good order.

Size: UK/US/FCI: Dogs 20-23 ins (51-58 cms); bitches 18-21 ins (46-53 cms).

Temperament, training and exercise: A loyal dog that is devoted to his family, the Aussie may show initial reserve with strangers. Training should start at an early stage for this highly intelligent breed, and it is essential to give him some purpose or activity to keep his mind occupied. Essentially a working dog, the Aussie requires extensive exercise on a daily basis.

Health issues: Check out Collie eye anomaly, progressive retinal atrophy and cataracts. Hip dysplasia and epilepsy should also be investigated.

Basset Hound

- **Comes from…**

France. It is believed he was bred by monks in the Middle Ages to hunt in heavy cover, with his nose to the ground. The French word 'basset' means low-set. The breed was then developed in Britain, where packs of Bassets were used for hunting hare.

- **Good at…**

Following a trail over long distances. In the US, the Basset is used to hunt racoons, and for trailing, flushing and retrieving birds.

- **Needs…**

A loving, securely-fenced home; a routine of regular exercise, with some long-distance hikes thrown in for good measure.

- **Loves…**

His creature comforts.

- **Hates…**

Being isolated.

- **Top tip…**

Make sure your garden is securely fenced. Although the Basset is a great family dog, he also has a roaming spirit.

- **Last word…**

The Basset is a true individual, and an owner must be able to appreciate his unique character, rather than trying to make him act in a more conventional 'dog-like' manner. Once you have become a Basset enthusiast, you will never want to own any other breed.

FACT FILE

Appearance: A favourite subject for cartoonists, the Basset cannot be mistaken for any other breed. The large, domed head is framed by wonderful, long velvety ears. Wrinkles, and dark or hazel-coloured eyes, combine to give a typically serious expression. The body is long, low-set and sturdy, with short powerful legs and massive feet. When moving, the tail is carried well up, curving gently in sabre fashion. A breed characteristic is the deep, baying bark.

Colours: Black, white and tan (tricolour) is the most common, but Bassets can also be lemon and white, or any other hound colour which includes: tricolour mottle; black and white; blue, tan and white; blue mottle; white; lemon and white; tan and white; lemon-pied; hare-pied; badger-pied; and liver, tan and white.

Coat/grooming: Smooth and short, easy to maintain. Regular attention is needed to ensure the ears are kept clean, and nails must be kept in trim.

Size: UK/FCI: 13-15 ins (33-38 cms), both sexes. US: Not to exceed 14 ins (35.5 cms). Weight: 50-70 lbs (22.6-31.75 kgs), both sexes, with bitches being slightly lighter than dogs.

Temperament, training and exercise: A kind, gentle, affectionate dog, the Basset gets on well with children, and soon becomes an integral member of the family. However, he does have a will of his own, and this can materialise into a stubborn streak when it comes to training. Patience and firmness is required, as well as a sense of humour. The Basset was bred to cover prodigious distances when on a trail, and this aspect of the breed should not be forgotten when it comes to exercise. He may not pick up great speed, but he will be a steady walking companion over many miles.

Health issues: Breeding stock should be eye-tested.

Beagle

- *Comes from…*

Britain. The Beagle is a scenthound, bred down from larger ancestors of Foxhounds to hunt in packs, followed by men on foot. Records of the breed date back to the 1300s, and, although still used as a hunting dog, its main claim to fame is as a family companion, and smart show dog.

- *Good at…*

Drag-hunting, also used as Quarantine Detector Dogs in North America and Australia, where they are used to sniff out anything from bees and reptiles to eggs, fruit and vegetables.

- *Needs…*

Exercise – although small in size, the Beagle is a sporting dog, and needs above-average exercise.

- *Loves…*

Food, being hot on the trail of an enticing scent.

- *Hates…*

Being deprived of human company for long stretches.

- *Top tip…*

The Beagle has an amazing sense of smell, even by canine standards. It is estimated that his olfactory sense is 100 times greater than ours. Give him the scope to follow his nose on interesting walks, but make sure you have worked hard at your Recall training.

- *Last word…*

A breed that is easy to keep and rewarding to live with. He suits all family situations – as long as someone in the family likes walking!

FACT FILE

Appearance: A sturdy, bold, active dog, the Beagle is compact and well proportioned. It is a breed without exaggeration, built to run for long distances. The head is quite powerful, with bitches being slightly finer in appearance. The skull is slightly domed, and the ears, which are set on low, are long with a rounded tip, hanging close to the cheeks. The Beagle's eyes, which can be dark-brown or hazel, have a mild, appealing expression.

Colours: Most people think of Beagles as tricolours (black, white and tan), but, in fact, they come in all hound colours (see Basset Hound colours).

Coat/grooming: A low-maintenance breed, the Beagle's short, dense coat needs no more than a weekly brush-through. Keep a check on the nails, as some Beagles have rapid nail growth, which will not be worn down with exercise. New owners should ask a Beagle breeder or a vet to trim the nails.

Size: UK/FCI: 13-16 ins (33-40 cms), both sexes. US: There are two varieties which are shown in different classes: 13 ins (33 cms) and under; and 13-15 ins (33-37.5 cms).

Temperament, training and exercise: The Beagle is one of the most amiable and even-tempered of all breeds, which makes him a pleasure to live with. Work hard at socialisation, and then your handy-sized Beagle really will be a dog you can take anywhere. Generally quick to learn, the Beagle can become a little hard of hearing when he is on a scent. Do not stint on the exercise – it is a must for this alert and active dog.

Health issues: No significant hereditary problems.

Bearded Collie

- **Comes from...**

Scotland, bred to gather and drive cattle and sheep to market. Evolved from an offshoot of the European shaggy sheepdog – which probably came to Britain by way of war or trade. References to the breed date back to the turn of the 19th century.

- **Good at...**

Agility, Obedience, some are still used to work livestock.

- **Needs...**

An energetic owner with a passion for grooming!

- **Loves...**

Being at the centre of things, playing the clown.

- **Hates...**

Being bored, lack of companionship.

- **Top tip...**

A Beardie's coat colour changes as the dog matures, so ask the breeder what you should expect – and what the final colour will be. A black or grey puppy will be a shade of black or grey as an adult. Brown or fawn puppies will be a shade of brown or sandy.

- **Last word...**

Intelligent and energetic, this is a breed for a get-up-and-go family – but don't forget the grooming...

FACT FILE

Appearance: A lean, active medium-sized dog, longer in the body than he is in height. Shoulders that slope back and strong hindquarters allow for supple, smooth movement, covering the ground with a minimum of effort. A long tail is carried low when standing, but in a happy manner when moving. The Beardie has a broad skull, a strong muzzle, and medium-sized ears that droop downwards. The eyes are set wide apart, and the colour tunes in with the coat colour; the expression is bright and enquiring, but soft.

Colours: Slate-grey, red-fawn, black, blue, all shades of grey, brown or sandy, with or without white markings.

Coat/grooming: The Beardie has a double coat – a harsh, shaggy topcoat, and a soft, furry undercoat. A distinctive feature is the beard, which has given the breed its name. It is the Beardie's shaggy appearance that attracts many would-be owners, but it is hard work to maintain. Daily brushing and combing is essential to keep the coat from tangling and matting, and baths will also be needed to keep your Beardie sweet-smelling.

Size: UK/US/FCI: Dogs 21-22 ins (53-56 cms); bitches 20-21 ins (51-53 cms).

Temperament, training and exercise: A self-confident, extrovert character, the Beardie is a wonderful family dog, who likes nothing better than to herd up his family when he is out walking. A bored Beardie is very often a destructive Beardie, so make sure you provide mental stimulation as well as plenty of exercise. Train with kindness and firmness, and watch out for a tendency to be boisterous.

Health issues: Breeding stock should be X-rayed for hip dysplasia under the recognised national scheme.

Bernese Mountain Dog

- *Good at...*

Carting, Agility, Obedience.

- *Needs...*

A safe, permanent, loving home.

- *Loves...*

Being the centre of attention, car travel, stealing the washing from the line, playing the clown.

- *Hates...*

Kennel life, being reprimanded.

- *Top tip...*

A fat dog is not a happy dog, so resist those pleading eyes, and make sure your Bernese never becomes obese.

- *Last word...*

A wonderful, steady companion that is biddable and a joy to live with. The only drawback is a relatively low life expectancy – most Bernese live betwecn 8-10 years – although some have made it to their teens. Not a dog for the house-proud (they can be great chewers, and their twice-yearly coat shedding causes havoc) but, like roses, they grow on you!

- *Comes from...*

Berne, Switzerland. Some 2,000 years ago the Romans invaded Switzerland, and their Mastiff-type guard dogs were crossed with the native flock-guarding dogs. The resulting dogs were developed to become general farmworkers, guarding the flock, and pulling carts full of dairy produce to market.

FACT FILE

Appearance: A strong, sturdy working dog, with a broad chest, a compact body, and muscular hindquarters. The tail is bushy, and is raised when the dog is alert or when he is moving. The Bernese has a strong, flat skull, medium-sized, triangular ears, and dark-brown almond-shaped eyes. The typical Bernese expression is one of gentleness and intelligence.

Colour: Jet black with rich tan markings on the legs, on the cheeks and above the eyes. White markings on the chest form an inverted cross and there is a white blaze extending from the top of the head down through the muzzle.

Coat/grooming: Soft, silky and lustrous. Regular grooming is essential. The ears should be given particular attention to prevent mats forming.

Size: UK/US: Dogs 25-27.5 ins (64-70 cms); bitches 23-26 ins (58-66 cms). FCI: Dogs 25-26 ins (66-68 cms); bitches 23-24 ins (60-63 cms).

Temperament, training and exercise: A kindly and devoted family dog, the Bernese gets on particularly well with children and other animals. He is intelligent enough to take on most training challenges, although speed is not really part of his make-up. The Bernese has a stubborn streak, and he may dig in his heels if there is something he really doesn't want to do. Strenuous exercise is not essential, but a routine of regular walks is important in order to keep him fit and active.

Health issues: Breeding stock should be hip-scored and elbow-scored. Osteochondrosis (OCD) can be a problem, as can bloat.

Bichon Frisé

- **Comes from...**

The Mediterranean area. Also known as the Tenerife Dog, as it is thought that these little white dogs were found on that island by sailors in the 14th century. The breed was developed in Europe, and soon became a favourite in the royal courts.

- **Good at...**

Companionship, looking glamorous, Mini-agility.

- **Needs...**

Regular trips to the grooming parlour, unless you are able to acquire the necessary skills.

- **Loves...**

Being the centre of attention.

- **Hates...**

Being uncomfortable, being neglected.

- **Top tip...**

Potential owners of Toy Dogs often make the mistake of thinking they are acquiring an ornament rather than a dog. A Bichon has lots of personality, and expects to be taken seriously as a full-blooded canine companion.

- **Last word...**

A delightful dog to own, he is kind and gentle and suits all family situations. However, a lot of attention is needed to keep your Bichon's pure-white coat in good order.

FACT FILE

Appearance: A small but sturdy dog, the Bichon is smart and proud-looking, with a well-muscled body and a plumed tail carried jauntily over his back. The head, which has a slightly rounded skull, is in balance with the body, set on an arched neck. The eyes are round, dark and forward-looking, with an alert, inquisitive expression. The ears hang close to the head, and are covered with fine, curly, long hair.

Colour: White. Some Bichons may have cream or apricot markings. Sometimes, but not always, these fade by the age of 18 months.

Coat/grooming: The coat is fine and silky with loose corkscrew curls, and it requires a huge amount of care to keep it in tip-top condition. Regular bathing is a necessity, and the coat needs to be scissored into shape. Presentation has now become something of an art-form in the show ring, but a general tidy-up is sufficient for most pet owners.

Size: UK: 9-11 ins (23-28 cms), both sexes. US: 9.5-12 ins (23-29.5 cms), both sexes. FCI: Not to exceed 11.8 ins (30 cms).

Temperament, training and exercise: A gay, lively, dog, the Bichon is playful in nature and loves to be part of everything that is going on. Like all puppies, the Bichon needs special patience and vigilance when it comes to house-training. However, in general, the breed is bright and intelligent, and can be trained to a surprisingly high standard. Although the Bichon was bred to be a lapdog, he does appreciate going out for walks on a regular basis.

Health issues: Legge-Perthes disease and patella luxation may be a problem.

Border Collie

- **Comes from…**

The borders of England, Scotland and Wales, where he was developed as the sheepdog par excellence. Now prized worldwide for his skills with livestock.

- **Good at…**

Everything from Competitive Obedience, Agility, to Working Trials (UK), Tracking, and Flyball. The Border Collie is quick-witted, agile and highly intelligent.

- **Needs…**

Lots of exercise, both physical and mental. A working sheepdog can run all day, and a quick walk around the block won't do. A Border Collie gets bored very easily.

- **Loves…**

Long walks, playing games, and, if you are not careful, chasing bicycles and cars!

- **Hates…**

Having nothing to do.

- **Top tip…**

The Border Collie's working instinct is very strong, and some individuals become obsessed by the urge to herd or chase. If you do not want your Border Collie to work livestock, channel his energies in a different direction while he is still young, and then the working instinct will not predominate.

- **Last word…**

The Border Collie is essentially a country-man's dog, not suited to life in a city apartment.

FACT FILE

Appearance: Athletic and well-proportioned, the medium-sized Border Collie is built on smooth, flowing lines, with the strength and substance of a dog that can work all day – often in harsh conditions. The ears are pricked (erect) or tipped (semi-erect); the eyes are set wide apart, and the typical Border Collie expression is alert and keen. The tail is quite long and is carried low.

Colours: Black and white, and tricolours are the most common, but red and white, blue and white, and blue merle are also popular.

Coat/grooming: Most Border Collies have a moderately-long coat, but some have a smooth coat. Both coat types have a dense undercoat to offer protection from the weather. Regular grooming is needed on the longer coat to keep it tangle-free.

Size: UK/FCI: Dogs 21 ins (53 cms); bitches slightly less. US: Dogs 19-22 ins (48-55.5 cms); bitches 18-21 ins (45.75-53 cms).

Temperament, training and exercise: The Border Collie is a highly motivated dog, and will not be happy without mental stimulation. This is the ideal dog for someone who wants to get involved in competition. Within the family, the Border Collie is generally good with children, but it is important to inhibit his chasing instinct in early puppyhood. Bred to work, the adult Border Collie will enjoy as much exercise as you can give him.

Health issues: Puppies and parents must be eye-tested.

Boxer

- **Comes from...**

Germany. This is very much a man-made breed, developed by a group of enthusiasts in southern Germany who wanted to create the ideal, all-round, guard, working and companion dog.

- **Good at...**

Guarding, Agility, Tracking, Competitive Obedience, Working Trials (UK).

- **Needs...**

Mental stimulation.

- **Loves...**

Playing the clown.

- **Hates...**

Being bored.

- **Top tip...**

The Boxer is a most appealing puppy, and it is all too easy to give into him, laughing off his unruly behaviour. However, your sweet little puppy will quickly grow into a strong, powerful dog, so it is essential to establish a regime of firm, kind, consistent discipline right from the start.

• *Last word...*

An adaptable breed, the Boxer will thrive in the town or in the country – as long as you are prepared to meet his exercise requirements, and spend the time training him.

FACT FILE

Appearance: A strong, noble-looking dog of medium size, the Boxer is square in build, with a deep chest and powerful hindquarters. The tail is customarily docked. The head is most distinctive with its broad muzzle, well-developed cheeks and undershot jaw. The nose is broad and slightly turned up; the eyes are dark and forward-looking. The ears are set wide apart on the highest part of the skull; in the UK, they lie flat, close to the cheek; in the US they are cropped.

Colours: Fawn (dark deer red to light fawn) or brindle (black stripes on a fawn background). White markings can be on the face, collar, chest and feet. White Boxers do occur in litters, and while they are perfectly acceptable as pets, they will not be successful in the show ring, as white is not an accepted colour.

Coat/grooming: A short, glossy coat that is very easy to care for.

Size: UK: Dogs 22.5-25 ins (57-63 cms); bitches 21-23 ins (53-59 cms).Weight: Dogs 66-70 lbs (30-32 kgs); bitches 55-60 lbs (25-27 kgs). US: Dogs 22.5-25 ins (57-63 cms); bitches 21-23.5 ins (53-60.25 cms). FCI: Dogs 22-24 ins (56-61 cms); bitches 21-23 ins (53-59 cms). Weight: Dogs 66 lbs (30 kgs); bitches 62 lbs (28 kgs).

Temperament, training and exercise: An extrovert dog with a lively disposition, the Boxer is a breed for energetic owners. He is a devoted member of the family, and will take his guarding duties seriously. He may be a little aloof with strangers. The Boxer is biddable and easy to train, as long as you establish your superior status at an early stage. Built on muscular lines, the Boxer needs regular exercise to keep in trim – but do not tax him too much while he is still growing.

Health issues: Heart conditions – breeding stock should be tested, deafness may occur in white Boxers. Progressive axonopathy, a debilitating disease which affects the nervous system, has been identified in the breed, and it is essential that only non-carrier stock is used in breeding programmes.

Bulldog

• **Comes from...**
Britain – famed as the national dog of this country, and recognised worldwide as a symbol of tenacity, determination and steadfastness.

• **Good at...**
Clowning around, protecting his family.

• **Needs...**
An owner who understands, and appreciates, the unique Bulldog character.

• **Loves...**
Children.

• **Hates...**
Being forced to do something against his will.

• **Top tip...**
Be inventive in your training so you do not set up situations of conflict where your Bulldog decides to dig his heels in – as then you will have a weighty problem on your hands.

• **Last word...**
A beautifully ugly animal, the Bulldog has his own very special charm – make absolutely sure this appeals to you before taking the plunge into Bulldog ownership.

FACT FILE

Appearance: Originally bred to bait bulls, the Bulldog is low in stature, with a broad, muscular body and a massive head. The shoulders are broad and very powerful, the back is short and strong, and the hindquarters are large and muscular. The tail is set on low, and juts out straight before turning downwards.

The skull is large in circumference, with high-set, rose-shaped ears. Round eyes are set well apart, the nose is large and broad, and the flews (chops) hang down, covering the sides of the lower jaw. A breed characteristic is the undershot mouth.

Colours: Brindle, red, fawn (of various shades), white, or white with any of the foregoing colours.

Coat/grooming: A short, close, smooth coat that needs minimal grooming. Attention should be paid to the nose roll and facial creases to ensure dirt does not accumulate.

Size: UK/FCI: Dogs 55 lbs (25 kgs); bitches 50 lbs (22.7 kgs). US: Dogs 50 lbs (22.7 kgs); bitches 40 lbs (18.1 kgs).

Temperament, training and exercise: A loving and affectionate dog, the Bulldog also has a strong sense of loyalty and can show great courage. He will respond to training – but it tends to be at his pace. Determined and strong-willed by nature, the Bulldog can be stubborn. There is no need to trudge for miles with your Bulldog, but he will appreciate regular exercise. Avoid exercising in hot weather, as the short-nosed Bulldog will find this a strain.

Health issues: Minor skin problems do occur in the breed. When it comes to breeding, the Bulldog is not suitable for the novice. Whelping difficulties may arise, and Bulldogs tend to be good but rather clumsy mothers.

Bullmastiff

- **Comes from...**

England, evolved from the Old English Mastiff and the Bulldog and originally used as a gamekeeper's dog, on the alert for poachers.

- **Good at...**

Guarding, faithfulness.

- **Needs...**

An owner who will establish his superior status, and give a sense of leadership.

- **Loves...**

Children.

- **Hates...**

Dogs trespassing on his property.

- **Top tip...**

For the first-time owner, it is wise to opt for a bitch, as she will generally prove to be easier to handle.

- **Last word...**

The Bullmastiff has many endearing traits: he is loyal and faithful, he loves to play the clown, and he gets on well with children. However, it must be remembered that this is a very powerful dog, and taking on the training required demands both time and experience.

FACT FILE

Appearance: Symmetrical in shape, the Bullmastiff is a dog of tremendous power and strength, while remaining alert and active. The chest is wide and deep, the back is short and straight and the hindquarters are wide and muscular. The Bullmastiff's head is large and square, with V-shaped ears, and dark eyes.

Colours: Brindle, fawn or red.

Coat/grooming: Short and hard in texture. Grooming requirements are minimal.

Size: UK/US/FCI: Dogs 25-27 ins (63.5-68.5 cms); bitches 24-26 ins (61-66 cms).Weight: Dogs 110-130 lbs (50-59 kgs); bitches 90-110 lbs (except for US). US weight for bitches 100-120 lbs (45.3-54.4 kgs).

Temperament, training and exercise: The Bullmastiff is a dog of exceptional loyalty, and makes a wonderful guard and companion. However, this is a breed with strong dominant instincts, and training must start right from the very beginning in order to establish control and discipline. Regular exercise is required to keep the Bullmastiff fit, but free-running should only be allowed under controlled circumstances when there is no chance of meeting strange dogs.

Health issues: Gastric dilation and torsion of the stomach must be guarded against.

Cairn Terrier

- **Comes from...**
The highlands of Scotland, where it was kept in packs to hunt and kill vermin.

- **Good at...**
Mini-agility, vermin hunting.

- **Needs...**
Regular exercise, companionship, coat care.

- **Loves...**
Digging, helping his owner (whether his assistance is needed or not!).

- **Hates...**
Having nothing to do, trespassing cats and pigeons.

- **Top tip...**
The Cairn has a deep, strong bark for his size. Being on the alert for strangers is one thing, but constant, uncontrolled barking is another. Train your Cairn puppy to "Be quiet" when he is told, ignoring him if he persist in barking, and rewarding him when he stops.

- **Last word...**
A dog with plenty of character, the Cairn lives happily with owners of all ages. Don't forget – he needs more exercise than you would expect for his size.

FACT FILE

Appearance: An active, natural-looking little dog, that looks ready for anything. He stands well forward on his forepaws, which are bigger than his hindfeet. The back is level, and of medium length, and the tail is short, and carried gaily. The Cairn's head is small, with a broad skull, and a powerful muzzle. The eyes are set wide apart, beneath shaggy eyebrows. The ears are small and pointed.

Colours: Cream, wheaten (the colour of wheat), red, grey, plus brindling in all these colours.

Coat/grooming: A weather-resistant coat, with a harsh, coarse topcoat, and a soft, dense undercoat. Grooming is needed on a routine basis. The coat also needs regular stripping. This can be done by a professional groomer, or you can ask an experienced Cairn breeder to give you lessons in hand-stripping.

Size: Height should be in proportion to weight. UK/FCI: 11-12 ins (28-31 cms), both sexes. Weight: 14-16 lbs (6-7.5 kgs), both sexes. US: Dogs 10 ins (25.5 cms); bitches 9.5 ins (24 cms). Weight: Dogs 14 lbs (6.5 kgs); bitches 13 lbs (6 kgs).

Temperament, training and exercise: A fearless little dog, with a gay, optimistic outlook, the Cairn fits in well with family life. He is quite assertive in his manner, so it is important to socialise him so that he learns to accept all situations. Bred to work, the Cairn will soon become bored and frustrated if you neglect his training and give him nothing to do. Despite his small size, the Cairn needs plenty of exercise.

Health issues: There are no known widespread hereditary problems within the breed, but if you are planning to breed from your Cairn, consult a vet first.

Cavalier King Charles Spaniel

the 15th century. It is thought that Henrietta of Orleans introduced her brother, Charles II, to these captivating little dogs. The king became a great enthusiast for the breed, and eventually they were called by his name.

- *Good at...*

Adaptability, giving affection, Agility, Competitive Obedience.

- *Needs...*

Daily grooming, companionship.

- *Loves...*

Family life and intelligence tests.

- *Hates...*

Solitude.

- *Top tip...*

Do not underestimate your Cavalier's intelligence. He is as bright as a button, and will thrive on being given a task to do.

- *Last word...*

One of the most adaptable and loving of breeds, the Cavalier is a fun dog to own for people of all ages, and all walks of life.

- *Comes from...*

Europe – a descendant of the Toy Spaniel, which was a favourite in the royal courts in

FACT FILE

Appearance: Although classed as a Toy Dog, the Cavalier is not one of the tinies. Elegant and well-balanced, the average Cavalier weighs between 12 and 18 lbs. An active little dog, the Cavalier is typified by his happy, wagging tail. The head is almost flat between the ears, and the eyes are large and dark with a gentle expression.

Colours: There is an attractive range of Cavalier colours which include black and tan, ruby (solid rich-red colour), blenheim (rich chestnut markings on a white background), or tricolour (black and white with tan markings).

Coat/grooming: The coat is long and silky and requires daily grooming attention, to avoid matting, particularly in the ear feathering.

Size: UK/US/FCI: 12-13 ins (30.5-33 cms), both sexes.

Temperament, training and exercise: The Cavalier is a gay, lively, little dog with an affectionate nature, and a surprisingly fearless outlook on life. He responds well to training, and enjoys working closely with his owner. Exercise is enjoyed, but it does not have to be too strenuous. The Cavalier tends to adapt to the amount of exercise he is given.

Health issues: A puppy should come from breeding stock tested and found to be clear of heart murmur up to at least five years of age. Parents and puppies should be eye-tested.

Chihuahua

• Comes from...

The origins of what is popularly known as 'the smallest dog in the world' are obscure. Its roots have been traced back to the Mediterranean area, before Christ. Smoothcoats were indigenous to Malta and longcoats to Melita. The breed was probably taken to South America by the early Conquistadors. Its name comes from the Mexican state of Chihuahua, where the breed came to prominence in the late 19th century.

• Good at...

Giving warning of strangers.

• Needs...

Mental stimulation, companionship and lots of love.

• Loves...

Fun games.

• Hates...

Being ignored, not keen on having nails clipped or teeth cleaned.

• Top tip...

The pocket-sized Chihuahua is extremely adaptable, and truly is the dog you can take wherever you go. Early training and socialisation will ensure that you can confidently take your Chihuahua (almost) anywhere!

• Last word...

A fun, long-lived dog that is an ideal companion for the elderly. Not a good choice for families with small children.

FACT FILE

Appearance: A dainty, compact little dog, typified by his brisk, powerful movement and saucy expression. The Chihuahua has straight forelegs set well under the chest, a level back, and muscular hindquarters. The head is well rounded with an apple dome; the eyes are large and round. The large, erect ears are set on at an angle of approximately 45 degrees.

Colours: All colours.

Coat/grooming: The smooth-coated Chihuahua (top left) has a soft glossy coat. Grooming is minimal, although special attention should be given to keeping the ears clean. The longcoat (top right) also has a soft coat, but with feathering on the ears, legs, hindquarters and tail. Regular care is needed to keep the coat tangle-free, but no trimming is necessary.

Size: UK/US/FCI: Not to exceed 6 lbs (2.7 kgs), both sexes. Very few weigh 2-3 lbs (0.9-1.4 kgs), and

they are often delicate. Most popular are those that weigh 3.5-5.5 lbs (1.6-2.5 kgs).

Temperament, training and exercise: A gay, friendly dog, the Chihuahua is inquisitive by nature and takes an active interest in everything that is going on. Quick-thinking and intelligent, he will enjoy the stimulation of training and playing games. The tiny Chihuahua will get as much exercise as he needs running around the house and garden, but will enjoy walks too.

Health issues: Patella luxation. This is a breed with large, lustrous eyes, and dust on hair can cause tears. The Chihuahua will often quiver, and sometimes snort, when excited – but this is usually nothing to be concerned about.

Collie (Rough)

- ### Comes from...
Scotland, bred from the native shepherd dogs that have been recorded since Roman times.

- ### Good at...
Herding, Competitive Obedience, Agility.

- ### Needs...
An owner with a passion for grooming.

- ### Loves...
Companionship – the Rough Collie is particularly fond of children and car rides.

- ### Hates...
Being told off, kennel life (but he will adapt if necessary), missing out on the action.

- ### Top tip...
The Rough Collie is more than capable of working in many disciplines but, all too often, he is treated as a 'dumb blond' of the canine world. Training is not as instant as with some of the other Collie breeds, but patience and perseverance will win the day.

- ### Last word...
A beautiful dog to own, who fits in well with family life – but coat care is a chore that cannot be neglected

FACT FILE

Appearance: The Rough Collie is a dog of great beauty, with a noble, dignified bearing, built on balanced, athletic lines. The head resembles a well-blunted wedge which is smooth and clean in outline. The eyes are set obliquely and have a sweet, dreamy expression. The ears are small and carried semi-erect when the dog is alert. The body is slightly longer compared with the height, and the long tail is carried low, or with a slight upward swirl at the tip when the dog is moving.

Colours: Sable (any shade from light gold to dark mahogany), tricolour (black with rich tan markings) and blue merle (silver blue splashed and marbled with black). All colours should have the typical white Collie markings. In the US, white is also recognised as a colour, which is a predominantly white dog with sable, tricolour or blue merle markings.

Coat/grooming: A well-fitting coat consisting of a soft undercoat and long, straight topcoat which is harsh in texture. There are no short-cuts when it comes to coat care, and the Rough Collie needs daily grooming sessions to keep his coat free of tangles and mats. Bathing is only needed when the coat is particularly muddy, or when shedding.

Size: UK/FCI: Dogs 22-24 ins (56-61 cms); bitches 20-22 ins (51-56 cms). US: Dogs 24-26 ins (61-66 cms); bitches 22-24 ins (56-61 cms). Weight: Dogs 60-75 lbs (27.2-34 kgs); bitches 50-65 lbs (22.7-29.5 kgs).

Temperament, training and exercise: The Rough Collie is a friendly, even-tempered dog which is responsive to training. He is loving and affectionate, and has a particular affinity with children. A part of his nature is to protect, without showing a hint of aggression. Some Rough Collie owners have noticed a 'sixth sense', where the dog seems to anticipate events – standing at the door to await the arrival of a loved one, long before the car has even entered the road.

Bred as a working dog, the Rough Collie should receive plenty of exercise – even on wet days when you will see his coat become muddy and bedraggled!

Health issues: Parents and puppies should be eye-tested.

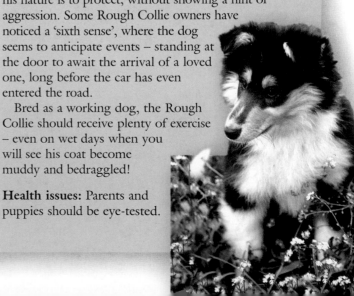

Dachshund

- ● *Comes from…*

Germany, where it is known as the Teckel. The German word 'dachs' means badger, and this distinctive breed was developed as a hunting dog that could burrow underground in search of badger, fox and rabbit.

- ● *Good at…*

Earth dog tests, Tracking.

- ● *Needs…*

Competent handling.

- ● *Loves…*

Following a scent.

- ● *Hates…*

Having nothing to do.

- ● *Top tip…*

The Dachshund is a sporting little dog but is prone to obesity, which can lead to serious health problems. Watch the diet carefully, and make sure you take your Dachshund for regular walks.

- ● *Last word…*

Spirited and intelligent, the Dachshund requires firm handling, but is an ideal and adaptable companion for a variety of home situations.

FACT FILE

Appearance: The Dachshund comes in six varieties categorised by size (standard and miniature), and coat type (smooth-haired, wire-haired and long-haired). There are minor differences between the varieties, but, in essentials, the breed follows very similar lines. The main characteristic is the low-set body with an exceptionally long back, which should be level, and just slightly arched at the loin. The tail continues the line of the spine. The head is long with high-set ears and almond-shaped eyes.

Colours: All colours including dapples.

Coat/grooming: The smooth-coated Dachshund has a dense, short coat that is easy to care for. Wire-hairs have a short, straight, harsh coat, with a beard and bushy eyebrows. They need stripping (like other Terrier breeds). Long-haired Dachshunds have a soft, straight coat with feathering on the ears, legs, underparts of the body and the tail. Regular attention is required to keep this coat in good condition.

Size: UK: *Standard:* 20-26 lbs (9-12 kgs). *Miniature:* under 10 lbs (4.5 kgs). US: *Standard:* 16-32 lbs (7.25-14.5 kgs). *Miniature:* under 11 lbs (5 kgs). FCI: *Standard:* under 20 lbs (9 kgs).

Temperament, training and exercise: The hallmark of the Dachshund temperament is bold, courageous and sporting. Training should cause few problems for this intelligent breed, but is it important to get the upper hand from an early stage. There are some differences in temperament between the varieties: the long-haired tend to be more docile whereas the wire-hairs and smooths are more feisty and outgoing. The wire-haired is generally the most extrovert. Bred as a hunting dog, the Dachshund retains his love of the great outdoors and moderate but regular exercise should not be neglected.

Health issues: Spinal problems, patella luxation, inherited eye conditions.

Dalmatian

• Comes from...

Greece, where they crossed a breed of small, spotted dogs with Egyptian and Cretan Hounds, which were used in the 13th century for hunting fallow deer. In the 17th century travelling gypsies were attracted by their unusual appearance, and they were incorporated into circus acts. In the early 1800s, young British aristocrats travelling in Europe brought the breed back to England, where they were best known as carriage dogs. It is thought that the name is derived from 'Damachien', a 13th-century corruption of *dama* (Latin for fallow deer) and *chien* (French for dog).

• Good at...

Agility, playing the clown, manipulating their owners, guarding the house.

• Needs...

A home where there is never-ending attention, interspersed with interesting walks.

• Loves...

To share a major slice of your life.

• Hates...

Being deprived of human company, meals being late, being cold or wet, being teased, being treated as a dog rather than a person.

• Top tip...

The breeds high profile can encourage the less than scrupulous, so always consult the national breed club to find a responsible breeder in your area.

• Last word...

Dalmatians have received huge publicity recently, but make sure you buy one for the right reasons, taking on board all his needs, before taking the plunge.

FACT FILE

Appearance: The Dalmatian is balanced and athletic, capable of trotting for long periods, as well as occasional bursts of speed. The chest is deep with plenty of heart and lung room, the back is level, and the hindquarters are well developed. The Dalmatian has a flat skull, fairly broad between the ears, which are carried close to the head. The eyes are bright and sparkling in expression – dark in black-spotted dogs, amber (the colour of sweet sherry) in liver-spotted.

Colours: Black-spotted or liver-spotted on a white backgrounds. The spots should be clearly defined and well distributed over the body. They vary in size between a dime (1 pence) to half a dollar (50 pence).

Coat/grooming: A short, sleek coat that is easy to maintain; a daily session with a rubber grooming glove helps with the constant coat-shedding. This continuous moult can affect asthmatics.

Size: UK: Dogs 23-24 ins (58.5-61 cms); bitches 22-23 ins (56-58.5 cms). US: 19-23 ins (48.25-58.5 cms), both sexes. FCI: Dogs 22-24 ins (56-61 cms); bitches 21.25-23 ins (54-59 cms). Weight: Dogs 59.5 lbs (27 kgs); bitches 53 lbs (24 kgs).

Temperament, training and exercise: Outgoing and friendly, the Dalmatian enjoys the hurly-burly of family life. Not the easiest breed to train, as they can be both stubborn and strong-willed but, with patience, you will get there in the end. Firm and kind discipline is needed, particularly with adolescent males. Bred for endurance, to hunt and later to run alongside carriages, the Dalmatian is not one for a sedentary life. Daily walks are the essential high spot of his life.

Health issues: Deafness is a major problem in the breed. Ensure that both parents and puppies have been BAER hearing-tested, and that you receive the correct certificate along with the pedigree documents. Unilateral deafness (in one ear only) is acceptable in a pet puppy which is not to be bred from.

English Springer Spaniel

• Comes from…

England, originally known as the Norfolk Spaniel after one of the Dukes of Norfolk who kept Spaniels of this type in the 19th century. The name 'Springer' comes from the ability to 'spring' game.

• Good at…

Springing game and retrieving it for the gun, Field Trials, Hunting Tests, Tracking, Agility. Highly valued as a sniffer dog, detecting drugs, arms and explosives.

• Needs…

An interesting, varied life, preferably with a family of growing children.

• Loves…

Family life, long country walks, toys and food (especially snitching it when your back is turned!).

• Hates…

Being bored, being ignored, missing out on a walk.

• Top tip…

Working lines tend to produce dogs that are more highly-charged, and they may become frustrated and unhappy if they are underused. If you want a companion dog, it is better to opt for show lines.

• Last word…

The Springer is happy dog who loves to be busy, so make sure you include him in all the family activities.

FACT FILE

Appearance: The tallest of the British land Spaniels, the English Springer is a medium-sized, compact strong dog, with a racy, athletic appearance. The chest is deep, the forelegs straight, and the hindquarters are muscular and well developed. The tail is customarily docked. The Springer has a beautiful head, with a slightly rounded skull, framed by long, feathered ears. The eyes are dark and almond-shaped, with a kind, alert expression.

Colours: Liver and white, black and white, or either of these colours with tan markings.

Coat/grooming: A close, straight, weather-resistant coat, with moderate feathering on the ears, forelegs, body and hindquarters. Regular grooming is essential to keep feathering tangle-free. This is especially important as the Springer loves nothing better than going through undergrowth, picking up seeds, twigs and brambles in his coat – particularly in his long, feathered ears.

Size: UK/FCI: 20 ins (51 cms), both sexes. US: Dogs 20 ins (51 cms); bitches 19 ins (48.25 cms).

Temperament, training, and exercise: A happy, friendly dog, the English Springer makes an excellent family dog. He is biddable, and loves being given a job of work to do. Bred to keep going in the field all day, the Springer has endless stamina which needs to be used up on long walks. However, take care not to overdo the exercise while your puppy is growing.

Health issues: Parents and puppies should be eye-tested.

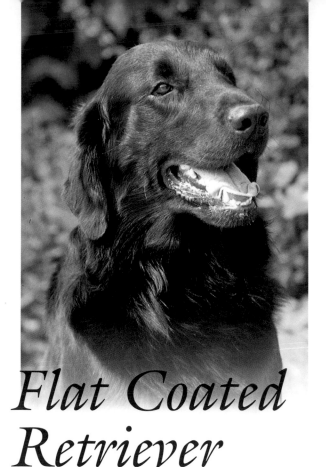

Flat Coated Retriever

• **Comes from...**

England (Warwickshire). Developed from the Wavy Coated Retriever by selective breeding, which may have included the Black Welsh Setter. The aim was to produce the 'perfect Retriever' to meet the changing pattern in the shooting field. The Flat Coat was highly prized and was the 'must-have' accessory of the fashionable shooting man.

• **Good at...**

Excels as shooting/companion dog. Reasonably good at Field Trials, Working Tests, Hunting Tests and Obedience. Enjoys Flyball and Agility.

• **Needs...**

A fit, caring, patient owner who enjoys 'togetherness'. Mental and physical stimulation is a must.

• **Loves...**

People and activities, but only a few reach the heights in competition due to a tendency to blow it at the crucial moment by playing the clown. (Known as the Peter Pan of the dog world).

• **Hates...**

Being alone and idle.

• **Top tip...**

The Flat Coat's boundless enthusiasm is typified by his ever-wagging tail – so clear all your precious ornaments when your Flat Coat makes an entrance!

• **Last word...**

A wonderful breed for the energetic owner who wants to go out and do things with his dog.

FACT FILE

Appearance: A medium-sized retriever with an active, racy appearance. The Flat Coat is without exaggeration, with a deep chest, straight forelegs, and muscular hindquarters. The tail is short and straight, and is never carried above the level of the back. The head is long, well moulded with strong jaws. Small ears lie close to the head, and the medium-sized eyes have an intelligent expression.

Colours: Black or liver.

Coat/grooming: A dense coat lying as flat as possible, with feathering on the legs and tail.

Size: UK/US/FCI: Dogs 23-24 ins (59-61.5 cms); bitches 22-23 ins (56.5-59 cms).Weight: Dogs 60-80 lbs (27-36 kgs); bitches 55-70 lbs (25-32 kgs).

Temperament, training and exercise:
A confident, optimistic approach to life is typical of the Flat Coat, who must rate as one of the friendliest of all dogs. He loves to be given a job of work, and will show great enthusiasm for all tasks. Competent handling is a must for this energetic dog, who will enjoy as much exercise as you can give him.

Health issues: Breeding stock should be hip-scored and eye-tested.

German Shepherd Dog

- **Comes from...**

Germany, where it was first used to herd and guard flocks of sheep. The breed was then developed and standardised, and has been adopted worldwide as the number one police dog.

- **Good at...**

Competitive Obedience and Working Trials in particular, but also enjoys Agility. The Shepherd will naturally act as family guard and protector.

- **Needs...**

Mental stimulation provided by a sensitive and understanding handler. Lots of exercise is a must for this big, powerful dog.

- **Loves...**

His family, free running, training challenges.

- **Hates...**

Being bullied or shouted at.

- **Top tip...**

The German Shepherd tends to form a bond with one particular person, so make sure that all members of the family take part in simple training exercises so that the dog learns to respond to everyone in the 'pack'.

- **Last word...**

A fabulous companion, but time and commitment are needed to bring out the best in this breed.

FACT FILE

Appearance: The German Shepherd is strong, agile and well muscled, and is slightly long in comparison with his height. Typically, the German Shepherd has free, elastic, far-reaching movement. The head gives an impression of nobility; and it is easy to tell male and female apart. The line of the back slopes slightly from front to back, and the tail is carried low.

Colours: A black saddle with gold, tan or light grey markings is probably the most commonly seen, but Shepherds can also be all-black, or sable (grey with lighter or brown markings), or predominantly black with tan points usually referred to as 'bi-colours'. White German Shepherds have an enthusiastic following, but they are not eligible for showing.

Coat/grooming: A straight, harsh outer coat, with a thick undercoat, which requires basic grooming care. Most Shepherds shed their coat twice a year – and you will know all about it! Most long-haired Shepherds do not have the correct undercoat, so would be faulted in the show ring. However, they are much loved as pets, although they do require considerably more grooming care.

Size: UK/US/FCI: Dogs 24-26 ins (60-65 cms); bitches 22-24 ins (55-60 cms).

Temperament, training and exercise: Loyal, watchful and courageous, the German Shepherd's skills as a defence and tracking dog are second to none. He also makes a devoted companion, although experienced handling – or access to expert help – is important. The German Shepherd is a sensitive dog and needs firm, but quiet discipline to get the best from him.

Health issues: Breeding stock must be hip-scored, stud dogs must be tested for haemophilia.

German Shorthaired Pointer

- **Comes from...**
Germany – a member of the versatile hunt, point, retrieve group of gundogs.

- **Good at...**
Rough shooting, Field Trials, Hunting Tests, Tracking, Working Trials (UK), Competitive Obedience, Agility, Flyball.

- **Needs...**
Plenty of things to do.

- **Loves...**
A day working in the field, or simply using his highly-developed retrieving instinct.

- **Hates...**
Kennel life.

- **Top tip...**
The GSP is receptive to training and has a particularly good memory. Structure your training programme to suit the individual – and if your GSP is struggling to understand, go back to basics.

- **Last word...**
Bright, intelligent, with bags of energy, the GSP needs a committed owner who wants to work with his dog.

FACT FILE

Appearance: A medium-sized dog that shows power, endurance and speed. The neatly-built GSP has a short back, but stands over plenty of ground. The chest is deep but not wide, the forelegs straight, and the hindquarters are broad and muscular. The tail is customarily docked. The GSP has a noble head, which is clean-cut. The eyes are soft and intelligent in expression, and the ears are broad and high-set.

Colours: Liver, liver and white spotted, liver and white, and ticked (black, black and white UK only).

Coat/grooming: Short and coarse in texture. Low-maintenance as far as grooming is concerned.

Size: UK/US: Dogs 23-25 ins (58-64 cms); bitches 21-23 ins (53-59 cms). US weight restrictions:

Dogs 55-70 lbs (25-31.75 kgs); bitches 45-60 lbs (20.5-27.3 kgs). FCI: Dogs 24.5-26 ins (62-66 cms); bitches 23-25 ins (58-63 cms).

Temperament, training and exercise: An even-tempered dog who is both gentle and affectionate. Biddable by nature, the GSP thrives on having something to do, and will take all training challenges in his stride. Bred to spend long days in the field, the GSP needs plenty of exercise.

Health issues: Breeding stock should be hip-scored.

Golden Retriever

• Comes from…

The highlands of Scotland, where the first Lord Tweedsmouth developed a breed of yellow, wavy-coated dogs to work as all-round retrievers. Today, the Golden Retriever is still widely used as a working gundog.

• Good at…

Retrieving (whether you want him to or not!), an enthusiastic competitor in Agility, Field Trials and Working Trials, also successful in Competitive Obedience.

• Needs…

A loving home, lots of exercise, the chance to work with and please his owner.

• Loves…

Carrying things in his mouth, children, a long muddy walk and a good swim.

• Hates…

Being left alone.

• Top tip…

The Golden Retriever has a sensitive side to his nature, and may dig his heels in if he is upset or confused. Make sure your Golden always understands what you want, and be lavish with the praise.

• Last word…

Kindly and fun-loving, the Golden Retriever is an ideal family dog, but he also has lots of energy, and must be given the opportunity to use it.

FACT FILE

Appearance: A balanced, symmetrical, medium-sized dog, the Golden Retriever has a deep chest and a level back. He is built on working lines, and moves with powerful drive. The Golden's head is broad, with a characteristic kindly expression. The tail, which is well feathered, is carried level with the back.

Colour: Any shade from pale to deep gold. In the UK, cream-coloured dogs are popular, but this is not the case in the USA.

Coat/grooming: The topcoat is flat or wavy with feathering, which makes daily grooming essential. The undercoat is dense and water-resistant.

Size: UK/FCI: Dogs 22-24 ins (56-61 cms); bitches 20-22 ins (51-56 cms). US: Dogs 23-24 ins (58.5-61 cms); bitches 21.5-22.5 ins (54.5-57 cms).

Temperament, training and exercise: Friendly, trustworthy and reliable, the Golden Retriever is an extrovert companion who is easy to live with. He is a real 'people' dog, and will be devoted to all members of the family. Training poses few problems for this intelligent breed, and any chance to retrieve is viewed with boundless enthusiasm.

Health issues: Breeding stock must be hip-scored and eye-tested.

Great Dane

• **Comes from...**

Germany – developed to hunt the packs of wild boar that roamed the forests of Europe in the Middle Ages.

• **Good at...**

Competitive Obedience, Agility, Tracking.

• **Needs...**

A spacious home.

• **Loves...**

His family.

• **Hates...**

Being excluded from the family's activities.

• **Top tip...**

The Great Dane takes 18 months to reach full maturity, so it is essential to provide a correctly balanced diet and limit strenuous exercise during this formidable growing period.

• **Last word...**

If you have the space, the Great Dane makes a wonderful companion. The only drawback is that, like many of the larger breeds, their life span is limited, and 8-10 years is the average life expectancy.

FACT FILE

Appearance: The most noble of dogs, the Great Dane has a look of power and daring. The head and neck are carried high, and the shoulders and hindquarters are muscular, combining strength and elegance. The muzzle is broad, and the eyes are fairly deep-set. In the US the ears are cropped – this is not the case in the UK.

Colours: Brindle, black, harlequin, fawn.

Coat/grooming: A short, sleek coat that is very easy to maintain.

Size: UK/US/FCI: Minimum height: Dogs 30 ins (76 cms); bitches 28 ins (71 cms). Weight: Dogs 120 lbs (54 kgs); bitches 100 lbs (46 kgs).

Temperament, training and exercise: The gentle giant of the canine world, the Great Dane is loyal, dependable and affectionate. Basic training is essential for this large dog, who is capable of competing in a number of disciplines. The Dane does not need enormous amounts of exercise, but he does appreciate the opportunity to stretch his legs and gallop.

Health issues: Breeding stock should be hip-scored; check out OCD and Wobblers Syndrome.

Irish Setter

- ### Comes from...

Ireland. Dogs were used to set birds from at least as early as the 14th century, and Ireland had its own bird dogs. Early Irish Setters were mainly white dogs with red patches, but, through selective breeding, a solid red dog was evolved.

- ### Good at...

Pointing and setting games, Hunting Tests, Field Trials, Agility.

- ### Needs...

An owner with patience and a keen sense of humour, routine and order.

- ### Loves...

Lots of exercise, fun and games, the sofa, being the centre of attention.

- ### Hates...

Being excluded from family activities.

- ### Top tip...

Take care with your training. Irish Setters are willing to learn, but are easily bored by too much repetition.

FACT FILE

Appearance: One of the most glamorous of all breeds, the Irish Setter is a racy, active dog that should appear elegant and full of quality. The chest is deep, the forelegs straight and sinewy, the back is firm and slopes down from the withers to wide and powerful hindquarters. The tail is set on just below the level of the back, and is carried level with the back. The Irish Setter's head is long and lean, with an oval-shaped skull. The ears are set on low, and hang close to the head. The eyes are dark with a kindly expression. The Irish Setter's free, flowing movement is a joy to behold.

Colour: Rich chestnut.

Coat/grooming: The body coat is flat and should be as straight as possible. There is silky feathering on the ears, chest, legs, underparts of the body, and on the tail. This requires regular brushing and combing. Trimming is required to keep coat and feathering looking neat and tidy.

Size: UK/FCI: No measurements given in the Breed Standards. US: Dogs 27 ins (68.5 cms); bitches 25 ins (63.5 cms). Weight: Dogs 70 lbs (31.75 kgs); bitches 60 lbs (27.2 kgs).

Temperament, training and exercise: The Irish Setter is extremely affectionate but can be quite boisterous especially when young. However, the Irish is responsive to training, although a fair degree of patience is required. Bred as a working gundog, the Irish Setter must have regular exercise.

Health issues: In the past, progressive retinal atrophy was a major problem, but due to the determined action taken by Irish Setter breeders after the Second World War, PRA was largely eliminated through test-matings. This was confirmed when a DNA test for PRA was developed, and a representative sample of all the major bloodlines was tested. Only one carrier could be found, and only genetically PRA-clear Irish Setters are eligible for registration with the Kennel Club. A second DNA test for canine leucocyte adhesion deficiency (CLAD) has become available, and the Irish Setter is the only breed fortunate enough to have two DNA tests available.

• *Last word...*

The Irish Setter, with his flamboyant good looks, makes a loyal and loving companion. While the breed is better suited to life in the country, Irish Setters will adapt to town life as long as the owner is prepared to work out a regime for essential exercise.

Jack Russell

• *Comes from...*

Britain's West Country, where the
Reverend John Russell, a clergyman with a
passion for hunting, gave his name to this
feisty little terrier. The Jack Russell (or
Parson Russell Terrier) was bred to go to
ground and run with the hounds and, to this
day, he retains a strong working instinct.

• *Good at...*

Going to ground and pleasing himself!
However, when his keen intelligence is
channelled, he has proved highly successful
at Agility, Flyball, Terrier racing, and Earth
Dog events.

• *Needs...*

Lots of variety, firm handling and
regular exercise.

• *Loves...*

A challenge.

• *Hates...*

Cats (he may be fine with those in his
family, but watch out for others); having
nothing to do.

FACT FILE

Appearance: The Jack Russell has a workmanlike appearance. He is built for speed and endurance with long, sloping shoulders, a strong, straight back, and muscular hindquarters. The head is moderately broad, tapering towards almond-shaped eyes, which have a keen expression. The ears are small and V-shaped, and the jaws are powerful. The tail is customarily docked.

Colours: White, or predominantly white with markings – tan, lemon, black. In the show ring, it is preferred if these markings are confined to the head and the root of the tail.

Coat: This can be rough, broken or smooth, but it is always harsh in texture. Smooth-coated dogs need basic grooming care; broken and rough-coated dogs will need stripping every spring. This is a process of removing the overgrown topcoat by plucking with finger and thumb.

Size: UK/FCI: Dogs 14 ins (35 cms); bitches 13 ins (33 cms). US: No Standard available.

Temperament, training and exercise: The Jack Russell is bold, friendly and courageous. There is no doubting his intelligence, but it takes hard work and patience to channel this in the direction you want. The Jack Russell loves being on the go, and the main problem is to keep his concentration on you. Variety is the spice of life, and this applies to both training and exercise.

Health issues: Breeding stock must be eye-tested. Talk to the breeder about the occurrence of patella luxation, atazia and deafness.

- ## *Top tip…*

Early socialisation with other dogs is always important, but particularly so with the Jack Russell who thinks that he should take on all-comers. Go to training classes, and meet as many different breeds as possible in a calm, stress-free environment. In this way, your Jack Russell will learn the correct code of canine relationships.

- ## *Last word…*

Do not be deceived by the Jack Russell's handy size and think that this is an easy breed to own. Energetic, fearless, independent-minded, the Jack Russell presents a challenge to his owner – but if you are prepared to take this on, you will never look at another breed.

Labrador Retriever

• Comes from...

The east coast of Canada where they worked as fishermen's dogs, dragging nets ashore and retrieving fish that had fallen overboard. The breed was developed on its arrival in the UK – history tells of Labradors swimming ashore from the boats that brought fish from Newfoundland – and it soon became recognised as the all-round gundog, retrieving game over land and water.

• Good at...

Retrieving, swimming, Working Trials and Field Trials. Enjoys Agility, and can be successful in Competitive Obedience, although most Labradors do not have the precision seen in some of the other working breeds. A calm, intelligent nature has made the Labrador the most popular breed used as a guide dog for the blind, and he is also one of the top 'sniffer' dogs, detecting drugs, arms and explosives.

FACT FILE

Appearance: A strongly-built, medium-sized, active dog with a deep chest, a short loin and a level back. The Labrador's head is broad, and the medium-sized ears hang close to the head. The 'otter' tail is a breed characteristic; it is thick at the base, tapering towards the tip and covered in thick, dense coat.

Colours: Black, yellow (varying shades) or chocolate.

Coat/grooming: Short and dense with a weather-resistant undercoat. Low-maintenance.

Size: UK/FCI: Dogs 22-22.5 ins (56-57 cms); bitches 21.5-22 ins (54-56 cms).

US: Dogs 22.5-24.5 ins (57-62 cms); bitches 21.5-23.5 ins (54.5-60 cms).

Temperament, training and exercise: Biddable with a strong desire to please, the Labrador is one of the easiest dogs to train. He is generally laid-back and, given the correct education, he will be a loving family companion. The Labrador is also more than capable of taking on advanced training. Exercise should be limited during the growing period, but thereafter there is nothing a Labrador likes better than a free run, or even better, a swim.

Health issues: Breeding stock must be hip-scored. Puppies and parents should be eye-tested.

• *Needs...*

Human companionship, lots of exercise, fun and games.

• *Loves...*

Water, food, people, lots of walks with interesting scents.

• *Hates...*

Being left alone, being told off.

• *Top tip...*

The Labrador is famous for his love of food, and as a direct result, obesity is a real problem in the breed. Resist those pleading eyes – remember a lean dog is a healthy dog.

• *Last word...*

The Labrador is one of the most adaptable of dogs, and loves to be at the centre of family life. Do not choose this breed if you cannot give the company he requires.

Lhasa Apso

• Comes from...
Tibet, kept as a watchdog in Buddhist monasteries and in family homes, especially more wealthy households. In Tibetan, Lhasa Apso means either 'moustached lion dog' or 'barking hairy dog' (depending upon the translation).

• Good at...
Keeping watch.

• Needs...
Constant grooming attention.

• Loves...
Playing games, keeping an eye on proceedings from a discreet distance.

• Hates...
Mindless Obedience exercises, having his coat tugged by young children.

• Top tip...
Stubbornness can be a problem, and if an Apso digs his heels in, he can take some shifting! Try to avoid confrontations, and be firm and consistent when it matters.

• Last word...
Undemanding in terms of exercise, the Apso more than makes up for this with the attention needed on coat care. Some Apsos get on well with children, but are probably better suited to a household without youngsters.

FACT FILE

Appearance: A jaunty little dog, built on sturdy lines. He is well balanced with a relatively long back, and a high-set tail carried over his back. The Apso's head is distinctive, with heavy head furnishings which fall over the eyes, pronounced whiskers and a beard. The skull is quite narrow, framed by heavily-feathered ears. The eyes are dark and placed frontally.

Colours: A stunning variety – golden, sandy, honey, dark grizzle, slate, smoke, particolour, black, white or brown.

Coat/grooming: The topcoat is long, straight and hard in texture. The undercoat is moderate. This is a breed for the dedicated groomer, as regular brushing and combing sessions are required, along with frequent bathing.

Size: UK/FCI: Dogs 10 ins (25.4 cms); bitches slightly less. US: Dogs 10-11 ins (25.4-28 cms); bitches slightly less.

Temperament, training and exercise: Gay and assertive, the Lhasa Apso also has an independent streak, which means training can be a question of give and take. Loving and affectionate within his family, the Apso can be slightly wary with strangers. He is entirely adaptable as far as exercise is concerned, and stays fit with short but regular outings.

Health issues: Breeding stock should be eye-tested.

Maltese

- **Comes from...**

The Mediterranean area, with particular connections with Malta. The Maltese has a very long history, and small white Toy dogs were used as gifts by the Phoenicians as they sailed from country to country.

- **Good at...**

Companionship, making a sensation in the show ring.

- **Needs...**

A dedicated groomer.

- **Loves...**

Having fun and acting the clown.

- **Hates...**

Neglect.

- **Top tip...**

Get your Maltese puppy used to the grooming table, and to the routine of being groomed from the moment you have him, and then he will learn to accept the attention without resentment.

- **Last word...**

A beautiful little dog that is easy to live with. However, the grooming care needed to keep a Maltese in peak condition should not be underestimated.

FACT FILE

Appearance: An enchanting Toy dog that is sturdy and long-lived. The Maltese is well balanced, with a short, cobby body, and short, straight legs. The tail is feathered and carried over the back. The Maltese has long ears that lie close to the head, and dark, oval eyes, with a sweet, sparkling expression. The Maltese has a short, very rapid, trotting gait.

Colour: Pure white, sometimes with lemon markings.

Coat/grooming: A long, straight coat that is silky in texture. The coat demands an enormous amount of grooming, and this applies to the pet owner, who will have almost as much work as the show exhibitor – but the end result is really worthwhile. The coat can be trimmed down, but will still require a daily brush and comb.

Size: UK: Not to exceed 10 ins (25.5 cms), both sexes. US/FCI: Dogs 8.25-10 ins (21-25.5 cms); bitches 7.75-9 ins (19.7-23 cms).

Temperament, training and exercise: A sweet-tempered little dog who is a loving companion, but will also take part in fun and games with great zest. The Maltese responds to basic training and life will be more enjoyable for dog and owner if house rules are taught and obeyed. Exercise requirements are minimal.

Health issues: Patella luxation can be a problem.

Mastiff

- **Comes from...**

England. Records of Mastiff-type dogs
go back to Roman times, and in the 15th
century, Mastiffs were used as dogs of war,
going into battle and attacking the enemy.

- **Good at...**

Companionship, and, in the US, Mastiffs
have gained both Obedience and Utility titles.

- **Needs...**

Plenty of space to stretch out.

- **Loves...**

His family.

- **Hates...**

Being in disgrace, the breed has a particular
dislike of cats.

- **Top tip...**

The Mastiff undergoes phenomenal growth
during the first 12 months. It is essential to
feed a balanced diet that is not too high in
protein, and to limit exercise during this
vulnerable period. Always go down to your
dog – do not let him jump up.

- **Last word...**

The Mastiff is tolerant of people and
other animals, and is highly prized for his
companionship. However, the Mastiff's size
and weight must be taken into consideration,
and there are few that can provide a suitable
home for this heavyweight of the canine
world.

FACT FILE

Appearance: A truly massive dog, the Mastiff
should be symmetrical in frame with an appearance
of dignity and grandeur. The chest is wide and deep,
the legs stand four-square, and the hindquarters are
broad and muscular. The Mastiff's head is large with
a great breadth of skull. The muzzle is dark, the lips
are pendulous, and the eyes are small and set wide
apart.

Colours: Fawn, apricot or brindle.

Coat/grooming: A short, coarse outer coat,
and a dense undercoat. Grooming should be on
a routine basis.

Size: UK/FCI: No measurements given in the
Standard. US: Minimum height: Dogs 30 ins
(76 cms); bitches 27.5 ins (70 cms).

Temperament, training and exercise: A dog that
combines a unique blend of grandeur, docility and
courage. The Mastiff is slow to rouse, but can be
formidable when he feels threatened. However, in
general, the Mastiff is easy-going and tolerant. There
is no doubting his intelligence, and, in the US,
owners have had some success in Competitive
Obedience but, for most, a slow but steady
compliance with house rules is the norm. Regular
exercise is required to keep the Mastiff fit and
healthy.

Health issues: Gastric torsion must
be guarded against, breeding
stock should be hip-scored.

Miniature Schnauzer

- **Comes from...**
Germany, bred down from the Schnauzer and the Affenpinscher.

- **Good at...**
Obedience, Agility.

- **Needs...**
The attentions of an experienced groomer.

- **Loves...**
Being a lively, alert companion.

- **Hates...**
Repetitive training, being intelligent enough to learn the first time around.

- **Top tip...**
The Miniature Schnauzer's coat needs to be kept in tip-top condition, so make sure you go to a groomer who is experienced in caring for the breed,

- **Last word...**
An adaptable companion who suits all ages – ideal for the urban owner with limited space.

FACT FILE

Appearance: A smart, stylish-looking dog, the Miniature Schnauzer is sturdily built, robust and sinewy. The length of body is equal to the height at the shoulder; the back is strong and straight, and is slightly higher at the shoulders than the hindquarters. The tail is customarily docked. The head is most distinctive with its powerful muzzle, beard and shaggy eyebrows. In the US the ears are cropped – this is not the case in the UK.

Colours: Pepper and salt, black, black and silver.

Coat/grooming: A harsh, wiry coat (which is essential for show dogs) needs stripping every 6-8 weeks (approx). For the smart pet, clipping is required every 8-12 weeks, although clipping often results in the coat becoming softer in texture. Daily care is needed to keep the coat in good order, paying particular attention to leg hair, underneath (skirt) and to the beard. If a Miniature Schnauzer's coat was left without attention for six months, it would

be just fluffy undercoat. Stripping would be highly traumatic and would probably result in a bald or very moth-eaten-looking dog.

Size: UK: Dogs 14 ins (35.6 cms); bitches 13 ins (33 cms). US: 12-14 ins (30.5-33 cms), both sexes. FCI: 11.8-13.75 ins (30-35 cms), both sexes. Weight: 8.8-13.25 lbs (4-6 kgs), both sexes.

Temperament, training and exercise: Alert and intelligent, the Miniature Schnauzer is a most reliable dog. He is quick to learn, and training poses few problems. Exercise requirements are moderate.

Health issues: Progressive retinal atrophy and cataract may be inherited.

Newfoundland

• Good at...

All types of water work, draught work.

• Needs...

An owner who is not too house-proud.

• Loves...

Water (including rain), car rides (anybody's car!), carrying objects in his mouth.

• Hates...

Solitude.

• Top tip...

A large, heavyweight breed is very vulnerable while it is growing. Do not over-exercise your Newfie at this time, and make sure he does not put too much strain on his joints by going up and down stairs, or jumping in and out of the car.

• Comes from...

Newfoundland – kept by fishermen, so that the dogs could swim out from the boats to spread the fishing nets.

• Last word...

An exceptionally lovable dog, but beware of the slobber, the coat-shedding and the Newfie's love of mud and water...

FACT FILE

Appearance: A majestic-looking dog, giving an impression of power and strength. The Newfie has massive bone throughout. The chest is deep, the back is broad, and the hindquarters are strong and well built. The tail is of moderate length, and carried with a slight upward curve. The head is broad with a short muzzle. The eyes are small and dark, and the ears are set well back.

Colours: Black, brown, landseer (white with black markings).

Coat/grooming: A double coat that is oily and water-resistant. There is feathering on the legs and tail. Regular attention is needed to keep the coat free of mats, and judicious trimming of the feet and the ears is recommended. Coat-shedding is prodigious, but can be controlled with daily grooming sessions with a slicker brush.

Size: UK/US/FCI: Dogs 28 ins (71 cms); bitches 26 ins (66 cms). Weight: UK: Dogs 140-150 lbs (64-69 kgs); bitches 110-120 lbs (50-54.5 kgs).

US: Dogs 130-150 lbs (59-69 kgs); bitches 100-120 lbs (45.3-54.5 kgs). FCI: Dogs: 132 lbs (60 kgs); bitches 119 lbs (54 kgs).

Temperament, training and exercise: The Newfie is famed for his devoted nature, which makes him a most endearing companion. He is docile and eager to please, and will respond well to training. Some may be a little 'intense' during their teenage period. Newfies enjoy their exercise, particularly when water is involved. Avoid strenuous exercise in hot weather.

Health issues: Breeding stock should be hip-scored. Check out OCD and congenital heart defects.

Old English Sheepdog

• Comes from...

Britain, although it is thought that the larger European herding sheepdogs played a part in its development. The breed, often referred to as the Bobtail, was used for driving and minding sheep.

• Good at...

Herding tests; in the US they have been successful in Obedience and Flyball.

• Needs...

An owner who loves grooming – a task that should start from the day you bring your puppy home.

• Loves...

Being a 'nanny' to children.

• Hates...

Harsh handling.

• Top tip...

There are no short-cuts to caring for the OES coat, but the sooner you start training your puppy to accept grooming, the easier it will be. Be firm, and your OES will get the message.

• Last word...

If you are house-proud, this breed is best avoided. Far too many puppies end up in rescue shelters because people have not thought about the needs of an adult dog. However, if you have the time and space for this lovable shaggy clown – go for it!

FACT FILE

Appearance: A strong, square-built dog that is symmetrical in outline. The body is pear-shaped when viewed from above, with a gently rising topline. The forelegs are perfectly straight, and the hindquarters are muscular. The tail is customarily docked. The OES's head is in proportion to his body with a strong, square muzzle. The ears are small and set close to the head, and the eyes, which can be dark or blue in colour, are set well apart. When walking, the OES has a characteristic roll to his gait.

Colour: Any shade of grey, grizzle or blue, with a white head, neck and forequarters.

Coat/grooming: A shaggy coat that is harsh in texture, with a waterproof undercoat. Grooming is pretty much a full-time occupation, unless you want to take the easy way out and have your OES clipped.

Size: UK/FCI: Minimum height: Dogs 24 ins (61 cms); bitches 22 ins (56 cms). US: Minimum height: Dogs 22 ins (55.8 cms); bitches 21 ins (53.3 cms).

Temperament, training and exercise: A faithful, trustworthy dog that is gentle and kindly towards all members of the family, but is particularly fond of children. Bred as a working dog, the OES is capable of reaching a reasonable standard of Obedience. A dog that enjoys the outdoor life – regardless of what it does to his coat!

Health issues: Breeding stock should be eye-tested.

Pekingese

- **Comes from...**
China. This aristocrat of the canine world has origins that stretch back to the Tang Dynasty when they were kept as the royal favourites of the Chinese Emperor.

- **Good at...**
Companionship.

- **Needs...**
To be appreciated for his own unique charm.

- **Loves...**
Investigating.

- **Hates...**
Being wet and bedraggled.

- **Top tip...**
The Pekingese has a will of his own, so do not get backed into a corner with training. Patience is the key – you will get there in the end!

- **Last word...**
The Pekingese loves his family and gets on well with children if he is brought up with them. The adult Pekingese, who is not used to youngsters, may be somewhat reticent.

FACT FILE

Appearance: The Pekingese is a small Toy dog, but is surprisingly sturdy. The neck is short and thick, the chest is short and broad, and the back is level. The forelegs are short and heavily boned; the hindlegs are lighter than the forelegs. The tail is set on high and is carried over the back. A rolling gait is typical of the breed. The leonine head and expression of the Pekingese is famous, and the large head, with the large, lustrous eyes gives a very special appeal.

Colours: All colours – both solid and particolours.

Coat/grooming: Long, straight, and harsh in texture, with a thick undercoat. The mane, which extends beyond the shoulders, coupled with the profuse feathering on the ears and legs, means that daily grooming is essential.

Size: UK/FCI: Not to exceed: Dogs 11 lbs (5 kgs); bitches 12 lbs (5.5 kgs). US: Not to exceed: 14 lbs (6.3 kgs), both sexes.

Temperament, training and exercise: The little lion dog truly has the courage of a lion, and this is coupled with great loyalty. The Pekingese can appear aloof to those outside his family circle. Stubbornness is a characteristic of the breed, so training can pose a challenge. The inquisitive Pekingese enjoys going out and about, and this will amply fulfil his exercise needs.

Health issues: Check out eye problems and back problems.

Pomeranian

- **Comes from...**
Germany, descended from the larger Spitz-type dogs of the Arctic.

- **Good at...**
Giving warning of the approach of strangers.

- **Needs...**
A secure home and garden – Poms can squeeze through the smallest of spaces.

- **Loves...**
Investigating.

- **Hates...**
Being shut away.

- **Top tip...**
A member of the Spitz group of dogs, the Pom shares the vocal characteristics of his larger relatives. This is fine up to a point; however, get in early with your training if you want a bit of peace and quiet.

- **Last word...**
A tiny dog that can give a huge amount of pleasure to his owners – particularly suitable for those getting on in years, as exercise demands are minimal. Beware! You never own a Pom – he owns you.

FACT FILE

Appearance: Small and compact, the Pom is neatly put together with clean shoulders, a short back, and fine-boned legs. The tail is high-set and carried over the back. The Pom has a foxy head, with small ears carried erect, and bright, dark eyes showing great intelligence. Characteristically, the Pom has a brisk, buoyant movement.

Colours: Orange, orange sable, cream, wolf sable, black, white.

Coat/grooming: A soft undercoat, and a straight topcoat that is harsh in texture. The coat grows in a mane around the neck to the shoulders, and there is feathering on the forequarters, the hindlegs, and the tail. Weekly grooming is required to keep the coat tangle-free.

Size: UK: Dogs 4-4.5 lbs (1.8-2 kgs); bitches 4.5-5.5 lbs (2-2.5 kgs). US: 3-7 lbs (1.4-3.2 kgs), both sexes. FCI: 7-8.5 ins (18-22 cms), both sexes.

Temperament, training and exercise: A bouncy, extrovert character, the Pom likes to be in the thick of things, investigating everything that is going on. Bright and intelligent, the Pom enjoys the challenge of training, and enjoys performing tricks. His exercise needs are moderate.

Health issues:
Patella luxation.

Poodle

Left: Standard Poodle

century in Germany that describe large Poodle-type dogs being used to disturb and retrieve game from the water.

• **Good at...**
Competitive Obedience, Agility, Canine Freestyle (Heelwork to Music).

• **Needs...**
Love and companionship, as well as regular attention to the non-shedding coat.

• **Loves...**
Participating with his owner in any chosen occupation.

• **Hates...**
Being chastised, dried food (which tends to make them hyperactive).

• **Top tip...**
Regardless of size, this is an intelligent dog and should be treated accordingly. Poodle owners must have a sense of humour.

• **Comes from...**
Russia, France, and Germany all lay claim to the evolution of this breed. Certainly there are records dating back to the 16th

Left: Four-month-old Miniature Poodle puppy.
Above: Toy Poodle.

• *Last word...*

The Poodle usually has it! An entertaining, kind breed to own – but one that is King. Do take all those trips to the groomer into account.

Left and below: Miniature Poodles.

FACT FILE

Appearance: There are three sizes of Poodle – Toy, Miniature and Standard. They all share the same Breed Standard (the written blueprint of the breed); it is size alone that separates the three varieties.

The Poodle is a well-balanced, elegant dog that is light on his feet, but has substance. The tail, which is carried at a slight angle away from the body, is customarily docked. The head is long and fine, with a strong, well-chiselled foreface. The eyes are dark and almond-shaped, and the ears are long and hang close to the face.

Colours: A wonderful range that includes white, cream, apricot, red, black, brown, silver, and blue. The colour is solid, but varying shades appear on the ears, and during the coat change from puppy to adult.

Coat/grooming: Unlike most dogs, the Poodle does not shed his coat, which makes him the perfect choice for those suffering from asthma or hair allergies. Routine daily grooming is required, and the coat needs to be clipped at 4-6 week intervals. There is a variety of clips to choose from, and this will mostly depend on whether you plan to show your Poodle. The Lamb trim is the most popular for the smaller variety, while the larger Poodle often sports the Utility/Sporting clip. Show dogs have a traditional style of their own.

Size: UK: *Toy:* Up to 11 ins (28 cms). *Miniature:* 11-15 ins (28-38 cms). *Standard:* Over 15 ins (38 cms). US: *Toy:* Up to 10 ins

(25 cms). *Miniature:* 10-15 ins (25-38 cms). *Standard:* Over 15 ins (38 cms). FCI: *Toy:* Up to 11 ins (28 cms). *Miniature:* 11-13.75 ins (28-35 cms). *Standard:* The FCI has two categories which fall into the UK/US 'Standard' category. They are: *Medium:* 13.75-17.75 ins (35-45 cms). *Large:* 17.75-24.5 ins (45-62 cms). All measurements apply to both sexes.

Temperament, training and exercise: The Poodle is a warm, intelligent dog of great character, giving equally as much affection as it receives. A good-natured dog who likes to entertain, is eager to please, and enthusiastic about joining in with everything that is going on.

The temperament and suitability for work varies with the size – the Standard Poodle tends to be more passive in his approach. All varieties are easy to train, but like to think for themselves.

Obviously exercise varies according to size – although walking and free-running is enjoyed by all Poodles. The Standard, a big, robust dog, needs plenty of exercise, but this should be regulated while he is growing.

Health issues: Inherited diseases are minimal and vary according to size. The smaller varieties should be eye-tested before breeding.

Pug

- **Comes from...**

China, where snub-nosed dogs found favour. The Pug came to Europe with traders of the Dutch East India Company, and was adopted as a royal favourite. When William of Orange went to be King of England in 1688, he took his beloved Pugs with him, and the breed's popularity soared.

- **Good at...**

Being attuned to their owner.

- **Needs...**

Companionship and warmth – a Pug is a people dog, and should never be left alone for long periods.

- **Loves...**

Being loved, food!

- **Hates...**

Walking through puddles, though many like a supervised swim.

- **Top tip...**

The Pug's short nose means that he overheats more quickly than other dogs, so never leave your Pug out in the sun for long periods, and do not exercise him when it is warm.

- **Last word...**

A friendly, adaptable dog who gets on well with people of all ages, and mixes well with other dogs. Most owners become terrific Pug enthusiasts, and would never consider owning another breed – despite the snoring!

FACT FILE

Appearance: A compact, cobby little dog that is basically square in shape. Although it is a Toy breed, the Pug has quite a thick-set appearance with strong legs and a wide chest. The tail is high-set and tightly curled. The Pug has a large, round head with a short, blunt muzzle. The eyes are large and lustrous, and have a melting expression, which becomes fiery when the Pug is excited. A breed characteristic is a slight roll of the hindquarters when moving.

Colours: Silver, apricot, fawn or black.

Coat/grooming: A fine, smooth coat which needs little more than a regular brush, particularly when the coat is shedding.

Size: UK/US/FCI: 14-18 lbs (6.3-8.1 kgs), both sexes.

Temperament, training and exercise: The Pug is an even-tempered dog which thrives on companionship.

He is alert and intelligent, and is perfectly capable of responding to training. Exercise requirements are moderate, but a Pug is very playful, and will enjoy periods of activity.

Health issues: Rare cases of hip dysplasia; patella luxation can be a problem.

Pyrenean Mountain Dog

- **Comes from...**
The Pyrenean mountains in France, where it was used as a guardian of the flock.

- **Good at...**
Carting, backpacking.

- **Needs...**
Plenty of space, and an owner who does not mind dog hair and slobber.

- **Loves...**
Human companionship.

- **Hates...**
The heat.

- **Top tip...**
The Pyrenean was bred to protect the flock, and this instinctive guarding ability is still very much apparent. Let your Pyrenean guard his home and family, but do not over-encourage this side of his nature.

- **Last word...**
A beautiful dog with a quiet, but distinctive personality. Definitely not for the apartment dweller.

FACT FILE

Appearance: An imposing dog of great size and substance, the Pyrenean Mountain Dog is strong and well balanced. The shoulders are powerful, the chest is broad, and there should be a good length of back. The hindquarters are strong and muscular, and the tail is long, carried low when the dog is in repose, and carried high above the back when he is alert. The head is strong, but with no hint of coarseness. The eyes are almond-shaped and dark amber-brown in colour, with a regal, kindly expression; the ears are relatively small and triangular in shape.

Colour: White, but they may have patches of pale yellow or wolf-grey on the head, the ears, the base of the tail, and a few on the body.

Coat/grooming: A profuse undercoat, and a longer topcoat that is coarse in texture. Daily grooming is essential – and when the coat sheds, you will know all about it!

Size: UK: Minimum height: Dogs 28 ins (70 cms); bitches 26 ins (65 cms). US: Dogs 27-32 ins (69-81 cms); bitches 25-29 ins (63.5-73.6 cms). FCI: Dogs 27.5-31.5 ins (70-80 cms); bitches 25.5-28.25 ins (65-72 cms). Weight: Dogs 132 lbs (60 kgs); bitches 99 lbs (45 kgs).

Temperament, training and exercise: A noble, confident dog, the Pyrenean is not one of the world's extroverts but gives quiet, loyal companionship. He is often wary of strangers until introductions have been made. Start training early, as the Pyrenean will grow into a very large and powerful dog, but do not expect lightning responses. Exercise is a must, and, although the pace is not fast, the Pyrenean thrives on long, interesting rambles.

Health issues: Breeding stock should be hip-scored.

Rhodesian Ridgeback

- **Comes from...**
Southern Africa, famed as a fearless hunter of lions and other big game but was also used as a guard on the big farms.

- **Good at...**
Guarding, Tracking, lure coursing, Agility.

- **Needs...**
Mental challenges, and a 'pack leader' he can respect.

- **Loves...**
Children, working with his owner.

- **Hates...**
Repetitive Obedience exercises.

- **Top tip...**
The Ridgeback has a very long memory, so think before you act. If you treat your dog unfairly, he will not forget.

- **Last word...**
The Ridgeback is a marvellous breed for the experienced, dedicated dog owner who understands the canine mind. An ideal family companion who should always be treated with respect.

FACT FILE

Appearance: Breed pioneers used the Dalmatian as the basis of what a Rhodesian Ridgeback should look like, and the athletic, symmetrical outline of the two breeds has much in common. The Ridgeback is a strikingly handsome dog, with dark, sparkling eyes that have a typically intelligent expression. Male and female characteristics are clearly defined. The most striking breed characteristic is the ridge – a symmetrical formation of hair growing in the opposite direction to the main coat on the back.

Colours: A range of shades from light wheaten to red wheaten.

Coat/grooming: A short dense coat that looks sleek and glossy. It is very easy to care for.

Size: UK/US/FCI: Dogs 25-27 ins (63-67 cms); bitches 24-26 ins (61-66 cms).

Temperament, training and exercise: A loyal companion who is devoted to all members of his human family, but tends to be aloof with strangers. The Ridgeback is a self-confident dog, and is a natural guard. However, he should show no trace of aggression towards people. This is a breed that needs firm and consistent handling from an early age. He will respond well to all training challenges, but has a short attention span and will become bored by too much repetition. Built on athletic lines, the Ridgeback needs exercise on a regular basis.

Health issues: Puppies must be tested for dermoid sinus.

Rottweiler

● Comes from...

Germany, named after the town of Rottweil in the Black Forest. Rottweilers were originally used as a herding or droving dog, taking cattle to market and guarding their master – and his money – on the way home.

● Good at...

Most things – Tracking, Working Trials (UK), Carting, Herding, Agility, Flyball, Competitive Obedience.

● Needs...

Extensive socialisation, i.e. exposure to the sights and sounds of the outside world, including people of all ages, sizes and cultural backgrounds; a clear sense of structure in the household – the dog is not No. 1; involvement with his family; mental stimulation.

● Loves...

Being given an important job to do.

FACT FILE

Appearance: A large, imposing-looking dog, the Rottweiler gives an impression of strength and power. Compact in build, he has a deep chest, a strong, straight back, and muscular hindquarters. The tail is customarily docked to the first joint. The Rottweiler's head is broad, with small ears set wide apart. The typical expression is calm, indicating good humour.

Colour: Rich tan markings on a glossy, black background.

Coat/grooming: Medium length, lies flat to the body and is coarse in texture. Easy to care for with basic grooming.

Size: UK: Dogs 25-27 ins (63-69 cms); bitches 23-25 ins (58-63.5 cms). US: Dogs 24-27 ins (60-69 cms); bitches 22-25 ins (56-63.5 cms). FCI: Dogs 24-26 ins (61-68 cms); bitches 22-25 ins (56-63 cms). Weight: Dogs 110 lbs (50 kgs); bitches: 92.5 lbs (42 kgs).

Temperament, training and exercise: Bold and confident, independent, dignified and self-possessed, the Rottweiler may appear slightly aloof with strangers. This is a highly intelligent dog with a strong guarding instinct, so kind, firm and consistent training, especially in manners, is needed right from the start so that your Rottweiler accepts that you are the pack leader. Bred as a working dog, the breed needs plenty of exercise – it is important that he stays fit and active, and that size and substance do not degenerate to bulk. Short walks daily will suffice until the puppy is about six months old. Thereafter exercise should be *gradually* increased.

Health issues: Breeding stock should be hip-scored and eye-tested. Puppies should be eye-tested. Watch out for Osteochondrosis (OCD) a condition that affects developing bones and joints in the heavier, fast-growing breeds.

• *Hates...*

Having nothing to do, limited contact with humans, being tied up or confined in a small yard.

• *Top tip...*

Harsh handling, shouting and threatening never wins the day – particularly if you are dealing with a highly intelligent Rottweiler, who will react to such behaviour with stubbornness and defiance. When it is needed, enforce discipline, quietly, calmly and consistently. Make training fun for your Rottweiler, then it will be fun for you too – and he will learn more quickly.

• *Last word...*

With his size, strength and noble looks, the Rottweiler is one of the most impressive of all breeds. Make sure you choose a Rottie for the right reasons: because you want a challenging dog to train as a useful, lifelong companion – not because you think a 'macho' breed will make you look good.

Samoyed

• Comes from...
Northern Russia where they were used to herd reindeer. They take their name from a nomadic tribe known as the Samoyeds.

• Good at...
Sled-pulling/racing with rigs, skijoring, weight-pulling, pack hiking, herding.

• Needs...
An owner who is prepared to give a daily five-minute brush, with an additional full grooming session of about an hour per week to keep the dense white coat in good order.

• Loves...
People (especially children), car rides.

• Hates...
Lack of attention, being left alone for any length of time.

• Top tip...
Excited yapping may greet visitors to the house, but this can be overcome with a firm command of "No" or "Quiet".

• Last word...
A marvellous family dog, but Sams do love to dig the garden. If this creates a problem, a special digging area should be allocated and fenced.

FACT FILE

Appearance: A medium-sized, well-balanced dog, the Samoyed is strong and active, but also gives an impression of gracefulness. The neck is strong and proudly arched, the back is broad and muscular, and the legs are straight and strong. The tail is long and carried over the back. The Sam's head is powerful and wedge-shaped. The ears are thick and set well apart, the eyes are dark and almond-shaped and the mouth curves up at the corners – all features combining to create the famous smiling expression that is so characteristic of the breed.

Colour: White; they can also be white and biscuit, and cream.

Coat/grooming: A soft undercoat with harsh hair growing through it to produce a weather-resistant topcoat. A certain amount of work is needed to keep the coat in top condition. This is an integral part of Sam ownership. Should be bathed for shows, but otherwise, only when really necessary, since the daily grooming should keep the coat clean.

Size: UK: Dogs 20-22 ins (51-56 cms); bitches 18-20 ins (46-51 cms). US: Dogs 21-23.5 ins (53.5-60 cms); bitches 19-21 ins (48.2-53.5 cms). FCI: Dogs 21.3-23.7 ins (53-59 cms); bitches 11-13.5 ins (50-56 cms).

Temperament, training and exercise: A superb temperament is a hallmark of the breed. Sams love people; they are cheerful, mischievous, and eager to please. Training should start early since Sams can sometimes be stubborn and require firm but gentle handling. Some have a tendency to pull on the lead. Regular exercise is a must for this lively dog who thrives on variety.

Health issues: Breeding stock should be hip-scored.

Shetland Sheepdog

• Comes from...
The Shetland Isles in north-east Scotland where they were used for herding sheep.

• Good at...
Herding, Competitive Obedience, Agility, Flyball.

• Needs...
To be treated as an active companion, rather than an ornament.

• Loves...
Pleasing his owner.

• Hates...
Lack of companionship. (The Sheltie is not a fidgety, busy-busy dog; provided his owner is nearby, he will be happy to lie peacefully for hours at a time.)

• Top tip...
Alert, vigilant and quick-thinking, the Sheltie can become overexcited, which is not desirable. Make sure you are calm and firm in all your dealings so you bring out the best in him.

• Last word...
Beautiful to look at, eager to please, and convenient in size, the Sheltie makes an ideal companion. However, it is important to remember that this is a working breed which needs companionship, regular exercise and a sensible diet.

FACT FILE

Appearance: A small working dog of great beauty, the Sheltie is a symmetrical dog, without coarseness or cloddiness. The chest is deep, and the body is slightly longer than the height at the shoulders. The tail is set on low, and reaches down to the hock. The Sheltie's head is refined with medium-sized, almond-shaped eyes that are set obliquely. The ears are small and set fairly close together on top of the skull; they are carried semi-erect when the dog is alert.

Colours: Sable (pale gold to deep mahogany), tricolour (black, white and tan), blue merle (silvery blue splashed with black), black and white or black and tan.

Coat/grooming: A soft, close undercoat with a harsh, straight outer coat, an abundant mane, and feathering on the legs and tail. This is a coat that needs regular weekly grooming, plus an occasional tidy-up, but the workload steps up when the coat is shedding.

Size: UK/FCI: Dogs 14.5 ins (37 cms); bitches 14 ins (35.5 cms). US: 13-16 ins (33-40.5 cms), both sexes.

Temperament, training and exercise: An affectionate dog that is always eager to please. The Sheltie shows a slight reserve towards strangers. Bred to work, the Sheltie thrives on training challenges, and will do well in most canine activities. Although relatively small in size, the Sheltie will enjoy a routine of regular exercise.

Health issues: Breeding stock should be eye-tested.

Shih Tzu

- **Comes from...**

China, with roots also in Tibet. In the Buddhist religion it was believed that a monk who had transgressed in his life was reincarnated in the form of a Lhasa Apso – one of the Shih Tzu's ancestors. Apsos were used as tribute gifts for safe passage from Tibet to China, where the Shih Tzu evolved as a separate breed.

- **Good at...**

Begging (a breed characteristic), retrieving, Mini-agility.

- **Needs...**

Dedicated grooming, unless he is put into a pet trim.

- **Loves...**

Being the centre of attention, playing games, taking his ease in comfort.

- **Hates...**

Being ignored.

- **Top tip...**

The Shih Tzu has a decidedly independent, mischievous streak. Watch out for that gleeful expression when your Shih Tzu decides to 'forget' his training and make a fool of you!

- **Last word...**

A fun-loving, adaptable dog, the Shih Tzu is an ideal companion – provided you can face the grooming. Getting on well with other dogs is a characteristic of the breed.

FACT FILE

Appearance: A sturdy dog with an abundant coat, and a chrysanthemum-like face. The Shih Tzu has an Oriental appearance and looks full of his own importance. The legs are short and muscular, and the back is slightly longer than the height of the dog at the shoulder. The tail is heavily feathered and is carried gaily over the back. The head is broad, the ears large and drooping, and the eyes are dark and round, placed wide apart.

Colours: All colours, both solid and particolours.

Coat/grooming: Long and dense with a good undercoat. Daily grooming sessions are essential. A dog must be checked thoroughly after every walk to ensure he has not picked up any debris in his coat, and regular bathing is needed to keep him fresh and clean. A pet trim reduces the workload drastically.

Size: UK/FCI: 10.5 ins (26.7 cms), both sexes.
US: 8-11 ins (20-28 cms), both sexes.

Temperament, training and exercise: Friendly and outgoing, the Shih Tzu has a positive outlook on life, and takes most situations in his stride. He is quick-witted and intelligent, and enjoys fun-training sessions. Exercise needs are moderate, but the Shih Tzu can keep going for longer than you would expect, and, given the opportunity, will enjoy a long ramble.

Health issues: Some breathing problems associated with tight nostrils – check with the breeder.

Siberian Husky

• Comes from...

North-eastern Asia. The breeed was developed by the nomadic Chukchi tribe to pull loads over long distances at a moderate speed.

• Good at...

Working in harness on snow, or on dirt where climatic considerations prevail.

• Needs...

Large amounts of exercise.

• Loves...

Free-running in harness in large, secure areas.

• Hates...

Being isolated and bored.

• Top tip...

The Siberian Husky has something of a wanderlust so, if you are thinking of owning one, security is the name of the game. The garden must be well fenced – and that does not just mean providing high fencing. A Sibe is quite likely to dig his way out.

• Last word...

A dog of striking appearance, with a great temperament, but think at least twice before you plunge into Sibe ownership. The need for extensive exercise must be taken very seriously. However, the Sibe must never be let off the lead because his natural hunting instincts mean he will kill for survival.

FACT FILE

Appearance: The fastest of the sled dogs, the Siberian Husky is light in build and quick on his feet. He is medium-sized, with a strong, straight back; the tail, which resembles a fox's brush, is carried over the back when the dog is alert. The head also has a fox-like appearance, with medium-sized ears set close together and carried erect. The eyes are a feature of the breed; they may be any shade of blue or brown, one of each colour, or particoloured.

Colours: All colours, often with striking markings on the head.

Coat/grooming: A soft, dense undercoat, and a straight, smooth-lying topcoat. Although the Siberian Husky appears well furred, his coat is relatively easy to care for. Extra attention is needed when the undercoat is shedding.

Size: UK: Dogs 21-23 ins (53-58.5 cms); bitches 20-22 ins (51-56 cms). US/FCI: Dogs 21-23.5 ins (53-61.2 cms); bitches 20-22 ins (51-56 cms). Weight: UK/US/FCI: Dogs 45-60 lbs (20.5-27.2 kgs); bitches 35-50 lbs (16-22.7 kgs).

Temperament, training and exercise: A sweet temperament is a hallmark of the breed; most people find the Siberian Husky a surprisingly friendly dog that is easy to live with. He has no instinct to guard, and shows no aggression with other dogs. Training and socialisation should begin at an early age, but should present few problems. A regime of extensive exercise is absolutely essential. A very vocal breed; if you keep more than one Sibe, they may well set up a chorus of howling – which could make you unpopular with the neighbours!

Health issues: Breeding stock should be hip-scored and eye-tested.

St Bernard

• Comes from...

The Swiss Alps, developed by the monks of the Hospice of the Great St Bernard, to rescue travellers lost in the mountains.

• Good at...

Search and rescue, and draught work.

• Needs...

Very careful rearing. Strict attention must be paid to providing the correct diet, and limiting exercise, during the vulnerable growing period.

• Loves...

Children.

• Hates...

Nail-clipping, so work hard at getting your Saint used to this routine from puppyhood.

• Top tip...

The St Bernard has a marked tendency to slaver. If a St Bernard shakes – take cover!

• Last word...

A wonderful, noble companion, but think twice before taking on a dog that will eat 4-5 lbs of meat and biscuits per day when fully grown.

FACT FILE

Appearance: A dog of great substance but the general impression should be of an animal that is well proportioned and symmetrical. The shoulders are broad and sloping, the chest is wide and deep, the back is straight, and the hindquarters are muscular. The tail is set on low. The skull has a huge circumference and, by comparison, the muzzle is short. The eyes are dark, with a kindly, benevolent expression, and the ears lie close to the cheeks.

Colour: Mahogany brindle, red brindle, or orange with white markings on the muzzle, blaze, collar, chest, forelegs, feet and tail end.

Coat/grooming: The rough coat is dense and flat with feathering; the smooth coat is short, and is tough without feeling rough to the touch. The rough coat needs more grooming attention to keep it in good order.

Size: UK: The Standard states, *"Taller the better, so long as symmetry is maintained"*. US/FCI: Min height: Dogs 27.5 ins (70 cms); bitches 25.5 ins (65 cms).

Temperament, training and exercise: The St Bernard is utterly trustworthy in temperament which makes him an ideal family dog as long as you have the space, and you are able to meet all those food bills! Some Saints can be over-enthusiastic, particularly if a loved one has returned home, so it is essential to teach basic manners, such as not jumping up, from a very early age. St Bernards do not require a great deal of exercise but it is important to keep to a routine of regular walks so as to guard against obesity.

Health issues: Hip dysplasia is a problem in the breed. Some predisposition towards heart defects.

Weimaraner

- ### Comes from...
Weimar, a republic of Germany, where they were used to hunt deer and wild boar, as well as ground game and birds.

- ### Good at...
Working gundog, Agility, Working Trials (UK), Tracking, Field Trials.

- ### Needs...
An owner he can love and respect.

- *Loves...*

Long rambles in the country with lots of interesting scents.

- *Hates...*

Being excluded from his family.

- *Top tip...*

The Weimaraner is protective of his home and family, which is a natural asset that

emerges without training. Do not attempt to over-encourage this aspect of your Weimaraner's behaviour or his instinct to protect will dominate his character.

- *Last word...*

A wonderful family companion that is intelligent enough to be successful at virtually all the canine sports. However, the Weimaraner's behaviour or his instinct to protect will dominate his character.

FACT FILE

Appearance: A medium-sized aristocratic looking dog, the Weimaraner should present a picture of power, stamina and balance. The head is long with high-set ears, and medium-sized, round eyes, which can be amber or blue-grey in colour. The neck is strong – a throwback to his hunting days when a Weimaraner could retrieve game as big as a fox with ease. The topline is level, and the tail is customarily docked.

Colour: The silver-grey colour is the Weimaraner's most distinctive feature, and this, with his pale eyes, led to him being dubbed the 'grey ghost' of the canine world.

Coat/grooming: Short-haired Weimaraners, which are seen most commonly, have a short sleek coat which is very easy to care for. The long-haired Weimaraner's coat (bottom left) is about 1-2 ins (2.5-5 cms) in length, with feathering on the tail and the back of the legs. This needs considerably more care, and regular brushing and combing is a must.

Size: UK: Dogs 24-27 ins (61-69 cms); bitches 22-25 ins (56-64 cms). US: Dogs 25-27 ins (64-69 cms); bitches 23-25 ins (58.5-64 cms). FCI: Dogs: 23.25-27.5 ins (60-70 cms); bitches 22.5-25.5 ins (57-65.25 cms). Weight: Dogs 30-40 lbs (13.6-18 kgs); bitches 55-77 lbs (25-35 kgs).

Temperament, training and exercise: Alert, intelligent and fearless, the Weimaraner also has a slightly protective streak in his nature. Mental stimulation is essential, and he will relish all training challenges. Bred as a working dog, the Weimaraner needs plenty of exercise, and is better suited to country living.

Health issues: Breeding stock should be hip-scored.

Welsh Corgi (Pembroke)

• Comes from…
South-west Wales, where it was used as a cattle drover.

• Good at…
Herding. In the US, these dogs are successful in Obedience and Tracking.

• Needs…
Something to occupy his mind.

• Loves…
Being the boss.

• Hates…
Missing out on the action.

• Top tip…
Obesity is a serious problem in the breed – generally the result of too little exercise, and too many treats. Make sure you never allow your Pembroke to become obese, as it will seriously impair the quality of his life, as well as leading to serious health problems.

• Last word…
An adaptable dog that will suit a variety of different lifestyles but, remember, a bored, idle Pembroke can become yappy and fail to show the excellent sound temperament that is truly typical of the breed.

FACT FILE

Appearance: A sturdy low-set dog that gives an impression of substance and stamina. The legs are short, the chest is deep, the back is level and the tail is short. The Pembroke has a fox-like head, with an alert, intelligent expression. The ears are pricked, and the eyes are round and brown, blending with the coat colour.

Colours: Red, sable, fawn, black and tan, with or without white markings.

Coat/grooming: A medium-length coat with a dense undercoat. Generally, the coat is easy to care for, but watch out for the seasonal shedding, which has to be seen to be believed.

Size: UK/US/FCI: 10-12 ins (25.5-30.5 cms), both sexes. Weight: Dogs 22-26 lbs (10-12 kgs); bitches 20-24 lbs (10-11 kgs). US weight restrictions: Not to exceed: Dogs 30 lbs (13.6 kgs); bitches 28 lbs (12.63 kgs).

Temperament, training and exercise: A breed of extrovert character; his bold approach to life often belies his small size. Bright and intelligent, the Pembroke is quick to learn – and is equally swift in his efforts to outsmart his owner! Despite his small size, the Pembroke relishes exercise, and regular outings should be part of his daily life.

Health issues: Health surveys reveal no major problems.

- **Good at...**
  Earth dog events, Mini-agility.

- **Needs...**
  To be treated like a proper dog; this is a terrier and he does not want to be mollycoddled.

- **Loves...**
  A chance to follow his nose on exciting rambles.

- **Hates...**
  Being excluded from family activities.

West Highland White Terrier

- **Top tip...**
  The more you wash a Westie's coat, the more quickly it gets dirty. The secret to a clean coat is regular brushing.

- **Last word...**
  The Westie is a deservedly popular breed to keep, and his adaptable nature is his greatest asset.

- **Comes from...**
  North west of Scotland, originally used for hunting fox, badger and otter.

FACT FILE

Appearance: A small sturdy dog with a relatively large head. The ears are small and erect, and the dark-coloured eyes have a bright, alert expression. The body is short with a level back and a good depth of chest. The tail is straight and carried upright, and is often referred to as 'carrot-shaped'.

Colour: A pure, sparkling white.

Coat/grooming: A short, straight outer coat which is harsh in texture, and a soft undercoat. The Westie's coat keeps on growing, and needs to be trimmed at least three times a year to keep it in good order. Show exhibitors get the best results by hand-stripping, which is a laborious process where the dead coat is plucked out between finger and thumb. This is done on an almost daily basis to achieve a neat, yet natural appearance.

Size: UK/FCI: 11 ins (28 cms), both sexes. US: Dogs 11 ins (28 cms); bitches 10 ins (25.5 cms).

Temperament, training and exercise: The Westie is a friendly, outgoing dog, who fits in well with most family situations. Originally bred as a working terrier, he has an independent mind and an active body. Establish the house rules and stick to them, and make sure you give your Westie something interesting to do. Exercise need not be strenuous, but it should be regular and varied.

Health issues: Legge-Perthes disease can be a problem.

Whippet

- **Comes from...**
Developed in England, probably from the Greyhound. The Whippet became popular for rabbit coursing in the late 19th century.

- **Good at...**
Lure coursing.

- **Needs...**
Love and affection, preferably from one 'special' person.

- **Loves...**
Comfort and warmth.

- **Hates...**
Being cold and wet, being frightened.

- **Top tip...**
The Whippet is a sporting dog, and his instincts and speed of reactions are fully intact. If you keep other small animals and birds, their safety cannot be guaranteed. Instinct will outweigh house rules.

- **Last word...**
The Whippet is adaptable – castle or cottage will do, as long as he has the same owner. The Whippet thrives as a fully integrated member of the family, but will select only one as his special person to whom he gives total devotion.

FACT FILE

Appearance: A medium-sized sighthound that has very similar conformation to the Greyhound. The Whippet is built for speed, but has an unmistakable air of elegance. The head is long and lean, tapering to the muzzle; the eyes are oval with a bright, alert expression, and the ears are rose-shaped. The chest is very deep, the back is broad with a distinct arch over the loin, and the hindquarters are strong and well developed. The tail is long and, when moving, it is carried in a delicate upward curve.

Colours: The Whippet can be any colour or mixture of colours.

Coat/grooming: The coat is fine and short, and so grooming is very straightforward.

Size: UK/FCI: Dogs 18.5-20 ins (47-51 cms); bitches 17-18.5 ins (44-47 cms). US: Dogs 19-22 ins (48.25-56 cms); bitches 18-21 ins (47-53.5 cms).

Temperament, training and exercise: A gentle, affectionate dog that is sensitive, although he shows exuberance in play and when greeting people. The Whippet is not a candidate for top-level Obedience competition, as endless repetitive training is not compatible with the breed. However, the Whippet is quick to learn many words he sees as appropriate to his daily life. The youthful Whippet is notorious for his energy and mischief, but, providing he is brought up with kindness and firmness, he will be easy to live with – eventually! Bred on sporting lines, the Whippet relishes the opportunity to free-run, and will need at least two miles of exercise per day.

Health issues: No specific problems, but the breed keeps in better health if fed on simple, unprocessed food.

Yorkshire Terrier

- **Comes from…**

Yorkshire in the UK, bred from a mixture of terriers that travelled south from Scotland with their owners to find work in the mines and factories at the time of the Industrial Revolution. The Yorkshire Terrier was a man-made creation, bred to keep rats at bay at home and at work, and to compete in the famous rat pits in public houses.

- **Good at…**

The glamour game, Mini-agility – some have also been successful in Competitive Obedience.

- **Needs…**

To be taken seriously, as befits a terrier breed.

- **Loves…**

Being given things to do.

- **Hates…**

Being left alone.

- **Top tip…**

Do not make the mistake of overindulging your Yorkie and turning him into a spoilt, pampered pooch. Treat him like a dog, and you will be rewarded with the companionship of one of the great characters of the canine world.

- **Last word…**

The diminutive Yorkie really is a dog that you can take anywhere; he will fit in with all family situations, and will thrive in the town or in the country.

FACT FILE

Appearance: A compact, neat little dog, with a great air of his own importance. The Yorkie's head is small, with V-shaped ears which are carried erect. The eyes are dark and sparkling with a sharp, intelligent expression. The tail is customarily docked.

Colour: Dark steel-blue with a rich tan on the head and legs.

Coat/grooming: The Yorkie's coat is his crowning glory – it is long and straight, and silky in texture. A Yorkie that is kept in full coat requires a phenomenal amount of grooming care and the long coat needs to be protected with crackers, which is a method of folding the coat in small packets of tissue paper and fastening them with rubber-bands. The pet Yorkie can be clipped and, although this coat is far easier to maintain, daily grooming care is still required.

Size: UK/US/FCI: 7 lbs (3.1 kgs). Pet Yorkies may well exceed this.

Temperament, training and exercise: A spirited little dog, the Yorkie's size belies his formidable personality. An alert guard, he will be quick to warn you when strangers approach. He is bright and intelligent, and is very quick to learn. Exercise needs are moderate, but if you fancy a long walk in the country, your Yorkie will be more than happy to come too.

Health issues: Patella luxation occurs in the breed.

3 PUPPY TEMPERAMENT TESTING

If you are looking for a puppy, the most dangerous thing you can do is to go and see a litter 'just to take a look'. Once you are actually in the presence of those fuzzy, squirmy, cute little creatures, all your common sense goes right out of the window. It is as if you become unable to make logical, rational decisions. It is also difficult, if not impossible, to walk away empty-handed. After experiencing a few moments of 'puppy love' most people do not want to go home alone. This is what causes people to make poor choices when choosing a puppy. Puppies are so sweet and appealing and we get caught up in the excitement of the moment. Rather than making a clear, considered, objective decision with our heads, we make an emotional one with our hearts.

The most important thing to remember, when you are considering bringing a puppy into your home, is that you are making a long-term commitment to another living creature. You may be sharing your life with this pet for the next 15 years, so it is important to choose very, very carefully. This is your chance to actually choose a family member, rather than taking whatever you get. A quick, ill-considered decision can lead to much heartache and unhappiness. However, a good choice can add much enjoyment and happiness to your life for years to come. So, the key question is,

how do you make a good choice? That is what this chapter is about; choosing the right puppy for you.

TEMPERAMENT TESTS

After doing background research you have probably narrowed your focus down to one or two breeds or types of dogs. Now you may actually be going to talk to some breeders and to look at some litters. At this point, your goal is to find the absolutely perfect puppy for you and your lifestyle. Pups of the same breed, even within the

Simple temperament tests may help you to find the ideal pup.

Temperament tests can help to identify shy, nervous or dominant traits in young pups.

same litter, can be very, very different from one another. One way to make an educated decision is to complete a series of simple behavioural tests on the puppies you are considering. Their responses to these tests will help you narrow down your choices.

Puppy temperament tests have been around for some time. The purpose of such testing is twofold. The first is to gain information about the pup's current personality and behaviour. These tests can help to determine how active, bold, or curious the puppy is at a particular moment in his development. The second is to make predictions about how the puppy may behave as an adult. These types of tests were first used by those who were breeding and raising 'service' dogs, such as Guide Dogs for the Blind, to help them decide which puppies were likely to be successful in their future work. For most pet owners, the purpose of puppy testing is to determine whether the pup is the right 'fit' for the owner's lifestyle.

Temperament tests are thought to indicate some of the personality traits and behavioural tendencies that the adult dog will possess. The term 'temperament' refers to inborn tendencies. Temperament can be thought of as the raw material that is inherited by the puppy from the parents. It gives behaviour a slight 'push' in a certain direction, but is not the only factor in determining how your dog will act as an adult. Temperament combines with environment and learning to form the actual behaviour of the dog. However, to have the best chance of a successful relationship with your dog, it helps to know about and to understand his basic temperament.

PARENTAL BACKGROUND

If possible, try to see the parents or other close relatives of the puppy. While their behaviour is individual and based on their environment and training as well as on their temperament, you can still gain some important information by seeing them. Because of the close genetic relationship between the pup, his parents, and his siblings, you can get a basic idea of the possible adult personality by seeing his close adult relatives. Besides personality characteristics, you can also get an idea of your pup's eventual size and coat.

TEMPERAMENTAL TENDENCIES

In humans, two characteristics that seem to be due to strong temperamental tendencies are activity level, and degree of shyness (introversion) as opposed to an outgoing personality (extraversion). It is possible that this is true in dogs as well. Very early in life you can see real differences in these characteristics between individuals. For most pet owners, a dog who is moderate on both of these characteristics would be the best choice. A dog who falls in the mid-range would be best suited to most homes: not hyperactive, not a couch potato, not a wallflower, not a social butterfly. For those who want performance dogs for work or sport, it might be desirable to choose a dog who is likely to have a higher activity level and a more outgoing personality.

PREDICTING BEHAVIOUR

In attempting to predict a puppy's possible future behaviour from his test scores we are performing what psychologists call an aptitude test. Aptitude tests measure the likelihood that the animal will be successful in his intended function. In humans, aptitude tests are used to measure the probability that advanced training in a particular area will be useful. For example, tests can be given to help people learn more about their talents and skills when deciding on career training. An aptitude test may indicate that you would be best suited for training as a surgeon or a teacher or an actor. In temperament testing puppies, we are typically trying to determine their aptitude to be good family companions and screen out those who will not.

GOOD PET CHARACTERISTICS

Before we begin puppy testing, we need to consider the characteristics that make a dog a good pet and companion. These are the characteristics we should test for.

GOOD FRIEND

First, even though it seems obvious, we want a dog who is comfortable around people and who is reasonably friendly. It is important to keep this critical characteristic in mind. Puppies who are shy may become even more fearful, and possibly aggressive, later on. Puppies who are overwhelmingly needy and clingy will have trouble adjusting to being alone, even for short periods. Puppies who are very pushy and

Consider a breed's known characteristics and needs when choosing your puppy. Collies make fabulous pets, but need lots of mental and physical stimulation.

domineering can end up frightening or harming people.

STABLE REACTIONS

Second, we want a dog who reacts to new or unusual events with reasonable caution, but who is also curious and confident. Strange things will happen to your dog. People dressed in unusual clothing or costumes may bend over to pet him. Someone may push a rattling pram (baby carriage) towards him. Children will run up behind him screaming and yelling.

In any of these cases, and in many others, we want a dog who reacts appropriately. If a puppy's first reaction is to snap, growl, or bite, someone will be hurt eventually. While it is acceptable, and reasonable, for a puppy to be startled by unusual events, he should recover from them quickly. Given a bit of recovery time, a pup with a stable personality should approach and investigate the source of what unsettled him.

HANDLING

Third, we want a puppy who can accept being handled and restrained as needed. Throughout their lives, dogs need to be comfortable with human contact and manipulation. They will need veterinary care, grooming, and day-to-day handling. It is no fun to live with a dog who is 'touchy'. Dogs who react to normal touch with undue fear or undue aggression will not make good family pets. They may always require careful and special handling.

TRAINABILITY

Finally, we want a puppy who enjoys learning and is relatively easy to train. A puppy who is curious and interested in the world around him, but able to focus on one task at a time, will be trainable. It also helps to have a puppy who enjoys a wide variety of food treats and toys (these can be used as rewards during training).

BREED BEHAVIOUR

While all dogs of a particular breed or type are not the same, they may have some similar behavioural tendencies. When testing puppies, it is important to keep in mind the characteristics typical of the specific breed and type.

For example, herding dogs (Border Collies, Shetland Sheepdogs, Belgian Sheepdogs, etc.) tend to be more reactive to sight and sound than some other types. They may display a more pronounced reaction. Be careful of over-sensitive or fearful dogs of this type. Also, herding dogs can tend to be noisy and barky. Avoid very vocal herding dog puppies.

GUARDERS

Dogs who have been bred to be guardians and protectors tend to be a bit more serious than some others (Rottweilers, Dobermanns, etc.) They may be bold and extremely confident. Be aware that these tendencies can, at an exaggerated level, become pushy and obnoxious. Dogs like this tend to 'take over' if given an opportunity. The boldest, most confident puppy of this type is not necessarily a good choice for the average pet owner.

TOY DOGS

Small, toy breeds can have a tendency to be barky and snappy. Do not choose a toy dog who is fearful and unsure. This dog will not be a good companion, and may become a fear-biter over time.

RETRIEVERS

Most retrieving dogs are energetic and active. Make sure your physical health and lifestyle allows you the time and energy for this type of dog. Also be aware that these dogs can be physically dangerous to young children and frail or older people. In their excitement and exuberance, they are not aware of their own strength. A retriever needs to learn physical limits and self-control at a young age.

Whenever you are testing or evaluating a dog, keep in mind the characteristics typical of his breed and type.

WHAT IS BEING TESTED?

Most currently available puppy temperament tests attempt to measure the same general personality and behavioural factors. These include (in no particular order):

1. Sociability and following (desire to be with humans).
2. Curiosity about novel events.
3. Shyness/outgoingness.
4. Reaction to, and ability to recover from, surprise or being startled.
5. Desire to work with people.
6. Reaction to restraint/discomfort/handling.
7. Desire to chase and fetch (prey drive).
8. Trainability.
9. Physical activity level.

PREPARING FOR THE TESTS

Most trainers and breeders agree that the ideal age for temperament testing is around seven to eight weeks of age. Puppies much younger do not have the mental and physical development necessary to complete the tests. It is possible to test older dogs and puppies, but keep in mind that the older animal has already had learning experiences which may influence the results.

You will probably be performing your puppy testing at the breeder's home. You will need to have a few pieces of equipment available, as well as some open floor space for the testing. To prepare for the testing you will need:

- A set of keys.
- A small squeaky toy or a small ball.
- An umbrella.
- A towel and a 6 ft piece of string or rope.
- Small, soft food treats.
- Pieces of different-coloured soft yarn or ribbon (one for each puppy tested).
- Copies of the test (one for each puppy tested) and a pencil.
- Watch with a second hand or a stop-watch.

Each puppy should be tested individually, out of sight and hearing of his or her littermates and other pets in the household. The day of the testing should be a calm, quiet one for the puppies. Puppies should not have grooming, veterinary care, or any other exciting activity on that day. Try to test the puppies when they are at their most active, before a meal.

BEGINNING THE TESTS

Begin testing each puppy by taking him or her to the testing area. Loosely tie one of the coloured strings around the puppy's neck, or on the collar, and note the colour

An eight-week-old pup makes the perfect subject for the tests.

on your score sheet. Also note the sex of the puppy and any distinguishing or unusual physical features of the pup. To make your test a valid one, handle each puppy in exactly the same way throughout the testing procedure. Perform each test and mark down the results before moving on to the next test. Make any comments on unusual behaviour or reactions at the bottom of the sheet.

When observing the puppy's reaction to each test, you are relying on your interpretation of the pup's behaviour. This can be a difficult judgement call. For example, it is sometimes hard to tell the beginnings of aggression from extreme playfulness. A thorough understanding of canine behaviour and body language can be quite useful here. If you are not sure how to categorise the response, test again while a knowledgeable dog person observes (breeder or trainer).

A good breeder can also be an excellent resource for further information about the puppies and their normal behaviour. Listen carefully to the breeder's advice.

For each test the puppy can score low (1), moderate (2), or high (3). A low score indicates an extreme reaction in either direction. For example, the puppy either does not react at all, or wildly overreacts. A moderate score indicates an acceptable and expected reaction. A high score indicates an ideal reaction.

THE TESTS

 Activity & Curiosity Level

Place the puppy in the middle of the testing area. Watch him without interference or interaction for at least two minutes. If the puppy approaches you, be still and ignore him.

Scoring:

Low score (1). Puppy does not move about or explore the environment. Puppy actively avoids you. Puppy displays extremely high level of activity by running wildly and/or jumping.

Moderate score (2). Puppy remains still for a few moments, then slowly begins to sniff and/or move about. Puppy approaches you or objects in the room cautiously.

High score (3). Puppy confidently moves about, exploring the new area. Puppy sniffs objects and may physically interact with them. For example, putting front paws up on a chair to further investigate. Puppy may approach you and attempt to gain attention.

2 **Social Attraction**

Take the puppy into the testing area and set him on the floor. Move at least 10 feet away, kneel down, clap your hands, and call "Here puppy, puppy" in a happy, inviting voice.

Scoring:

Low score (1). Puppy ignores you, attempts to hide, approaches slightly then retreats, looks around frantically, tries to escape testing area.

Moderate score (2). Puppy approaches you slowly and cautiously, but deliberately.

High score (3). Puppy quickly and happily runs to you with tail up and wagging.

3 Following

Quickly move away from the puppy, calling and encouraging him to follow. Move at least 10 feet away.

Scoring:

Low score (1). Puppy runs in other direction, ignores you, sits still and watches you without moving, sniffs the ground. Puppy runs to you and jumps on you, growling and/or nipping.

Moderate score (2). Puppy cautiously moves towards you but may not actually reach you. Puppy shows great interest, but is slightly cautious in approaching.

High score (3). Puppy quickly and enthusiastically runs after you. Puppy may jump up on you in excitement.

4 Restraint

While sitting on the floor, entice the puppy close to you and wrap your arms around his chest, gently preventing him from moving away. Hold puppy for 30 seconds.

Scoring:

Low score (1). The puppy panics and struggles violently. Puppy scratches and/or attempts to bite. Release the puppy immediately! Puppy trembles and shakes the entire time you hold him.

Moderate score (2). Puppy struggles initially, but quickly relaxes in your arms.

High score (3). Puppy immediately relaxes in your arms. Puppy may lick you and voluntarily move closer.

5 Handling

While sitting on the floor, stroke and pet puppy. Puppy may be held in your lap or on the floor close to you. Gently stroke the head and ears, down the spine, the tail, and each leg and foot. You may talk softly to the dog during this test.

Scoring:

Low score (1). Puppy actively resists and attempts to escape. Puppy attempts to bite or nip. Release the puppy immediately! Puppy remains still, but stiff. Puppy trembles and shakes.

Moderate score (2). Puppy initially resists, but quickly relaxes. Puppy may have one or two 'sensitive' areas, but does not actively object to the handling.

High score (3). Puppy relaxes and allows all handling. Puppy seems to enjoy the attention.

6 Sound Sensitivity

When the puppy is not looking at you, drop a set of keys at least 12 feet behind him.

Scoring:

Low score (1). Puppy jumps, shakes, trembles. Puppy attempts to run and hide. Puppy attacks the keys growling and biting (the puppy seems intensely focused and his body is stiff, his tail may be held straight up). Puppy barks uncontrollably.

Moderate score (2). Puppy is startled, but recovers within 20 seconds. Puppy looks, but does not approach the keys or approaches keys very cautiously.

High score (3). Puppy is startled, but recovers within 10 seconds. Puppy approaches and investigates keys (sniffing and/or pawing) without fear.

7 Sight Sensitivity

Tie a string or rope around the towel. Quickly pull the towel on a string across the floor in front of the puppy. Once puppy moves towards the towel, stop pulling and let it be still.

Scoring:

Low score (1). Puppy looks at towel, but shows no active interest. Puppy does not move towards the towel. Puppy runs or backs away from the towel. Puppy viciously attacks the towel, growling, barking and/or biting. The puppy's body is stiff. His tail may be held upright and still, or he may make quick jerky motions with it.

Moderate score (2). Puppy approaches the moving towel. Puppy may grab and shake the towel. Puppy ignores towel once it stops moving.

High score (3). Puppy playfully and enthusiastically chases and grabs the towel. He may jump and pounce. Puppy may continue to play with the towel once it stops moving.

8 Fetch Test

Show the puppy a ball or squeaky toy. At a pinch, a wadded-up piece of paper will do. Attract the puppy's attention to the object by bouncing the ball, squeaking the toy, or crumpling the paper. Make sure the puppy is paying attention to the object before it is thrown. Throw the object six to eight feet in front of the puppy and verbally encourage him to "Get it!"

Scoring:

Low score (1). Puppy completely ignores thrown object. Puppy watches object, but does not show any interest in moving towards it. Puppy seems fearful of object. Puppy approaches object and guards or protects it with a stiff stance and possible growling.

Moderate score (2). Puppy shows interest in object. Puppy begins to approach thrown object, then stops. Puppy approaches and investigates thrown object.

High score (3). Puppy shows great interest in thrown object. Puppy chases object and picks it up. Puppy may run around the room or return towards the tester with the object.

9 — Reaction to a Surprise or to Being Startled

About six feet away, and slightly to the side of the puppy, open an umbrella and place it on the floor. DO NOT approach the puppy with the open umbrella or wave it at him.

Scoring:

Low score (1). Puppy runs in fright. Puppy seems 'frozen' and stiff. Puppy attacks umbrella while barking or growling. Puppy backs away from umbrella while barking or growling. Puppy is not startled, but does not show any interest in the umbrella either.

Moderate score (2). Puppy is startled at first, but recovers within 20 seconds. Puppy shows interest in the umbrella, and may approach cautiously.

High score (3). Puppy is startled at first, but recovers within 10 seconds. Puppy shows great interest in the umbrella and approaches without fear.

10 — Trainability

Have several small, soft food treats in your hand. Feed several to the puppy. Then show him a treat and hold it slightly over his head. Next, show him a treat and hold it on the floor in your fingers.

Scoring:

Low score (1). Puppy ignores food treats. Puppy does not follow the movement of the treats with his eyes. Puppy moves away from the tester and the treats.

Moderate score (2). Puppy shows interest in food treats, but loses it quickly. Puppy follows food treats with his eyes. Puppy moves slightly towards food treats, but may become distracted. Puppy nips, jumps, and/or scratches at your hand in an attempt to get the treats.

High score (3). Puppy quickly and enthusiastically approaches the food treats. Puppy follows the food treats with his eyes and body. Puppy focuses intently on the hand holding the treats.

* Note: If the puppy shows no interest in the food treats, re-test using a squeaky toy.

SCORE SHEET   **SCORE**

SEX _____

COLOUR _____

MARKINGS _____

Test 1. (Activity & Curiosity Level).   _____

Test 2. (Social Attraction).   _____

Test 3. (Following).   _____

Test 4. (Restraint).   _____

Test 5. (Handling).   _____

Test 6. (Sound Sensitivity).   _____

Test 7. (Sight Sensitivity).   _____

Test 8. (Fetch Test).   _____

Test 9. (Reaction to a Surprise or to Being Startled).   _____

Test 10. (Trainability).   _____

TOTAL SCORE: _____

INTERPRETING THE SCORE

Each puppy's score can range from a low of 10 to a high of 30. The higher the score, the more ideal the puppy's responses on the tests.

10-14 No way! This puppy will NOT make a good companion. All his responses are inappropriate.

15-19 Low. This puppy's reactions are slightly better, but not great. He will require lots of work and effort, and may never have appropriate reactions and behaviour patterns.

20-24 Average. While the responses are in the normal range, this puppy may need some extra effort, so may be best for an experienced owner.

25-30 Great! This puppy had appropriate and ideal responses to the tests. He should make a good family companion.

CONCLUSIONS

While puppy testing is not a strict scientific endeavour, it can be very helpful for making a decision about which puppy to adopt. Keep in mind that puppies can test differently on different days, or even at different times of day. If you are unsure about a particular puppy, repeat the test in a day or so. The current owner or breeder can provide more information by answering questions about the puppy's normal and usual behaviour and personality as well.

Remember, adopting a puppy is a big commitment of time, energy, and money. Make your choice wisely and thoughtfully. The right pup for you is out there. Do not be in a big rush. Take your time. A good choice will bring you enjoyment for many years.

The Ultimate Puppy

4 *SETTLING IN*

Once you have made the decision to buy a puppy, have researched, thoroughly, your chosen breed, and have booked a puppy from a responsible, reputable breeder, there are a few points to consider before taking your puppy home.

PUPPY SAFEGUARDS

Is your garden puppy-proof? Your garden should be securely fenced, as most puppies seem to be expert at squeezing through the smallest of holes, and any potential hazards should be removed, such as slug pellets, which are highly toxic.

Many puppies like to 'have a go' at redesigning your garden at some point, and take great delight in digging holes in the lawn, digging in ornamental pots, pruning the rose bushes, and digging up your lovingly-tended flower beds! When your puppy is spending time outdoors, supervise him while he is still small, or he will dig you a hole where you did not want one. If you have a fish pond, can your puppy climb out if he should fall in? Ideally, do not let your puppy near it unsupervised. The same applies to swimming pools.

A few precautions should be taken in your home too. Electrical flexes can have fatal consequences if chewed, so these need to be boxed in, where appropriate. As with children, all cleaning fluids, such as bleach and disinfectant, should be kept out of the reach of your puppy.

Your garden should be made as safe as possible, but sessions outside should always be supervised.

All puppies chew, so it is advisable to use a cardboard box or hard plastic bed to begin with.

Your pup should get used to wearing a collar for short periods throughout the day.

To keep your puppy away from any hazards, or just for when you need time out from your puppy, but do not want him to be excluded altogether, for example when you are busy, are eating dinner, or have visitors, a baby's stair-gate across a doorway can be useful.

EQUIPMENT

BED
Your puppy will need an area to which he can retreat for rest, and where he will feel safe and secure. It is best not to spend too much money, initially, on a bed, as they are easily ruined by a chewing puppy.

A cardboard box, with warm, washable bedding, will do at first, or a rigid plastic one, which is fairly chew-proof and easily cleaned. Wicker baskets are dangerous if chewed, so these are best avoided.

FEEDING BOWLS
Your puppy will need two feeding bowls: one for food, and one for water. There are many different types to choose from, made of plastic, stainless steel, or pottery – the choice is yours. In the interests of hygiene, they should be cleaned thoroughly after each use.

COLLAR AND LEAD
An inexpensive, soft, lightweight puppy lead and collar is all that is required. You will soon need to replace them as your puppy rapidly outgrows them.

Your puppy can get used to wearing a collar straight away, and you will need to check, regularly, that it is not too tight. Put the collar on your puppy for short periods at first, gradually increasing the length of time it is worn as the puppy gets used to it. Do not allow the puppy to wear the collar

The toys you provide should be safe and durable.

unless he is supervised, as it can get caught up and choke him.

BRUSH AND COMB
A soft brush will be ideal for getting your puppy used to being groomed. Grooming is essential for all dogs, but even more so for long-haired breeds. A few gentle strokes of the brush is all that is needed to start with, keeping the sessions short and enjoyable. This should be done on a daily basis. If your puppy tries to chew the brush, distract him with a tidbit or a toy.

IDENTIFICATION
Your puppy should wear a collar and tag, with your address and telephone number on it (a legal requirement in the UK) in case you should lose him.

Other means of identification are tattooing and microchipping. Some breeders tattoo or microchip their puppy

before they go to their new homes. The microchip is implanted in the loose skin just above the shoulder blades, and your puppy wears a tag to say he has one.

If your puppy should get lost, most rescue centres, dog wardens etc., will automatically scan dogs to see if they have a microchip implanted. Swift identification means you can be quickly reunited with your pet.

TOYS
All puppies need to chew. If you do not provide your puppy with something appropriate on which to exercise his jaws, he will find something inappropriate.

There are many different doggy toys from which to choose. It is worth spending a bit of money on toys of good quality and they should last a long time when compared to the cheaper variety. The best, and safest, ones are made from hard rubber, or nylon,

The crate is a great training aid, and most puppies regard it as their own special den.

and cannot be shredded or swallowed – later having to be removed from your pet's stomach by your vet.

Balls should not be too small or they may be swallowed, causing an obstruction. Toys can be found which, when moved around by your puppy, dispense food randomly as they roll. These toys provide excellent mental stimulation for your puppy and some toys make weird and wonderful noises as they roll about, which is great fun.

Some hard, rubber toys have a hollow cavity which can be stuffed with food. These will also keep your puppy busy and stimulated. Avoid giving your puppy old shoes and slippers to play with, as he will not know the difference between old and new!

It is a good idea to rotate chew toys, on a daily basis, to prevent your puppy from becoming bored with them. Keep some interactive toys in a box, or on a shelf, for you to play with your puppy when you want to; for example, tug toys, such as knotted ropes, and toys to play 'fetch' with (retrieve articles). Keeping these toys out of

reach of your puppy makes them more interesting to him, as he does not see them all the time.

Never use yourself as a toy, encouraging your puppy to bite and tug on your arms or clothing, as this type of play can quickly get out of control. If you teach your puppy that it is okay to play this way, and he decides to play with a child, for instance, like this in the park, a frightened child's parents will not understand that your puppy is 'just playing!'

CRATES, CAGES OR PLAYPENS
A folding crate (cage) can be of great use when training your puppy, as can a playpen. These can be bought from good pet shops. Your puppy should look upon his crate as his 'den', somewhere to which he can retreat, away from the hustle and bustle of family life.

Your puppy should gradually become accustomed to being in his crate. Put his bedding in there, feed him in there, and put toys and chews in there, and he will soon feel at home. You can then get him used to being in the crate with the door shut. This is best done for short periods, while he is asleep.

The crate, or pen, will teach your puppy self-control, and to relax in the house, so learning not to demand to be the centre of attention. Once your puppy is used to being in his crate, with the door shut, you will not have to worry about leaving him in a room unsupervised, to chew all the furniture and generally get into mischief. You can cover an area of the crate with newspaper while your puppy is very young, in case of toileting accidents. Crates help immensely with house-training (most puppies do not like to foul their sleeping areas), and help to prevent accidents on carpets.

If your puppy barks and whines in the crate, ignore him, and on no account let him out (unless you are sure he needs to relieve himself). Only let him out when he is quiet, or you will end up with a noisy, demanding dog.

Crates can be a godsend if you take your puppy to stay in hotels, or with friends or relatives. They also make car travel much safer, both for you and your puppy, as having him loose in your car is, potentially, very dangerous. Alternatively, fit a dog guard, or buy your puppy a special harness that attaches to your car's seatbelt.

VETS
It is best to find a good veterinary surgeon, if you do not already know of one, before bringing your puppy home. Ask friends and relatives to recommend one, and go along to pay them a visit. Ask for advice as to when your puppy will need to start his vaccination programme, worming, flea prevention, and insurance (some breeders insure their puppies for the first six weeks that they are in their new homes). Some veterinary surgeries run 'puppy parties' for very young puppies to attend. These get your puppy used to being at the surgery, meeting the staff, playing with other puppies, and having a good time.

PUPPY SOCIALISATION/TRAINING CLASSES
It will be very worthwhile enrolling your puppy on a training course. This should be done as soon as possible, as the better ones become booked up very quickly. Your vet, or other dog owners, may be able to recommend one to you.

Ask to go to watch a class before taking your puppy along. Look for small, friendly classes with reward-based training methods, such as food and toy rewards. There should be no shouting or choke-chains, as these methods are now out of date, thankfully, but beware, some classes unfortunately still exist that use these methods. All the puppies should be of a similar age and, usually, under five months old, when the course starts.

Help and advice should be given on such things as house-training, biting, jumping up, digging, barking, etc., and you will be shown how to teach your puppy to sit, stand, lie down, and come when he is called.

Puppy classes should not be free-for-alls with puppies off-lead all the time, and out of control. Puppies should be let off the lead for short play sessions, more often than not two at a time, with the puppies evenly matched. This ensures that your puppy should not be scared, initially, by a more confident, bolder puppy. If you are not happy with what you see when you visit the class, try elsewhere.

THE RIGHT AGE TO ACQUIRE YOUR PUPPY
Puppies need to spend enough time with their mother and littermates in order to

A towel may come in useful for the journey home.

learn discipline and the correct communication skills, which they will need in order to get along with other dogs later in life.

Puppies that leave the litter too soon, or have been hand-reared, often miss out on these vital experiences, which can cause problems later on. Between the ages of six and eight weeks is thought to be the best time to get your new puppy. Most breeders let their puppies go at around eight weeks. If puppies stay together too long, they can become more interested in, and more comfortable around, other dogs rather than people.

If you do consider buying a puppy older than eight weeks, ensure that he has been well socialised by the breeder and has been given lots of individual attention, and not just left in a kennel, as he will have missed out on so much.

COLLECTING YOUR PUPPY
Before leaving with your puppy, ensure you have the necessary paperwork – pedigree certificate, worming and vaccination record, and diet sheet (if relevant). Some breeders also provide a factsheet that contains lots of help and advice. Take newspapers or old towels with you, for your journey home, in case your puppy vomits. This is very common, so do not worry.

Take your puppy home at a time when the house is suitably quiet, if possible, and at a time that gives your puppy enough time to settle in, before you go to bed at night, as he may be frightened and confused at being taken away from his littermates and left alone for such a long time, overnight, so soon. It is always best to introduce your puppy to any older dogs in your household on neutral territory, rather than taking him straight indoors. Do not be surprised if your older dog is none too impressed, or completely disinterested. It might take a while for the older dog to get used to the idea of having the puppy around.

After meeting any other dogs, take your puppy into the garden to explore his new surroundings. He should also want to relieve himself after the journey home. Then take your new puppy indoors. Show him his bed/sleeping area, water bowl (he will probably be thirsty after his journey), and offer him some food, which should be the same as the breeder's, to avoid the puppy getting an upset stomach. If your puppy refuses the food, do not worry, as he may be unsettled due to the new surroundings. Offer him some later on.

If using a crate, leave the door open, put his bed and bedding inside, and encourage him to settle down and sleep there, if he is tired.

NIGHT-TIME

Take your puppy out into the garden at bedtime so he can empty himself. Do not let him get too excited beforehand, or he will be too awake and 'full of beans' to go to sleep. Make sure that he is not hungry either. An old T-shirt or jumper of yours, preferably one that had been left with your puppy when he was still with the breeder, can be left with him in his bed. Some puppies settle down to sleep straight away, others bark and whine, which can sometimes go on for what seems like ages. This is understandable behaviour as your puppy has had the upsetting experience of leaving his mother and siblings, and should not, of course, be punished in any way.

There are different schools of thought on how to deal with this. Some people say it is best to go and reassure your puppy and leave him again once he has settled, but this may teach your puppy that, if he cries, it gets the desired attention he craves, so making the problem worse. Whether or not this will work will depend on the individual puppy.

Ignore the night crying altogether and it usually lessens each night. Using this method, the majority of puppies settle into their night-time routine very quickly. You might like to have your puppy sleeping with you, in his crate, in your bedroom. Once he has got used to sleeping in the crate, you can move it elsewhere, if you so wish.

MEETING THE FAMILY

It is important to teach any children, either your own, or those that visit regularly, not to overpower your puppy or be constantly picking him up. He is not a toy! Never leave a small child, or baby, alone with your

Tempting though it will be to let the puppy sleep with you, he must learn a night-time routine where he sleeps alone.

Dogs and children can share a very special relationship but the foundations should be established from the beginning, during the pet's puppyhood.

puppy (or any dog for that matter), as either can be hurt, albeit accidentally. Some children can be unintentionally clumsy, and puppies have very sharp teeth. Children can be knocked over and puppies can be dropped from tiny hands. In order to avoid accidents, puppies and children should be supervised at all times.

CATS

When your puppy meets your cat for the first time, restrain the puppy, if necessary, and not the cat, so that the cat can make a quick exit, if he wishes to do so.

Confident cats will stand up for themselves and often hiss and spit, which will teach your puppy that the cat in question will not take any nonsense! Some cats run away at the sight of this strange 'intruder', so prevent your puppy from giving chase or this becomes an exciting game to play. Use a toy, or a tidbit, to distract your puppy if he gets too excited, and give him something else to do. Do not leave your puppy and cat, or cats, together unsupervised, at first; put him in his crate, or playpen, out of harm's way.

OTHER PETS

Your puppy will need to be introduced to any other pets that you have, such as rabbits and guinea pigs, as early as possible. He should soon accept them as other family members.

Always remember that small, furred and feathered creatures running around can bring out the predatory instincts in your puppy, so never leave them alone together.

HOUSE-TRAINING

Most puppies are not house-trained when they leave the breeder, although some may be well on the way to that target. It is up to you to teach your puppy where he can go to the toilet, and where he cannot.

It is important to take your puppy outside, letting him follow you, rather than you carrying him, so he knows which door he has to go out of. This needs to be done after your puppy has eaten, when he wakes up, after a play session, first thing in the morning, and last thing at night. Most puppies need to go to the toilet about every hour.

Puppies can learn to relieve themselves

The success of your pup/cat introductions very much depends on the animals' personalities and your own careful supervision.

Punishing a puppy when he has an accident in the house is never appropriate.

on command. Let your puppy have a good sniff around the garden, then, when your puppy squats to 'go', you can tell him what he is doing. Say something like: "Hurry up", "Toilet", "Be quick", Be busy" etc. – the choice is yours. Do not use words like "Good boy" as you will use these at other times and confuse him. When he has finished what he has to do, you can then give him lots of praise. Eventually, you can take your puppy into the garden, say the magic words, e.g. "Hurry up", and he will automatically want to 'perform' – bingo!

If you discover your puppy about to squat indoors, interrupt him, maybe by shouting, but being careful not to frighten him, and quickly get him outdoors, again preferably by getting him to follow you out rather than him being carried out.

If you find a puddle or mess on the floor, say nothing. Clear it up and blame yourself, as the puppy had to 'go' and you were not there to let him out into the garden. Be careful about what you use to clean up with. Bleach and disinfectant can make the area more attractive, so use a solution of

biological washing powder, or a special cleaner available from pet shops and veterinary surgeries.

Scolding your puppy is counter-productive, often resulting in a puppy who will not 'perform' in front of you and hides behind the sofa or piano to do it instead! Some owners say things like, "But he knows he's done wrong because he looks so guilty". What the puppy is displaying is submission (at the negative, sometimes angry, response they receive), which we wrongly interpret as guilt.

If you are busy and cannot keep a close eye on your puppy, confine him to a smaller space, e.g. crate, playpen, kitchen or utility room, so preventing accidents. The majority of puppies are unable to control themselves through the night, so you may want to put newspapers down on the floor in case of accidents, which are likely. Do not rely on paper training all the time as, often, you will make such a good job of doing so that, when you take the paper away, your puppy will still 'go' where the paper used to be.

HANDLING

Your pup should learn to accept thorough handling – to have his paws touched, ears checked and mouth inspected.

You might like your puppy to sleep in a bed, or crate, in your bedroom, so that when he wakes in the night you can get up and take him outside, reducing, even more, the likelihood of 'accidents' indoors.

It takes some puppies a long time to become completely reliable in the house, so a lot of understanding and patience is needed. Punishment is *never* appropriate.

Some puppies are prone to leaking a little bit of urine when frightened, or excited, often when greeting people and other dogs. This is perfectly normal and is the puppy's way of saying, "I'm only a baby and no threat to you, so please don't hurt me". This behaviour is best ignored, as telling your puppy off makes things worse because it merely serves to make him even more submissive.

HANDLING EXERCISES

Puppies need to be taught to accept people wanting to touch and stroke them, as this can be quite frightening at first, especially when people loom over them and pat them on the head. This can seem threatening to a young puppy.

As part of your daily routine with your puppy, gradually get him used to you calmly, and gently, stroking and touching him all over. Get him used to you looking in his ears, touching and lifting his paws, and looking into his mouth. Some puppies are a bit sensitive at having certain parts of their body looked at, for example, mouth and paws, so you will need to desensitise him gradually, by first of all teaching him to accept you putting a finger into his mouth, or just under his lips, and building up the procedure slowly to having his mouth opened. Putting a little peanut butter on your finger often does the trick, and makes the whole thing much more acceptable!

Your puppy will, at some time in the future, need to have his mouth opened to be given medication, have something taken from it (maybe because it is harmful), be examined by a vet, or at a dog show.

Once your puppy is used to you handling him, you need to ask others to handle him as well. Start with people he is familiar with and then those he is not. If he is not used to having children around, the experience of having one loom up and pat him on the head can be terrifying, and cause him to growl, or snap, in defence, so carefully get him used to children too.

FOOD-BOWL GUARDING

It is perfectly normal behaviour if your puppy growls at you, at first, if you approach him when he is eating. He believes you want to take the food for yourself! So, in order to stop, or prevent, this behaviour occurring, you will need to teach your puppy to relax when you approach him at mealtimes, and that it is a positive, not a negative, experience. If your puppy does display this behaviour, never use aggression to counteract his, as this just reinforces the reason why he felt he needed to guard his food from you in the first place.

Start by putting his empty food bowl on the floor, add some food to the bowl and let the puppy eat it. Add some more food to the bowl and repeat several times. When your puppy is happy with having this done, you will be able to approach him, and the bowl, from across the room, again adding food to the bowl. Soon, your puppy will have learnt that having you, and your family (all members of your family need to practise this exercise – children always being supervised) around him at mealtimes is a positive, rewarding experience, and he will welcome you approaching him.

Your pup must learn that you are not a threat to his food.

Once your puppy is relaxed at mealtimes, you should get him used to being touched and stroked while he is eating as well. This same approach can be used when your puppy is chewing on a bone or a toy. Approach your puppy with a tasty tidbit, or another chew item. Distract him with it, give it to him, and then let him go back to chewing his bone. Once he welcomes you approaching him when he is chewing, you can teach him to accept having his bone, or chew, taken from and given back to him. You can make a game of it by swapping one chew for another, and so on.

If you have another dog, or dogs, in the house, you will need to watch him with your puppy to avoid him stealing, or attempting to steal, your puppy's food or vice versa, so avoiding squabbles.

PLAY-BITING
When puppies are with their breeder, playing with their littermates, and one bites the other too hard, the puppy on the

Puppies first learn to inhibit their bite by interacting with their littermates.

Play-biting can be redirected on to toys.

receiving end of the needle-sharp teeth gives out a high-pitched yelp. This tells the other puppy that he used his teeth too hard, and he learns to regulate the strength of his bite. When the puppy is older he will have learnt to play with other dogs without hurting them, no matter how rough the game. He will have learnt what is called 'bite inhibition' – how not to damage others, even if frightened, or provoked.

Your puppy will naturally want to play-bite and will need to be taught that this is unacceptable behaviour where people are concerned. Your puppy may respond to you emitting a high-pitched 'ouch' if he bites, or touches you with his teeth. The 'ouch' needs to be instant, and withdraw attention and walk away if this does not get the point across immediately.

Your puppy may have a certain time of the day, often in the evening, for a 'mad half hour', when he rushes around like 'something possessed'! This is perfectly normal puppy behaviour and is your

puppy's way of getting rid of any excess energy. It can sometimes escalate into attention-seeking behaviour, with your puppy biting at members of the family, which can be scary for children, even though he is only playing. If this happens, put him in another room to cool off. Your puppy may look on children as playmates and 'fair game', and like to bite at their trousers and ankles. This needs to be interrupted at once with a sharp reprimand. Praise him for stopping the 'game' and give him an alternative game to play instead.

Play-biting can be redirected on to toys, so if your puppy starts using his teeth on you, tell him, "Don't bite me, bite this" and give him a toy to chew, instead of your tender flesh! Those teeth hurt and your puppy needs to know so.

Never encourage your puppy to use his teeth on you in play, as he will be totally confused when you tell him off for trying to play this way with Great-Aunt Maude when she pays you a visit!

Smacking your puppy's nose when he bites is not a good idea as this may lead to him becoming hand-shy and frightened, and this can cause him to react aggressively in return.

CHEWING

Your puppy will have a need to chew, especially when losing his baby teeth later on, so it is up to you to provide him with bone (always raw, never cooked), toys etc., and to teach him to chew these, and not your furniture. Play with the chew articles with him, giving him lots of praise when he does settle down to chew them. Redirect his attention back to the chew toy if his attention turns to the kitchen table legs. Your puppy may learn not to chew certain things when you are with him, but there is no one to stop him when you are not with him. In this instance, you need to put him in the crate, or playpen, to deny him access to these things, or put a bitter-tasting spray on them (available from pet shops and vet surgeries), which will teach him that the consequences of his actions are not very pleasant.

Your puppy may learn that if he chews the coffee table, for instance, he gets the attention he wanted, when one minute earlier he was being ignored. Do not make too big a deal out of it when he chews, or steals things, as chasing your puppy makes it into a great game. Interrupt the behaviour and redirect it on to something else. Be very 'matter-of-fact'. A chewing puppy will quickly teach children to put away their toys, and other family members to be tidier! If you do not want your mobile phone or TV remote control destroyed, put them up out of your puppy's reach – simple solutions are always the best.

Just when you think you can relax because your puppy has lost his little needle teeth, think again! This is when they have a secondary chewing phase, as the new teeth settle into their adult positions in the jaw. Most damage can be done at this time because he will now have big teeth. Some breeds of dog can be worse than others,

Puppies require hard chews when teething.

but even the smallest of breeds can do lots of damage in a relatively small amount of time. This damage is usually done when dogs are left alone.

Providing your puppy with more stimulating objects to play with can help a great deal, but make sure that they are safe for your puppy. Some puppies like to 'beat up' cardboard boxes, these being cheap and easy to replace frequently, but your puppy should be supervised with things that were not intended as toys for dogs.

ENCOURAGING INDEPENDENCE

Problems can occur with dogs that have not learnt to be independent puppies. They become anxious, and chew, dig, urinate, and defecate. Chewing can have a calming effect on stressed-out dogs.

To avoid this problem at a later date, teach your puppy to accept being on his own and happy with his own company. This is especially important if you and your puppy live alone and spend a lot of time together during the day, and night, as the relationship can become overpowering, and the puppy may become overdependent on you. If you use a crate or playpen for your puppy, this will help immensely, as he will be used to being separated from you, even if you are still in the same room as him.

Get him used to your leaving him a little at a time. Choose a time when he has been to the toilet and is sleepy, after a meal perhaps. Leave the room and ignore any whining, scratching or barking, or you will be rewarding his behaviour. Only return to your puppy when he is quiet. Practise this for short periods at first, building up to him being left for gradually longer periods. Soon he will accept being left while you go shopping, want to take a bath in peace, or wish to entertain guests.

Never punish your puppy whenever you

Crates can be used to teach your pup to be independent of his owner.

return to him, whatever the circumstances, as this can lead to major problems. Teach your puppy to accept being left in your car, gradually, and give him something wonderful to chew to keep him occupied, or he'll chew the interior of the car in no time at all!

Words of warning: *never* leave your puppy alone in your car for long periods and *never* leave him in your car in hot weather, even for a few minutes and even with the windows open, as he will rapidly overheat. Many dogs, unfortunately, still die each year as a result of being left in cars. Their owners face prosecution.

DIGGING

Some dogs have an instinctive need to dig, indeed, some breeds have been bred to do so.

Most puppies, at one time or another, will have a go at landscape gardening! Leave your puppy outside on his own for long periods and he will get into mischief, just as a toddler would.

Some pups, particularly terriers, enjoy tunnelling.

Distraction is a good way to stop your puppy digging, by giving him something else to do instead. Telling your puppy off will stop him digging temporarily, but he will wait until you are not watching and dig again, or slope off to dig somewhere else.

You can provide your puppy with somewhere he is allowed to dig – a 'digging pit'. This can be a small area, or corner of your garden, where you let your puppy watch you dig and bury interesting items, such as biscuits and chews, and encourage him to dig there himself. He will be more likely to dig there in future, where he found it very rewarding, than in your prize flower beds!

You will find that your puppy may find digging less attractive as he grows older, so much patience and perseverance is needed.

BARKING
Some puppies bark at the slightest provocation, such as strange noises or objects, so do not encourage your puppy to

do so. Ignore barking as much as possible, or your puppy will learn to bark for attention – he will bark and bark until he gets what he wants. If your puppy barks at mealtimes, do not give him his food until he is quiet. If he barks in anticipation of a walk, do not put his lead on, ignore him until he is quiet, and then attach the lead. Shouting at a barking puppy may be rewarding his behaviour. He might also think you are joining in!

Barking becomes a real problem if your puppy is doing it when you are out and the neighbours are complaining on your return. Try leaving a radio on as background noise for your puppy, and do not allow him access to doors and windows if he is barking at dogs, people, bikes, etc., that pass your house. Your puppy may bark because he is a social animal that does not like being left behind when you go out without him. All the more reason to teach him to be independent of you.

A well-socialised, relaxed puppy will bark at the threat of an intruder, for instance, so not encouraging your puppy to bark at other times will not stop this natural guarding instinct.

JUMPING UP
Jumping up to greet people is a normal puppy behaviour and one that you may encourage your puppy to do, without realising it, while he is small. When your puppy scrambles up your legs to say hello, you reward him, albeit unintentionally, by stroking and speaking to him. Suddenly, it becomes an unwanted behaviour. Maybe your puppy is wet, muddy, or just getting too big, and is in danger of knocking someone over and hurting them. Your puppy does not understand 'sometimes I can, sometimes I can't'. It is up to you to prevent, as much as possible, this unwanted

behaviour from occurring in the first place, from day one of bringing your puppy home.

Your puppy will quickly learn that jumping up gets attention, be it negative or positive, so ignore it completely. Teach your puppy that he needs to be sitting, or have his feet planted firmly on the ground, before you pay him attention. Bend down to greet him rather than letting him jump up to greet you.

People in the street, or visitors, will not appreciate the fact that you are training your puppy not to jump up, so it is up to you to restrain him, on a lead, or by his collar if necessary, and ask your puppy to sit before the other person may pay him attention.

Children can very quickly undo all our good work, so supervise them at all times and teach them to do the same as you and not encourage your puppy to jump up.

EARLY BASIC TRAINING – COMMUNICATION

It is human nature to sometimes ignore good behaviour and moan at bad or undesirable behaviour. Therefore, our dogs and children soon figure out what it is that 'gets us going' (for example, jumping up gets your attention – be it positive or negative).

Prevention is always better than cure, so distract your puppy (interrupt his behaviour) and give him something else to do. Reward him, whether with verbal praise, food, or a toy, when he is behaving as you wish, that is, sitting quietly and not barking, or chewing a toy rather than the leg of a chair. If your puppy finds something rewarding, whether it be from your point of view good or bad, there is a pretty good chance that he will try it again. You will therefore need to look at what 'turns your puppy on'. Some puppies will work for a plain piece of biscuit/kibble, some will

Your pup should be taught more appropriate ways to greet people than simply to mug them on arrival.

Good behaviour must always be rewarded in the early stages of training.

'sell their soul' for a piece of cheese or sausage. Others would rather have a toy as a reward. You will need to discover what works best for *your* puppy. Start training with low-value rewards, such as a biscuit, and keep high-value, more interesting rewards for when you need extra 'ammunition', for example when you are working amid the distractions of other dogs, or during advanced training.

REWARD OR BRIBERY?

Reward training is not bribery if used correctly. It should be seen as payment for a job well done – would you go to work for nothing? Reward training teaches your puppy to think for himself and enjoy learning, rather than getting him to do what you want by using force and compulsion (or punishment for not doing something right).

When you are first teaching your puppy a new exercise, reward each correct response immediately. It takes between 20 and 50 repetitions before the exercise is learned properly, and then it is very important to give the reward on a random basis – sometimes he will get it and sometimes he will not. This keeps your puppy guessing as to when the reward is coming, and gets him working harder for it (if he knows he can have what he wants anytime he likes, why work for it?).

Eventually, once the exercise is learned thoroughly, you only reward on the odd occasion. This is vital, otherwise you will still have a puppy that expects a reward every time he is asked to do something simple, like sitting, and you will need to carry a wheelbarrow of food around with you. Your puppy may also demand the reward, give up when he does not get it, or throw a tantrum, like a spoilt child, if he does not get it!

Puppies, like children, need to learn rules and have boundaries put in place – just what is acceptable and what is not; this results in happier puppies and happier owners too!

Sitting, for instance, becomes the canine equivalent of 'please'. Your puppy will learn to sit patiently for his dinner, sit calmly to have his lead put on, and taken off again, sit at the kerb, or sit for a thrown toy. Communicating to your puppy the importance of sitting teaches him good manners.

Initially, your pup will need rewards as a training incentive, but they can gradually be phased out.

TIMELY INTERRUPTIONS

Sometimes, a behaviour needs to be

Keep training sessions short and always enjoy a fun game at the end.

Clicker training is becoming increasingly popular, and is an effective way of training dogs.

interrupted immediately. A sharp word in a stern tone is all that should be needed to convey your disapproval to your puppy. Smacking or shaking your puppy is not necessary, and, indeed, would be detrimental to your relationship with him. You need to be firm but kind. If you need to shout in an emergency, or if you need your puppy to stop in his tracks (maybe he is about to do something dangerous), he will not take any notice if he is used to being constantly shouted at. The quieter and calmer you are with your puppy, the better he will respond to training, and to you and your family generally. Avoid constantly 'nagging' and moaning when you are training. Ignore unwanted behaviours/responses and reward

what you do want. Too much chatter will confuse your puppy.

CLICKER TRAINING

You may like to find a dog-training class that uses 'clickers' to train the dogs. Using a clicker toy is a very effective way of communicating with your puppy, without confusing him. When your puppy hears the 'click' sound, he knows exactly what it is he is being rewarded for and the food reward comes after the 'click'.

RULES OF REWARD

When you start training your puppy to do the basics (this can be as soon as you wish, do not wait until he has learned bad habits), keep the training sessions short and enjoyable for both your puppy and you. A few minutes, several times a day, is better than half an hour once a day, as your puppy's concentration span will probably be very short to begin with, and he will soon get bored or tired.

Reward-based training is very effective, and there is no need to push and pull your puppy around. Your puppy will learn what to do because he wants to, and not because he is forced to. The philosophy is to wait until he does something right, and reward him, as opposed to waiting until he gets it wrong, and punishing him.

Choose tidbits which are small enough to be eaten quickly, or it will take a very long time to reward each correct response. After waiting for your puppy to eat a large, hard biscuit, for instance, he will get full up too quickly and may also forget what it was he was being rewarded for. You need to be able to string several correct responses together at a time. Ensure that your puppy is hungry, not full up after a meal, and not too sleepy, when training him.

BASIC TRAINING

When your puppy is first learning an exercise, do not ask him to Sit for example, until he has learned what Sit means. Your puppy will follow your hand as a lure and you can reward him instantly he assumes the position you want him in. Once your puppy is understanding what it is he has to do, e.g. say "Sit" as his bottom hits the floor, release the reward at the same time. Timing is very important. Remember, whatever you are teaching your puppy, use lots of verbal praise too.

SIT

With your puppy in a standing position and the tidbit (or lure) between your fingers, hold the tidbit on his nose (imagining that the tidbit is glued to it!). Slowly move your hand backwards over his head. As his nose follows your hand, his head should tip backwards and his bottom should automatically hit the floor. As he sits, release the tidbit. If you hold the tidbit too high, he will jump up.

Once your puppy is understanding what it is he is being rewarded for (remember it takes between 20 and 50 repetitions, and sometimes more), you can include the word "Sit", the second his bottom touches the floor. Soon you will no longer need the tidbit on your puppy's nose and he will sit for just the word, the hand signal (lifting your hand), or both. You can practise Sit in different situations (different rooms in the house, in the garden, out on a walk etc.), and with you in different positions (sitting, kneeling, standing etc.), for your puppy to learn it properly. To teach your puppy to sit from the Down position, hold a tidbit on his nose and lure him up into Sit.

DOWN

This is easier to teach if you begin with your puppy in a sitting position. Hold the tidbit on his nose and slowly bring your hand down, in a straight line, until it reaches the ground. Your puppy should follow the lure. Keep the tidbit hidden and the puppy will investigate it. Be patient, and eventually he should lie down and you can immediately release the reward. If he does not lie down and jumps back up, put him in the sitting position and try again.

Once your puppy understands how to earn the reward, make him wait for a second or two, take the tidbit away from his nose, and say "Down". Bring your hand back to him and release the reward. This is very important, or your puppy will learn that "Down" means lie down, touch your

BASIC EXERCISES

Your pup will soon lie down if he thinks he'll receive a treat as a reward for his efforts.

With practice, your pup will sit whenever the command and/or hand signal is given.

The Stand is essential for dog shows, vet visits, and grooming sessions.

The Down-Stay (above) is a little easier than a Sit-Stay (below), as the dog must make more effort to break the Stay.

The Stay can be a difficult exercise, as pups like to be close to their owners.

hand and get a tidbit, thereby not focusing on the word. When you come to teach him to lie down at a distance, he will struggle to get to your hand as this is what he will have learned.

If you are going to teach your puppy that the word "Down" means to lie down, do not use the word "Down" when he jumps up or climbs on the furniture, as you will confuse him and weaken your Down command. Use the word "Off" instead, to mean do not touch. Alternatively, use the word "Lie" or "Flat", instead of "Down".

STAND

The Stand position is important for show dogs; it is helpful when your puppy is being groomed, and it makes a veterinary examination much easier.

With your puppy in a Sit position, offer him a tidbit and slowly lure him forward, keeping your hand level with his nose. He should follow the tidbit forwards, and, as he stands in the correct position, release the reward. If you move the reward forward too quickly, your puppy will learn to walk forward and not to Stand.

STAY

When teaching any exercise it is important to remember to progress at your puppy's own pace and not yours. If you rush him, the exercise will not have been learned properly. This is especially so when teaching the Stay position.

Your puppy should learn that "Stay" means to sit or lie still, until you release him from that position. In other words, not to move from where you have left him until you say he can.

Start with your puppy sitting in front of you, or beside you. Have a food reward tucked away in one hand and show him the other hand. Hold the empty hand out flat in front of him, as if stopping traffic! Ask your puppy to "Stay", wait a second or two, and reward him for patiently sitting still. You must not move away from your puppy at this early stage, since you are teaching him that "Stay" means still.

If your puppy jumps up, ignore him, wait until he sits, and then try again. Once he is beginning to understand what it is he has to do to get the reward, increase, gradually, the length of time that he has to sit still. Always give a clear release command so your puppy knows that the exercise has ended, such as "Okay".

When your puppy has learned to Stay for, maybe, a minute, you can then take a small step away. Return and reward him if he has not moved. Always return to your puppy when training the Stay. Do not call him to you, as the Stay should be seen as permanent. If you want to leave him and then call him to you, say "Wait" instead, because the word "Wait" should be seen by your puppy as meaning 'wait there until I ask you to do something else', e.g. wait while I throw a retrieve article, wait in the car until I say you can get out. "Wait" is temporary, "Stay" is permanent.

Gradually get your puppy used to you moving further and further away before returning to him. You can then start moving away in different directions, for example sideways and around him in a circle, increasing the size of the circle a little at a time.

If your puppy should move when in the Stay position, put him back (lure him with a tidbit) from where he strayed, and start again. If he keeps moving, you have probably progressed too quickly, so you need to go back a step to where your puppy was successful.

As with any exercise, always finish with your puppy succeeding at what he was doing, and leave him still interested and wanting to do more. If you push him too far, and he becomes disinterested, the behaviour will start to deteriorate.

LEAD-TRAINING

The golden rule with leadwork is *never* to allow your puppy to pull you along on a tight lead. Always keep the lead loose. If the lead is tight, your puppy will have something to pull against, and the more the lead tightens, the more your puppy will pull.

The following exercise should be taught without a lead on your puppy to start with, which makes it much easier for you both when the lead is introduced.

When your puppy is used to wearing a collar (never use a choke-chain), attach his lead and gain his attention with a tidbit. With your puppy sitting by your side, keep the lead loose (but not too long), and encourage him to walk forward with you. You can hold a tidbit in the hand without the lead (hold your hand across your body, close in by your stomach), as an incentive to watch you. If your puppy lunges forward – stand still. He must learn that, if the lead is loose you keep moving forward, if the lead tightens he gets nowhere. Do not shout or pull him back. Hold the tidbit on his nose and lure him back into the correct position and start again. Praise him verbally when he is doing what you want – walking nicely – and reward him.

If your puppy jumps up and tries to reach the tidbit, hold it higher, towards him but across your body, tucking it in by your waist but where he can see it. Never reward him when he jumps.

It is best to practise lead-training in short

The lead should always be kept loose.

bursts and to reward your puppy for taking a few steps in the correct position and building it up gradually. This should be practised in the house and in the garden to begin with. Once your puppy is able to go out for walks on his lead, only aim to go for short distances to begin with and always stand still if he pulls, as all the new sights and smells will be very distracting for him.

If you need to get from A to B quickly, for example, to the shop before it shuts, or walking the children to school and you are late, and you have not got time to train your puppy on the way, either leave him at home (or you are in danger of undoing all your good work), carry him there, (if he is small enough), or use a correctly fitted head-collar on your outward journey, and let him walk on the way home when you *will* have time to train him.

RECALL

Your puppy needs to learn that the word "Come", or "Here" (the choice is yours), means to sit in front of you. So, with a tidbit in your hand, hold it in front of your puppy's nose, at his eye-level, and take a step or two backwards with him following the tidbit. Stand still and give your puppy his Sit hand signal. When his bottom hits the ground say, "Come" or "Here", in a happy tone of voice, and reward him at the same time. As he takes the tidbit from your hand, gently take hold of his collar with the other hand (do not grab at your puppy). This way he will learn to be restrained in a positive way, essential in an emergency.

Repeat this exercise and, when you are sure he has understood it, you can say "Come" as he is coming towards you, as well. Never tell your puppy off when he comes back to you, no matter what he has done beforehand, or he will be much more reluctant to come back to you the next time you call him. Never use the word "Come" or "Here" when you want to do something your puppy does not like, (e.g. cutting his nails, putting him in the bath). Go and fetch him to you instead. The word "Come" should always be seen by your puppy as being positive, never negative.

Do not call your puppy to you if he is completely engrossed in something, as, chances are, he will not hear you and may learn to ignore you when you call.

When your puppy is coming when called, in the house and out in the garden, you will need to practise recalling him when out on a walk. Find somewhere safe and without too many distractions. Let your puppy off his lead and encourage him to explore his surroundings. Call him to

A game of Fetch encourages your pup to return to you.

you, reward him for coming, and, after a suitable pause, let him go to play again. Always call your puppy to you often on a walk. Do not leave it until it is time to put on his lead and go home, or he will look on the Recall as being the end of his fun, and avoid coming back to you. You can also practise calling him to you, put his lead on and walk him on it for a while, ask him to "Sit", take off his lead, and let him go to play again.

If you let your puppy off his lead, on a walk or to play, without interacting with him at all, he will become 'self-employed'! He will be having too much fun sniffing, rolling in dead things, and playing with other dogs, to be interested in you. So, play with him on a walk – throw a toy for him to fetch, play 'hunt the tidbit', generally make yourself just as, if not more, interesting than whatever else is on offer!

When your puppy is coming to you every time you call him, you will need to practise it in more distracting circumstances, such as training classes. You will also need to practise calling your puppy when he is playing with other dogs. Call him, reward him, let him go to play again, and repeat, so as not to teach him that "Come" means no more fun.

The Ultimate Puppy

5 THE OUTSIDE WORLD

The best family dog is one that is outgoing without being brash, and compliant without showing shy or fearful behaviour. Research firmly indicates that a puppy's temperament and personality are well on their way to being established by the end of the first few months of life. So, your puppy is going to learn during this period. He, or she, can learn what he picks up on his own or what you teach him. It is up to you. It is in your best interest to help him learn appropriate behaviour from the start, rather than allow him to get into bad habits. Hopefully, you have been training and socialising the pup from the day he joined your family. Now that he is a bit older and it is safe to venture afield, let us talk about some additional steps to take to help you raise the 'ultimate puppy'.

Pups mature quickly. A few days in a puppy's life equates to several months in a human youngster's experience. The clock is running, so let us get started. This chapter begins by outlining a few homework exercises. Rather than taking your puppy out and expecting a safe and fun time for all, do some preparation work first. Showing your pup how to respond confidently and appropriately to his environment is more important than teaching specific obedience exercises.

However, having said that, it is so easy and such fun to teach basic manners with

Your ultimate training aim is to have a dog who is confident in all situations he may face.

motivational methods that I heartily encourage you to do so! Having a puppy that loves to sit or lie down in anticipation of a reward is an ongoing advantage for both you and the dog. Instead of scolding for inappropriate behaviour, you can simply cue one of these control behaviours and reward your puppy for his excellent 'decision'.

LEARNING WHO IS LEADER

A puppy is a social animal who needs to belong to a group. Ideally, this group (pack) should be your family, with *you* playing the role of pack leader. It is especially important that your pup is willing to take your lead now that you are, together, about to go out into what will be, to the puppy, the unpredictable and sometimes frightening world. Give him a sense of security by showing him that you are a capable leader. Assuming the leadership role does not, however, mean that you need to be heavy-handed or domineering. Puppies of all personalities can benefit from a gentle, fair and consistent leader.

THE HIGH-ENERGY PUP

An active, attention-seeking pup will learn that, as leader, you give attention on your terms, not always when the pup demands it. A leadership programme combined with obedience training helps get all the wiggles under control, or at least gets the wiggles going in the right direction!

THE PUSHY PUP

Prevent a pushy pup getting the idea of 'running for higher office'. Teach him early on that you are a capable leader and in charge. You do this by earning the pup's respect from some of the simple exercises below, not by demanding it by force and intimidation.

THE BORED PUP

One of the biggest problems in dog-owning society today is coming up with enough time to be with our canine companions. Commitment to a structured leadership and/or training programme will remind you to find time to spend with your dog, who will be happy about the special attention, and will learn skills to help him be a good puppy.

THE ANXIOUS PUP

A shy or distrustful dog especially needs to know he can depend on his leader. He does not have all the worries of the world on his own shoulders. You are there to help him take care of the scary things in life. Leadership, especially for a worried puppy, does not come without responsibility. You must demonstrate that you are a reliable leader and, if your puppy trusts you, you will indeed keep him safe. Balance the leadership work with confidence-building exercises so the pup does not become over-dependent and unable to function without you!

LEADERSHIP CONCEPTS

Here are several leadership concepts taken from a well-established programme entitled *How To ALPHAbetize Yourself*! The following points were adapted specifically for the purposes of *The Ultimate Puppy* book, and will blend well with traditional training exercises.

KEEPING THE PUPPY'S ATTENTION

Young puppies are born followers, but do not necessarily stay that way. The information in Chapter Four will help guide and train your puppy into appropriate, rewardable behaviour. Your puppy might be well on his way to taking direction from you readily and happily, but do not let him lull

The pup must be willing to follow, and to respect his leader.

not a relapse into juvenile delinquency. You just forgot that training is an ongoing process! Positive reinforcement in training is extremely successful. One of the most helpful rewards to use is the puppy's belief that his leader is the key to all the fun and good things in life. Here is how to start getting him to think about you in that way:

MAKING EYE CONTACT
Several times a day in your distraction-free home, help your puppy to make eye contact with you by tracing a line with your hand between his face and yours. You can make your hand more interesting by holding a small squeaky toy. As that eye-to-eye lock is made, even if for one second, say the puppy's name in a pleasant tone of voice and praise him as if he had just made a monumental step forward in training. He has!

It is the beginning of a communication channel between you and your dog and an important step in future training. When you call the dog by name this should mean "Pay attention, something great is going to happen". Be sure something great does then happen. Does he like food, balls, going for a walk? Give him the tidbit, throw the ball, snap on the lead and take him for a walk. Phase the luring out quickly – once he catches on he will look up without help when he hears his name. He will want to pay attention to see what fun you will provide next!

Do not expect this to work during walks right away. Start by adding distractions around the house. Put one of the puppy's favourite toys in your pocket. Get a friend to help by passively offering a different toy to the puppy. Call the puppy by name. If he looks at you, bring the toy out and have fun. If he investigates the toy your friend is offering, the friend should quietly with-

you into a false sense of security. He is probably a confident, curious puppy by now – just the type of puppy to be drawn to new and different situations. Dogs are not good at generalising. Cues and responses learned in one environment do not always carry over to a different context. What used to be black and white some-times diffuses into shades of grey in a new situation. Your comment "But he obeys perfectly at home" is of no consequence if he becomes incorrigible on walks. This is

129

Eye contact between dog and handler is an essential part of communication.

In order to avoid bowl-guarding, your pup should be shown that people bring food, they do not take it away.

draw the toy. Eventually, without saying his name again, the puppy will look at you. Jackpot!

In order to keep his name a powerful tool for attention, do not say it in conjunction with any sort of adverse command. Do not call his name to take him away from fun. Do not use his name in conjunction with the word "bad". We want him to love it when you call his name.

THE LEADER IN CHARGE
A candy wrapper lying on the ground during a walk is a valuable find, one that

might be difficult (but necessary) to get away from the puppy. Teach him that it is quite OK, in fact it is in his best interest, for you to take food or even toys away from him. Here's how.

Get extra training mileage from the puppy's dinner time. Instead of putting his meal down all at once in the bowl, put his empty food bowl on the floor within view. Walk over to the bowl and place a small portion of his dinner in it. Go about your business. When the food is gone, place a little more into the empty bowl. In addition to ALPHAbetizing yourself, you are conveying a subtle message of "Don't worry about people getting near your food bowl – people turn empty bowls into full bowls". An ounce of prevention is worth a pound of cure. Dogs seldom get into a guarding mode when fed this way. Up the odds in your favour. Place two or three bowls down and rotate putting portions of food in them, waiting for one bowl to be empty before you place a portion in the other.

You might turn play time into a lesson too. Give the puppy one of his toys to play with. In your pocket, conceal a toy he likes better. Offer to trade with him and have a game with the great toy. At other times you can trade a toy for a favourite treat. The benefit of food as a reward is that you do not ever have to take it away.

Put your dog in a Sit-Stay while you open the door.

PUPPY RELATIONSHIPS

It is time for a walk. Do not allow the puppy to demonstrate to the whole neighbourhood who is in charge at your house by dashing out the door ahead of you. Not only is it dangerous for him and you, it gives him the impression he is in charge of what is going on out there. He is not. The puppy should go through doors on the invitation of his leader. Have him Sit-Stay while you open the door. If he does not do this, take off the leash and hang it up. Wait a few minutes and try again. Another option is to open the door and, if he gets up, close the door. Try again. Have him wait until you pass, or at least walk through together on a slack leash.

You have already learned how to teach the puppy to walk nicely on a leash. Keep it black and white. Some dogs tend to get excited when people approach on the pathway and pull ahead, anxious to greet them. Often the owner will give in and allow the dog to pull over to the person, because everyone is happy to see each other.

Once you have walked through the door, you can invite your dog to follow.

Whether it is a control issue or simply a nuisance, make sure the puppy stays at your side unless released for a turn to say hello. Dogs learn best with clearly defined lines, not fuzzy areas where they must figure out for themselves what might be appropriate. That is what leadership is all about.

ENCOURAGING SELF-CONFIDENCE

HOME ALONE

Due to our busy lifestyle, separation anxiety is a common problem for dogs. Every puppy should have 'independence' lessons early in life. Being confident while home alone not only balances the leadership programme, but will add to the dog's overall confidence. The poise that puppies need in all unpleasant or new situations can start with these home-alone exercises:

Get the puppy used to a crate. Put him in it next to you while you read a book. Find time each day to place him in the crate while you are there, but progress to the point where you might be in a different room, or at least sitting watching TV with your back to the crate, or with a blanket covering the crate.

If you do not have a crate, place a baby gate as a temporary see-through barrier across a doorway to an adjoining room. Keep the puppy on one side for a minute or so, ignoring him. If he is quiet he should be let out and no fuss made. If he is noisy, say or do nothing, wait for a quiet pause, then let him out.

Help the puppy to look forward to being apart from you. Acquire a selection of sturdy washable rubber toys, the kind that are chew-proof and designed with cavities where food can be placed. Start stuffing a toy in the puppy's presence. Pay lots of attention to the toy, not to the puppy. Talk

Your dog must be taught to accept periods of separation.

to it, pat it, add more food, all while the puppy is watching. Put it in the crate and shut the door, or put it on the other side of the room separator where the puppy cannot reach it. Yes, this is teasing. Then put the puppy and the toy together on the other side of the enclosure and go and sit down for a minute or two. End the exercise while the puppy is still engaged in the toy by opening the gate and removing the toy. Do not praise him for coming out. The toy was rewarding him for staying in! If this seems to be working well, the distance between you and the puppy could be increased, or you could sit with your back to him next time.

Try the same exercise by going into the bathroom and closing the door. Come out again within a minute if all is quiet. This has a built-in insurance policy because the puppy realises that you rarely spend all day in the bathroom like you do when you go out of the front door to work. Be random about the times spent behind the closed door. A breakthrough has been achieved when the puppy's period of quiet outlasts his interest in the toy.

If you are really into dramatics and worried about possible home-alone anxiety, you could do the above exercises, but before the puppy is put away, walk around the house as if you are getting ready for work: pick up your briefcase, open the coat cupboard door, jingle your car keys.

Slowly progress to very short departures out of the front door, coming right back to keep the puppy guessing.

As you become enthusiastic and creative about planning the puppy's away-from-home adventures, make it a point to teach him that home is a good place. Do not always go to the park for a play session then return home to ignore the dog. Sometimes go to the park and then return

A crate helps to engender confidence in a clingy pup.

home to play in the house. Do not raise the puppy to think the house is a good place to get away from.

OVERNIGHT VISITS

It is improbable that your dog will always be by your side. Prepare now for the day that you might be separated, not for the daily routine, but perhaps for an extended absence, for instance, overnight at the vet's or staying with a friend while you are on a trip. Talk to some friends about hosting your dog for an overnight stay.

Consider how your dog will interact with the puppy-sitter's family, pets, and the environment. Do the children in the family need lessons on the correct behaviour around dogs? Will the children be supervised when around your dog? Are there cats in the family? A good cat friend for a puppy is one that does not run and teach him the fun of the chase.

Tolerant adult dogs can be good role models for your pup. It is fair enough if the adult 'teaches' the puppy by walking away if the pup gets rambunctious or even gives a more overt warning about good manners. In most cases this display will be beneficial to your pup, so allow it to happen. It goes without saying that interactions with other pets while on the visit will be supervised.

HOME SOCIALISATION CHALLENGES

Introduce a different obstacle and/or a novel item into your home every few days. Think always of safety. The idea is gradually to introduce, at home, as many unusual sights and surfaces as possible and have the dog accept them with confidence. Do not go overboard and wait for an adverse reaction from your dog. Read him as you go along and do not allow him to step over that threshold from curiosity to fear. After successful challenges at home, be looking for safe and reasonable challenges around the neighbourhood. Here are some ideas to get you started:

- Place a ladder flat on the floor in an opening between two rooms where your dog has to step through it to pass. The pup will learn agility and the fact that no bogey men lurk in the 'holes'.

- When he's happy with that, you might replace the ladder or find additional openings where you might place a large plastic bag to walk over, the vacuum cleaner, a large stuffed animal with big black eyes, a suitcase, a plastic bag filled with newspaper.

- Ask the delivery man in for a chat. Teach him good manners with dogs!

- Find a mirror and place it against a wall where the dog can see himself. Do not leave the dog alone with it for fear he might try to make friends and hurt himself.

- In the spring, small plastic children's swimming pools are reasonably priced. Fill one with a little water and let the puppy go 'fishing' for toys – some that float and some that sink.

- Invite a friend with a nice dog over to visit. Supervise the dogs.

- Make a ramp with a large sheet of plywood or an old door, and prop one end up a few inches with a sturdy board. Help the puppy walk over it.

- Find a box just the puppy's size. Take off

Teach your pup not to be scared of his own reflection.

Saturate your puppy with different experiences and he will not develop phobias when he is older.

the lid and bottom to form a tunnel. Get help or prop it up securely. Call (do not pull or drag) the puppy through. Luring with food is legal.

- Make or purchase a variety of hats. Make the family members wear them!

- Have someone keep hold of your puppy while you make a big deal of saying goodbye and leaving. Go and hide. At first you might just go into another room, later into a closet with the door partially opened, or behind a chair. Say the puppy's name. Have lots of fun at the reunion at the end of this search-and-rescue game.

- Invite a friend over with a well-mannered child. Teach the child appropriate interactions. Supervise.

LEARNING ABOUT SOUNDS
Start now in getting your dog used to various environmental sounds. Special CDs are made for this purpose. Compact discs can be ordered which have a full hour of various selections on a specific theme. For instance, a CD of babies will have every conceivable sound a baby might make. Perhaps you are interested in thunderstorm sounds? Get a CD that has the whole range from beginning to end, rain on the roof, the sound from inside the house, from outside the house. A CD is a good way to get the pup used to the sounds of traffic, before he has to see and smell it as well. A sound CD made especially for dog training will come with instructions. Care must be taken not to frighten the dog with your good intentions.

Use your imagination (and common sense) for other activities.

Children and puppies learn a lot from supervised interaction.

BUILDING IN EMERGENCY CONTROLS

STRENGTHENING THE RECALL
Do not use the word "Come" unless you are sure the puppy will come! Dogs learn from association. If your puppy has a history of hearing "Come, Come" while he is running laps in the field, you have inadvertently 'abused' one of the most important words in your dog's vocabulary. For all we know, he might now believe "Come" means "Run" or "Faster". It might be wise to start over using a new cue word and make sure the puppy is clear on its meaning.

What does the puppy do when you make a sudden grab for his collar? This can be a life-or-death issue should he get into the

Reliable recalls can be life-savers.

The pup must be comfortable with you reaching for, and touching, his collar.

unfortunate situation of being panicked and off-leash. Stack the emergency deck in your favour. Here is what to do.

- Touch Release: Make it a policy, when you call the puppy, often to call him at a time when you can snap on the leash, touch the collar, then release him back to his activities. It will teach him that coming or the leash does not always end his fun. In fact, you might unsnap the leash and play ball with him – if that is what he likes.

- Grab and Treat: The next step to the touch release game can be done at odd times around the house, not necessarily after a Come command. Make a grab for the puppy's collar with one hand, gently at first. Within a second of the grab, thrust your other hand, in a very similar manner, toward his face with a yummy tidbit in it. Remember, first do this very slowly and gently, then progress to a more animated grab and treat. Teach your dog that hands reaching for him will do no harm, more likely they will do a lot of good!

ESTABLISHING THE EMERGENCY DOWN

You have already learned how to teach your puppy to lie down on command. If he has a history of ignoring this cue, start training over again, using a different word. Once he is dropping consistently with you nearby, a bit more practice can turn the exercise into one of distance control. Train the puppy to drop into a Down position, quickly, no questions asked, no matter what. Wow! If he will drop willingly, even if you are at a distance, even if he is into the garbage, even if he is trotting away in the other direction – that could save his life some

Practise the emergency Down until your dog is responding promptly – even at a distance.

day. The emergency Down is a good alternative to "Come". Once again, make your puppy think it is all his idea.

Start when he is bored, tired and there are no distractions. Start in your home or garden, on-leash, with you standing very close to him. Call his name and say "Down" and when he obeys, reward him. Do not fall into the habit of rewarding for the release from the Down position. That does not do much for the Down exercise. Remember to think about what you are rewarding. And do not forget about the principle of random reward. Sometimes he gets a treat, sometimes a thank you, sometimes a smile.

Then start to build distance. If you take the leash off, be sure you are in a fenced area. A retractable leash works well for this exercise. Do not allow the puppy to take even one step forward, the dog must drop on the spot. Tying the dog to a stationery object and then moving away to give the command will help keep him in place during training. Another idea is to practise with your puppy on a slightly raised platform so that creeping forward is not really an option. Reward him at random by going up and praising or by tossing a treat in front of his nose.

Another way to help with training the emergency Down is to cue the puppy to lie down while in motion walking with you. In a cheerful voice say "Down" and then immediately stop yourself and help him down. He can be released to go on with your walk. Your emergency Down will have even more power when you get to the point of being able to drop your puppy as you are walking, and he stays put, even if you keep on going.

IDENTIFYING SIGNS OF STRESS

Stress is a normal part of everyday life and learning. Some stress is good in that it helps us perform to our maximum. Too much stress can lead to long-term illness, as well as poor behaviour. Because stress is subjective, your puppy needs to tell you if he is starting to become unable to cope with his new environment. Owners would be well advised to observe their dogs for precursors, the signs that all is not well. The dogs will tell you what you need to know; however, identifying the signs of stress can be tricky. The signs are ambiguous. It is important to look for clusters of indications, rather than just one. And please, talk to your vet about possible other physical problems causing these symptoms.

A dog that pants when cool and at rest may be stressed.

Here are some red flags.

- Barking without an apparent reason may be compulsive behaviour caused by stress. This may be the dog's way of masking or ignoring the unpleasant situation.

- Diarrhoea or a sudden lapse in house-training is often one of many subtle signs of a dog under stress.

- A dog that pants when not hot or being exercised may be stressed. It is also an indicator of physical problems.

- You might see damp paw prints on the floor even though it is not wet outside. Consider stress. Dogs perspire through their paw pads.

- Rigid body tone is an indication of a stressed dog. Sometimes you have actually to touch the dog to feel the tension. At other times you can see tension just by the way the dog holds his body or in stiff movements. Also, look for a clenched mouth and tight, drawn lips.

- The shaking-off motion is often seen after a dog is released from a tense situation – as if a way to say "Phew, glad that's over, now I can relax". Some dogs, when excited, raise the hair on their backs a little. Perhaps the dog is getting his coat back in order or, perhaps, trying to get back to normal after a tensing-up of the skin and muscles.

- If your dog is 'wide-eyed' but it is not particularly dark out, the dilated pupils could be a sign of stress. The eyes of some very frightened dogs will show more white than normal.

- A dog might perform a 'cut-off' signal by averting his eyes and, perhaps, turning his head or entire body away from a source of stress.

- Drooling can be related to anticipation of food, sexual arousal, an upset stomach or a more generalised cause of stress.

- A dog might tremble from the cold, but if it is not cold outside, a different stress factor could be at work.

'Silliness' can be the result of anxiety.

- Some dogs will yawn when things are getting tense. Perhaps the deep inhalation and subsequent exhalation of a yawn produces calm in the way deep breathing does in humans.

- A quick little forward flick or stretch of the tongue might go unnoticed. It is another sign that all might not be well with the dog.

- A dog that scratches himself even though he does not have itchy skin may be defusing stress. A dog that is in conflict, that cannot make a decision on what action to take, for instance to run or fight when frightened, will often engage in a third inconsequential, unrelated displacement activity.

- Sniffing for no apparent reason is another form of displacement. Dogs use their noses to explore their environment, but excessive sniffing can be a show of

indifference about what is going on, to defuse a tense situation.

- Comic relief. We do it too! We laugh or act silly when we are most nervous or embarrassed. Dogs may act silly by leaping into the air for no apparent reason, doing little spins or rolling vigorously on their backs.

DEALING WITH STRESS

Dogs are non-verbal communicators. They readily pick up on human body language. Most people realise how an obvious posture such as facing the dog and making eye contact can be a worry – much more so than standing sideways and averting our eyes. We can also use more subtle body language to communicate with them. For example, some owners might intensify their dog's stress reaction by focusing on it and trying to reassure the dog with pats and kind words. Instead, the owner should be unreactive and demonstrate calmness. It helps to show the dog that all is well by breathing deeply and relaxing your body. If the dog looks at you, blink your eyes slowly, yawn, turn away, and avoid eye contact. Assume a ho-hum attitude. Then plan a programme to help your dog using some of the following concepts:

ELIMINATING THE CAUSE OF THE PROBLEM

Though it is not always possible, the simplest solution to stress is to remove the cause. For example, if your dog is absolutely petrified about walking over a bridge, just do not do it – not for now anyway. Take your walks where there are no bridges. This is an easy, first-aid solution to the problem. Consider the experience a tip-off to be alert for other situations that might frighten your dog. An overall leadership and confidence-building programme will be helpful as well as a programme of counter-conditioning and systematic desensitisation. Examples of those two techniques are given next.

Dogs learn by association. A lot of dog training boils down to changing the dog's association with a particular stimulus. Use a strong and pleasant association to overcome a stressful association. By now you pretty much know which food treats, toys and interactions rank high with your puppy. If, for example, on your last walk you discovered that the puppy was afraid to get close to a road construction area, be prepared next time with some high-ranking rewards. Watch closely. As soon as the puppy realises you are approaching the problem but *before* he shows too many stress signals, take one more small step toward the problem and then call the puppy's name. As soon as he looks at you, turn and walk away several steps, play

tug-of-war, give him the biscuit or do whatever you have planned to counter-condition him to the fear. Watch for those stress signs or your plans might backfire. If you are too late with your reward, the puppy may be afraid of construction areas and now be wary of the tug-of-war game too.

Here is how to use systematic desensitisation for a dog that is afraid of riding in a car. You might start getting him over the fear by walking around your driveway and around the parked car. Since exhausts, vibrations or sound may be a meaningful

A car phobia can be prevented (and overcome) by repeated exposure.

part of the problem, the car should not be running at first. If all is well, place the dog on the seat of the parked car and allow him to jump out. Open doors on both sides and call the dog through. Then do it again with the engine running, being careful not to get close to the exhaust. Systematic desensitisation works best in combination with other tools – improve the dog's association by adding Counter-condition. For example, play ball in the drive, circle the car while giving the puppy treats, place the dog's favourite toy and rug on the seat of the car, feed dinner in the car, sit in the parked car with the dog and read a book. Little by little, expose the dog to ever-increasing intensities of the car problem. Your first drives should be short, only a few minutes. Hopefully you can find a good place to stop off for fun, like a park. Do not let every car ride end at the vet's office.

PLACES TO GO, THINGS TO DO

If you have done your homework, your puppy should be a well-mannered, self-assured dog when venturing forth. Do remember that obedience commands are not a substitute for a leash. No dog has 100 per cent recall. Always have some sort of ID on the puppy. And do not forget your plastic bag.

Now is the time to get the puppy into more varied situations. We are not trying to make the dog endure a situation, but to introduce novel stimuli gradually as the dog builds confidence in new surroundings. Be ready to ignore adverse reactions, and to counter-condition them (bring your toys and treats) or use calming signals, just in case. Let the following examples help you think of even more advanced outings for you both.

- Go for a drive and buy an ice-cream. Give your puppy a lick. Then go home.

- Drive to the vet, let the receptionist give your dog a treat. Leave.

- Ride in a lift with your dog.

- Stop off and visit some farm animals, keeping the puppy on the leash of course.

- If your dog is brave, have him accompany you through a drive-in car wash.

- Walk past a school yard.

- Invite people you meet on a walk to pet your dog (coach them on body language).

- Find a shop that will allow you to walk through.

- Find a legal escalator ride (you might want to carry the pup over the first step).

- Stop in at a child's soccer game.

- Go to visit another nice dog – but supervise!

- Visit the parking area of an airport, or supermarket, or train station.

PUPPY CLASSES

Investigate: puppy training classes are not all alike. Before enrolling, ask the instructor if you can visit a class currently in progress. Here are some things to look for and think about before signing up.

LEARNING BY EXPERIENCE

A puppy that is exposed to a wide variety of situations will mature into a well-balanced adult.

Attending a well-organised training class is a must for all puppy owners.

A good instructor will be addressing relevant topics of socialisation, care-taking and a bit of obedience as well. Can the instructor tell you the goals for the class and the steps that will be taken to attain the objectives? Are the exercises that are being taught useful for your lifestyle or consistent with your expectations?

A good instructor will have a variety of positive training techniques. Are the exercises taught by reinforcing good behaviour rather than waiting for and punishing a mistake? A good puppy class teacher will structure the exercises to avoid or ignore mistakes. Are the owners getting individual attention and coaching, or is the instructor simply calling out general directions? A ratio of more than five students to one instructor is pushing the limit for a quality class. Are the instructor's directions clear to you? Do the people and dogs seem to be catching on with ease or are either confused? Is there reasonable control of the class? It should be clear to you right away who the instructor is and what is happen-

ing in the class. However, do not confuse lack of class control with enthusiasm and animation! A good class can have both.

Families should be welcome, but the class should not turn into a wild party. Children especially should be carefully supervised or pups could learn the wrong things about kids. Free play among small groups of carefully selected puppies is beneficial to their social skills, but should not comprise the majority of the time in class. The puppies accepted into class should be in a very tight age range. Adolescent pups can overwhelm young ones. Care must be taken not to allow bully dogs to overly dominate the quiet ones. Training class should be the highlight of your week. It should be a good night out with your best friend. Be brave – if you do not like what is going on in an obedience class, do not participate.

Puppy or human, the experience gained in early childhood will influence that individual more than at any other period of life. Consider time spent with a puppy as an investment in a savings account. Some effort must be put in at first, but later you can sit back and reap the benefits.

The puppy pupils should be approximately the same age, so that equal, well-matched play can take place.

The Ultimate Puppy

6 GROWTH AND DEVELOPMENT

The new puppy, with his bright eyes and wagging tail, is really a wonder of nature's organisation of the body into different 'systems' for many activities. The desire to play, to eat and to sleep is controlled by the brain cells. Messages are sent out and received by the nerves, while hormones are sent in the blood circulating round the body to give additional messages. The arrangement of the body into different systems starts within hours of the egg being fertilised inside the mother so that, by the time the puppy is born, most of the body is working harmoniously.

THE FUNCTIONS OF THE PUPPY'S BODY

The new-born puppy differs from many young animals. The puppy is in the nest and totally dependent on the mother for at least the first 10 days. The eyelids do not open, so the puppy cannot see at first, the ear openings also develop after birth and the puppy has no way of controlling his own body temperature.

As animals that once hunted for their food, this arrangement allowed the parents of the puppy to go off to find food and provide nourishment at the same place where the puppy birth took place. There is no temptation for the puppy to wander away from his birthplace in the early weeks. Puppy development, taking place over the

first six to 12 months, commences, with the period of the first 10 days after the birth being a time of total dependency on the mother. About 90 per cent of the time is spent sleeping but the puppy is able to move to find his mother's milk by pushing with his legs, rather like a swimmer in the sea might move. Within a few days, as the muscles and bones get stronger, the puppy can lift himself more off the ground and start crawling between the sleeping area and the food source.

As soon as the new-born puppy opens his eyes, he starts exploring the new world around the birthplace. The bold pup will make little journeys away from the warmth of the bitch and the littermates but returns quickly to the sleeping area, or the bitch's body that he associates with food and with warmth. Although the puppy was at first born helpless, from 10 days onwards the development of his senses and the ability to explore and move away from the birthplace is tremendously important

After 14 days, puppies will react to noises and, by about three weeks, tails will wag, perhaps as a sign of contentment with feeding rather than pleasure. Puppies also dream, as is seen in twitching and facial expressions while fast asleep. This is a vital period in growth and behaviour before becoming an adult dog.

After four weeks the puppy will be

SKELETON STRUCTURE

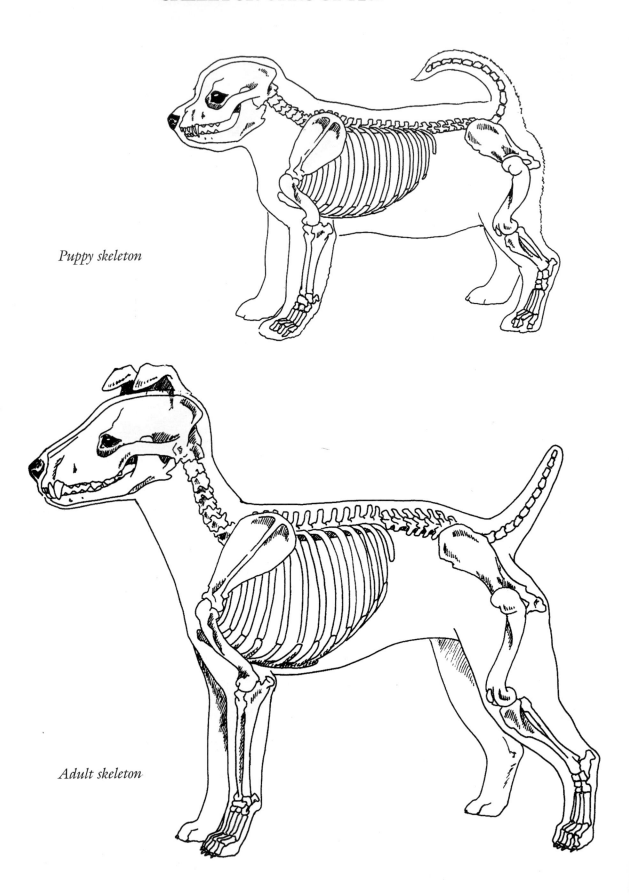

Puppy skeleton

Adult skeleton

walking around the pen on his own, he will recognise, and even fight with, his brothers or sisters but will always respond to any corrections made by the mother. If play gets too rough and noisy, or if the puppy pulls too hard at the teats of the bitch during feeding, a nudge with the nose is often enough to chastise the over-bold puppy. When slightly older, the mother will give a warning growl when the puppy goes too far. The puppy soon recognises the posture of the bitch's body when she is displeased but, if this is not enough, the puppy may be pinned to the ground with paw or nose until he learns to submit to correction. This is the first stage of socialisation: recognising the mother as leader and also being able to associate with and relate to other puppies. The importance of the puppy learning submission and dominance, as shown by the parent, is that it prepares the dog for the skills of adult life. Single puppies, and those reared in isolation, could well end up with behaviour problems by missing these early lessons.

The puppy, before he leaves his mother, goes through another important stage of development. After five weeks or so, the puppy becomes very interested in the world outside the nest where he was born. That is the time when it is very good for the pups to be exposed to normal domestic sounds like the doorbell, telephones, the vacuum cleaner, or radio and TV noises. This helps to develop their hearing sensitivities and will, therefore, lessen the chance of them exhibiting worries about noises later in life.

Getting used to people is equally important. It is advantageous to handle each pup and to weigh them at least once a week. You can take the guesswork out of whether the puppies are growing, monitor their progress when you handle each one and inspect them more closely at the same time. While they are away from the mother, time spent grooming each puppy with a very soft brush on his body, and giving a quick grooming hand massage once the puppy has been weighed, is beneficial.

As the puppies develop, the bitch gradually loses her obsessive attachment to them and allows them out of her sight. She will spend less time with them, until approximately six weeks when she may only want to visit them for additional feeding and cleaning. If the puppies' mother does not follow this pattern, it may be necessary to encourage her to leave the pups for longer periods so as to prepare for weaning. Doing this lessens the impact of the puppies leaving her, which will normally take place at six weeks, although some can certainly stay another 10 days, even when you consider that at six weeks they are fully weaned from the mother's milk.

DIGESTION

At first the new-born puppy is dependent on a milk diet then, after a few weeks, the mother will be able to bring up the puppies on a semi-solid diet. By the time the puppy is ready to leave the mother at six weeks or so, his digestive tract will be able to deal with foods such as meat, egg and cereals. Milk remains a useful source of fluids and calcium for the puppy during growth. Growing puppies need a much greater food intake for their size than an adult dog. The new-born puppy will increase his size forty-fold or more by the time he is adult.

Proteins are needed for body growth, energy foods such as fats and carbohydrates are needed for replacing the calories burnt up when the puppy races around. Calcium and phosphorus are needed for bone growth, the vitamins D and E are especially

THE DIGESTIVE SYSTEM

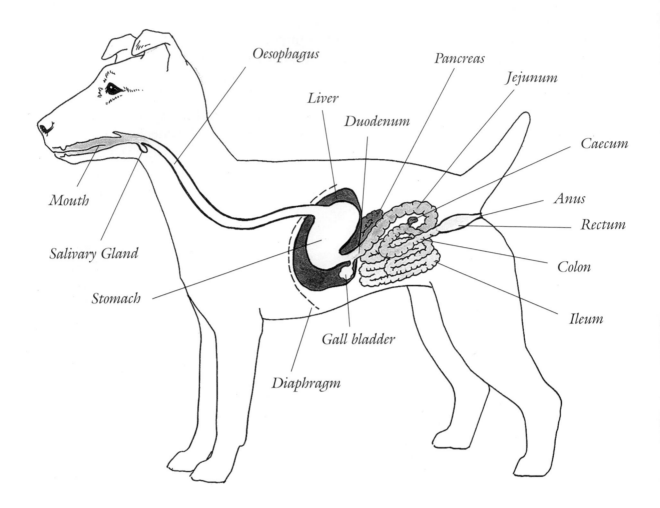

required in the young animal, but all the range of vitamins and minerals are required too in moderation. The amount eaten, and the balance of the nutrients, are equally important. If there should be too rapid a growth rate, often associated with a high-protein diet and oversupplementation, abnormalities of bone growth and joint development may result.

ELIMINATION OF THE BODY'S WASTE

The puppy born in a helpless state has to rely on his mother to keep the nest clean as there is no control over bladder-emptying, nor is there bowel control (defecation). The muscles at the exit to the bladder and at the anus are known as sphincters. These

are, at first, under automatic control and there is no brain connection working that allows the tiny puppy to know when these things happen or how to stop it ! This should be remembered when first house-training the puppy as, at birth, the mother has stimulated defecation and urine voiding by licking around the puppy's tail area after each time the puppy has fed.

Provision for this sort of stimulation may have to be used in the hand-reared bottle-fed puppy when the mother is absent. While still with the mother in the nest, a puppy, once he can walk, is able to go to a part of the pen away from the sleeping area for defecation, as there is a natural desire to keep the sleeping area clean.

These instincts to keep the sleeping area

clean can be used during the house-training of the puppy. Chapter Four describes how puppies can be trained to use newspaper pads in the room as a toilet area away from the preferred sleeping area. After waking from a sleep, and during or immediately after a play period, are the times the puppy is most likely to want to empty his bladder or bowels. Anticipation of such times, and a study of the puppy's facial and body expressions, will allow the owner to place the puppy in the right part of the room for elimination of waste to occur. If this is on newspaper, it is much easier to clear away but, if some of the smells are left remaining on the paper, it will help to remind the puppy that there is a right place and a wrong place to do this.

The nerve control of elimination is through the sympathetic and para-sympathetic nervous systems (the autonomic) supplying the bladder and rectum. As the puppy reaches four, or even as late as six months, there is another control through the conscious brain that stops elimination when the place or time is inappropriate, or the opposite, which is when the brain is sending messages that defecation or urination should take place immediately. A well-trained adult will seem as if he or she can read your mind without the words of command.

When you are with the puppy, you must observe closely the body language, the emotional expression and the habits, to anticipate when defecation or urination is about to occur. Such commands as "Be clean", "Busy", "Be quick" etc. are heard and processed by the brain so that the appropriate part of the autonomic nerve system gets into action. Some puppies learn quickly, and a clean start in life and an attentive mother help a lot. Other puppies cannot connect their messages and the new

owner will have to put up with 'accidents' of elimination up until six months of age. If, at this point, there is no control, then a veterinary opinion should be sought for a possible health disorder. Disease should be looked for too, as conditions such as ectopic ureter, pancreatic insufficiency and small intestine bacterial overgrowth, or worms in the intestine, can cause break-downs in house-training. With these disorders, the signs are quite severe and the ill puppy will have been brought in earlier than at six months to see the vet.

DIET
The type of food given to the young puppy is important, as the most rapid growth period is between birth and six months. Four meals a day should be given from six weeks to between three and four months. These smaller meals do not overstretch the stomach and they allow the digestive juices to penetrate all the food, breaking it down into finely divided components such as simple sugars, amino acids, and small fat droplets. In this state the components can be absorbed through the wall of the intestine to be carried away in the bloodstream to places where they are most needed.

With coarse foods, the puppy's stomach may become full before sufficient nutrients have been taken in. The energy needs are twice those of the fully-grown dog. After six months the growth rate reduces a little and the three meals a day from four to six months can be replaced with only two larger meals each day. Most puppies will not want to eat the breakfast meal at the beginning of the day. These two meals a day from six months to maturity are then sufficient.

The puppy will have reached half his final body weight by six months, but this time can be critical, as overfeeding leads to over-

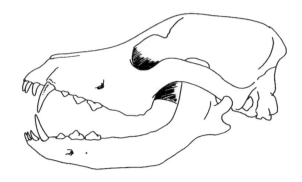

A two-month-old puppy's deciduous (milk) teeth.

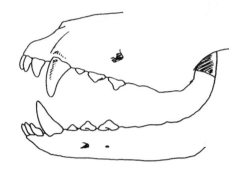

A five-month-old puppy with some permanent teeth (incisors, canines and premolars).

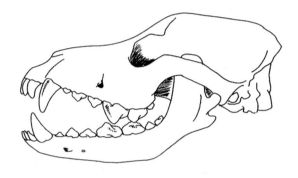

An adult dog's permanent teeth.

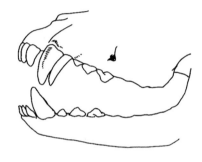

A dentition problem – there is a retained deciduous incisor behind the permanent incisor.

rapid bone growth and possible joint disorders such as osteochondrosis of the elbows or shoulders, and hip dysplasia. The greedy puppy, too, can become the overfat adult dog with all the subsequent problems of obesity. Once a guzzling approach to eating food has been learnt, the adult dog, even after dieting, will revert again to becoming overweight and there can be a constant battle to stop excessive weight gain.

Young puppies have smaller mouths and fewer teeth than adults, so they may gulp down food to fill their smaller stomachs, leading to a greed for food carried into adult behaviour. Feeding by an all-day access to food 'ad libitum' is to be discouraged. It is suggested that only 85 per cent of the food amount that a puppy could manage to eat is quite sufficient for normal growth. At the end of each meal the puppy should be looking for a little more, and earning his next meal by licking the bowl clean and looking for any spilt food remains on the floor.

The correct diet will be balanced. A commercial diet sold for 'growth' will contain more energy food and essential nutrients than an adult maintenance diet. Protein content too will be higher, to provide an adequate intake of amino acids. The percentage of protein will be listed on a bought food contents list, 22 per cent to 29 per cent might be expected in a formulated ration. Calcium and phosphorus

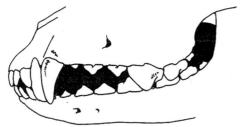

Scissor bite.

Level bite

Overshot

Undershot

are needed to form strong bones, the scaffolding for the healthy adult's body.

Puppies of the large breeds do not need extra calcium but they should have the normal amount fed in the balanced diet. Calcium levels between 0.8 per cent and 1.2 per cent should be looked for and the phosphorus level of between 0.7 per cent and 1.2 per cent is equally important for bone growth. A calcium phosphorus ratio of 1 to 2.1 is ideal. The larger puppy eats more food, so he will get a proportionately higher intake. Extra calcium or Vitamin D supplements will unbalance any pet food manufactured and specially formulated for the growing dog, so they should be avoided.

Nearly all puppies are reared on bought

dog foods and manufacturers can be relied upon to provide a balanced diet for growth and puppy energy needs. The commercial diets designed for puppy growth are advised, and such diets need no further supplementation. Variety of diet can be introduced by adding cooked eggs (fried, scrambled, boiled, or poached), occasional raw egg, pasta, toasted bread, meat, offal, cheese, fish and poultry. Milk is allowed in moderation, but the puppy loses the ability to digest lactose, and too much milk and dairy foods can lead to diarrhoea. When a change of main food is decided on, then the digestive system will adjust better if the old food is mixed in with the new food and the change is spread over a fortnight.

CONSTRUCTION OF BONE (PUPPY)

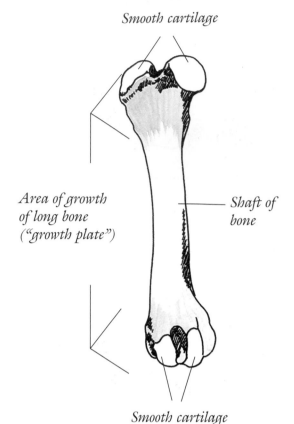

Smooth cartilage

Area of growth of long bone ("growth plate")

Shaft of bone

Smooth cartilage

STRUCTURE OF BONE

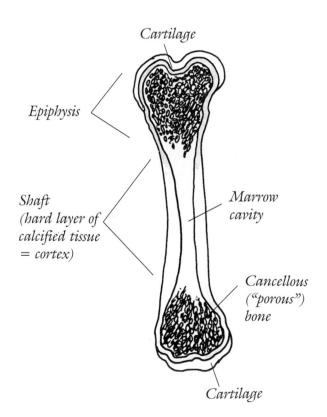

Cartilage

Epiphysis

Shaft (hard layer of calcified tissue = cortex)

Marrow cavity

Cancellous ("porous") bone

Cartilage

When a home-made diet is preferred, food composition tables should be looked at to make sure there is no excess of an ingredient that could harm the puppies' growth. A diet based on largely vegetarian foods could lead to a protein-deficient diet and the risk that some essential amino acids could be lacking. Supplements of vitamins, and some of the minerals, will almost certainly be needed, and some skill is needed in feeding a dog this way. Larger breed puppies do not have an increased calcium requirement.

A guide for constructing your own diet for a Labrador-size puppy might be:

Breakfast: half a pint of milk with some cereal such as 'Weetabix' mixed in, or a milk pudding, such as rice or semolina, provide variety and are well liked.

Lunch: quarter of a kilo (half a pound) of cooked meat (or less for smaller dogs) minced or cut up fine. This meat should be mixed with about 70 g (2-3 oz) of puppy meal or brown bread soaked in a gravy.

Beef, lamb, chicken, rabbit, and cooked fish (bones removed) can all be given. Lean, cooked pork is an alternative but it was once discouraged because of the risk of tapeworm cysts and other parasites. Pork is relatively cheap protein and need not be fatty if trimmed.

Alternatively, canned dog meat can be used but the content should be checked to see if it already contains cereals.

Teatime: the same as breakfast, or a more crunchy rusk food can be given with less milk than in the morning, since too much lactose will cause diarrhoea in some puppies.

Supper: the same combination as the lunch meal.

The aim, when feeding growing puppies, is to have a weight gain of 2 to 4 g (0.07-0.14 oz) per day per kg of the adult weight i.e. for a Labrador puppy 60 to 120 grams (2-4 oz) each day or half a kilo in a week. A 58.5-lb (26.5-kg) Golden Retriever about 1 year old might be seen to be getting fat on 13 oz (368 g) a day of a proprietary complete diet but, when cut down to 10 oz (283.5 g) a day, becomes a slimmer dog at 57 lbs (26 kg).

The supplements should be given in moderation; there are many powders, tablets and fish oils that find favour with various breeders. If bone meal is used, one teaspoonful a day is quite adequate. A large marrow bone can be given and the chewing will exercise the jaw and perhaps help teething. Warming food in the microwave stimulates the appetite of some dogs, as more aroma increases the palatability.

DO feed the puppy on the same food as he was weaned on to before leaving his mother. Any change in the diet should then be made 2-3 days after moving to the new home.

DO NOT feed puppies on a 'help yourself' system. Puppies tend to overeat and this can lead to over-fat puppies and bone growth defects that will last into adult life.

DO remove any uneaten food, but either offer it again later if still fresh or dispose of it.

DO NOT overfeed a very young puppy but be even more careful not to underfeed a rapidly growing one. A puppy nosing the dish for more, but not acting ravenously, may be a sign of adequate food intake.

DO feed the puppy from your hand initially as this will get him used to you touching his food and he will associate your smell with the food reward.

DO NOT feed the bones of chicken, poultry or fish. Lamb chop and neck bones are lethal if they should become stuck in the oesophagus.

DO NOT feed large portions of potatoes; the raw starch in potatoes is indigestible.

DO NOT feed treats from the meal table, nor should snacks be fed between the dog's set feeding times.

DO NOT feed foods straight from the refrigerator; milk should have the chill off it before pouring it into the bowl. Ice cream should be fed in moderation as it is high in fat but is enjoyed by dogs.

DO NOT worry if a pup is slow to feed when placed in strange surroundings. Two dogs feeding together will usually mean that both eat their food quicker but one of the pair may become a 'shy' feeder.

DO allow other persons to feed the puppy from time to time. This can be useful when a puppy shows nervousness with a member of the family. Once he has been given food by this person, it will

Small, frequent meals will not overstretch a young pup's stomach.

change the response to that person in the puppy's mind.

LOCOMOTION

Puppies start off in life very helpless, but 'rooting' for their food, which is the nose and neck action to find the teat of the mother, supplies a rich and warm instant energy source. The reflex is present at birth and is one of the signs used by breeders looking for normality in a litter of newly born pups. Puppies also propel themselves with their front and back legs to move to the required place and this is the first voluntary locomotion made.

As the puppy grows, the muscles develop to support the leg bones and the joints can then bend to allow the puppy to propel himself. Activities such as puppy play-fighting over scraps of paper, or pulling at the bedding, bring all the muscles of the body into use. Once they learn to stand and run, puppies then jump and may pounce on things as harmless as blown leaves. Games with toys, or safe objects from around the house, bring into use the puppy's awareness in preparation for adult retrieving and hunting.

PLAYING GAMES

Once the puppy is six weeks old, new owners should encourage playing games. Exercise should not exhaust a puppy and should be matched to the size and strength of the young one. Sleep after play is important to restore energy levels. Once protection with a first vaccine has been given, a six- or eight-week-old puppy can be carried in the arms out of the house and put down on a clean surface to walk a few paces back in the direction of the home. Only at 12 weeks of age should the puppy be allowed to run and only on soft surfaces such as earth or grass. Twenty to forty

minutes of walking a day would be sufficient for an older puppy, and the risk of excessive exercise causing concussion of developing bones and joints should be avoided.

EXERCISE

Most adult dogs are underexercised, as owners can be expected to have limited time (except at weekends and holidays). There are fewer and fewer places where dogs can be let off the lead and the anti-dog lobby wants dogs banned from all those open spaces used by children. In the USA, a 1995 study of diet and exercise in dogs less than three years old found that only 65 per cent of owners regularly exercised their dogs and more than 70 per cent of dogs were confined in some type of fenced-in area. Some 40 per cent of the dogs were exercised with others but 20 per cent were exercised on their own, probably reducing the amount of energy needed.

Thought should be given as to where and when the dog can obtain the necessary exercise. Collar and lead training comes first to allow the dog to walk safely in public places. Later, the voice recall will be established as a method of control and, provided there is a safe exercise area for free running, this will greatly assist you in providing plenty of exercise. The Sit, lying down in one place and the Stay to a voice command, are all things your older puppy can be taught. Long 'flexileads' may be the best way of giving the dog more freedom without losing total control of your dog.

'Fun and games' is the other sort of exercise. Making the pup give you his paw may not exercise much more than the prescapular muscle but rolling over gives opportunities for many body muscles to stretch and flex. Compare the actions of a horse let out into a field after a long period of stabling: it gets down on the ground and has a good roll with all four legs in the air,

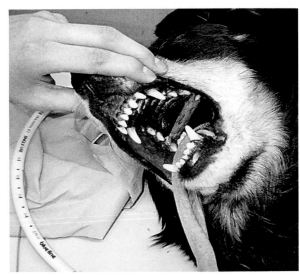

Dogs love sticks (above left) but they can cause life-threatening injuries if lodged in the back of the throat (above right).

then it gets up and shakes itself. These activities stimulate all the muscles of the body. Other activities such as opening or closing doors, and searching for hidden objects, will all provide exercise and stretch the dog's natural instincts. Ball games are generally encouraged but try to avoid any wooden stick games; unhappily, if wood becomes impaled in the dog's pharynx, expensive and often repeated surgery may be needed before all the wood can be removed from the throat. In the USA exercise study, more than half the dogs played retrieving games which included throwing balls to be fetched and retrieving a flying disc.

NAIL AND FOOT CARE

Toe nails can be very sharp in the eight-week-old puppy. When the puppy is presented for his first vaccination and health check, some vets will gently trim any sharp nails. However, it may not be an appropriate time to cut the nails of all puppies, as the most important thing is to have a gentle inspection and get the puppy vaccine injection in, without any pain or distress. The vet will judge by the puppy's manner whether nail-clipping should be done at this time. As a form of training, the dog should come to the surgery and have such things as the mouth looked at and the nails cut; it is best to start off when quite young and offer a small food reward at the end of the inspection. Some puppies will have already worn their nails short by running on concrete or paved enclosed areas. Other puppies may have been brought up on paper and carpets and have had little chance to blunt their nails, as they will not have been allowed out of doors until at least the first vaccine has been given.

Long nails in older puppies may lead to toe joint injury from sprains. In cold weather, the longer nail may be brittle and, if the outer nail shells off, a painful exposed quick or inside of the nail may have to be cauterised. The feet should be inspected after a puppy has been in muddy fields, as balls of mud can build up around the hairy parts of the toes. In wintertime, when salt and sand has been used to treat roadways, the feet should be washed with warm water to prevent skin irritation known as 'pedal eczema'.

EXERCISING YOUR DOG

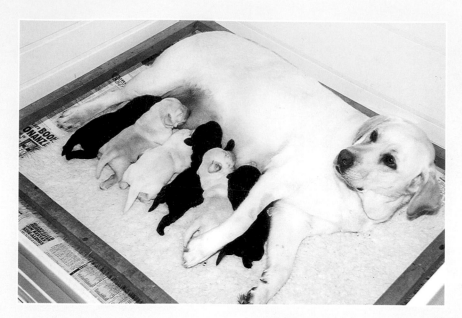

Young pups may appear helpless but have sufficient locomotion to find their dam – their chief source of food and warmth.

To begin with, a puppy will get all the exercise he needs playing in the garden.

Exercise is essential but a pup should never be allowed to overexert himself – particularly if he is a large breed, such as the St. Bernard, pictured.

Swimming is greatly enjoyed by some breeds. Make sure the water conditions are completely safe before allowing your dog to swim.

Playing games provides mental stimulation as well as physical exercise.

Free running, if possible, is of great benefit.

THE RESPIRATORY SYSTEM

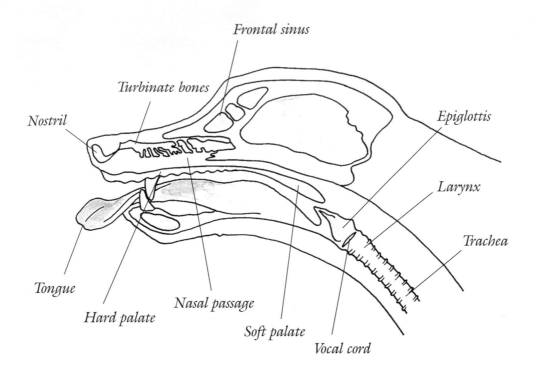

Frontal sinus

Turbinate bones

Nostril

Epiglottis

Larynx

Trachea

Tongue

Hard palate

Nasal passage

Soft palate

Vocal cord

PATH TO THE LUNGS

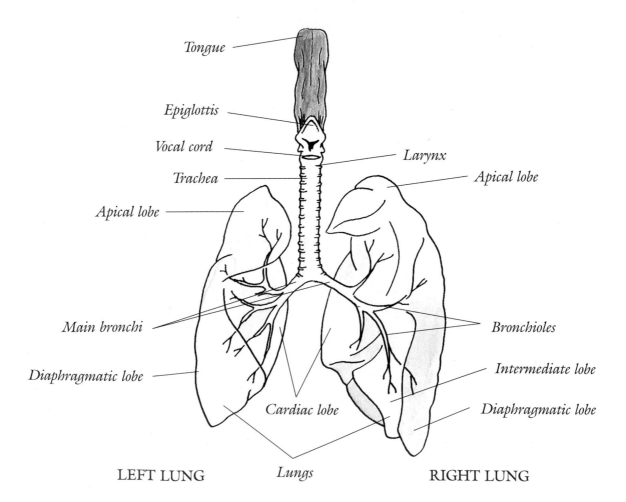

Tongue

Epiglottis

Vocal cord

Trachea

Larynx

Apical lobe

Apical lobe

Main bronchi

Bronchioles

Diaphragmatic lobe

Intermediate lobe

Diaphragmatic lobe

Cardiac lobe

LEFT LUNG

Lungs

RIGHT LUNG

RESPIRATION

Newly-born puppies start off life with independent breathing as soon as the birth membranes are broken and the lungs expand to draw in air. The resting puppy will breathe easily, and will not be seen to make a forceful effort, but after vigorous play, the mouth will be wide open, the tongue hangs out and the air is drawn in gulps until the body again obtains sufficient oxygen. A rate of 10 to 30 breaths a minute is normal but an over-hot puppy, or a puppy in pain, will breathe very rapidly until his situation improves e.g. he is cooler or the pain goes away.

Not only is breathing necessary to remove waste carbon dioxide from the body and bring in more oxygen, but the exhaled breath carries some body odours and can be used to find out what is happening inside the pup. The puppy's breath will usually smell of the last meal eaten. The new puppy in the home may have a milky odour, which is a sign to other dogs that he is barely weaned and is not a threat if brought into a house where there are already older dogs. A puppy's breath may smell of urine when there has been a disorder of the bladder.

REPRODUCTION

Puppies show no effective sexual activity until five months or a few months later when puberty occurs. Some of the robust games played by younger puppies may involve puppies of either sex mounting each other and, occasionally, male dogs show more visible signs of their excitement in their play. At six months or so, male puppies sometimes jump up and grip the trouser leg of anyone they are attracted to; this is another form of play relating to future mating experience but it can be discouraged by a sharp word of reprimand. At a young age, the male mounting is more a sign of trying out dominance behaviour rather than sexual activity.

The dog puppy starts raising his leg to urinate about the same time as he becomes sexually mature. This territory-marking device of using vertical objects to deposit urine on has a complex hormonal basis for activity, often stimulated by the presence of other dogs that have left urine trace marks in the street, or even in the home.

The bitch is only sexually active just before and during her season; she will come on heat usually twice a year. The earliest sign of a heat may be a tendency to run away more and deposit urine in the vicinity of the house or kennel which she had lived in quite contentedly until the moment of the onset of the heat.

The first oestrus or 'heat' in the bitch puppy can occur as soon as six months of age but is more likely to be at 9 to 10 months of age in the medium to large breeds. This first heat seldom lasts as long as the full three weeks of the adult bitch's season, although the older the bitch is when she first starts, the greater the blood loss in the first 10 days is likely to be.

The first visible signs of heat may be in the behaviour but, soon after, the vulva is seen to swell and you may see some blood spots on the floor. Some females lose quite a lot and become distressed at the amount of mess they cause in the home, others bleed very little and can clean up all the discharges by licking the area clean. The first heat is most likely to cause the least upset to the routine but care should still be taken to avoid males gaining access, as a pregnancy could happen. A six-month-old puppy should never be allowed to breed: not only will it cause restricted body

FEMALE REPRODUCTIVE SYSTEM

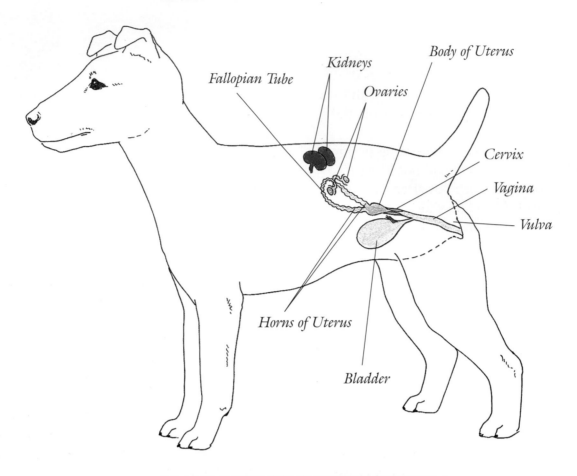

Fallopian Tube

Kidneys

Ovaries

Body of Uterus

Cervix

Vagina

Vulva

Horns of Uterus

Bladder

MALE REPRODUCTIVE SYSTEM

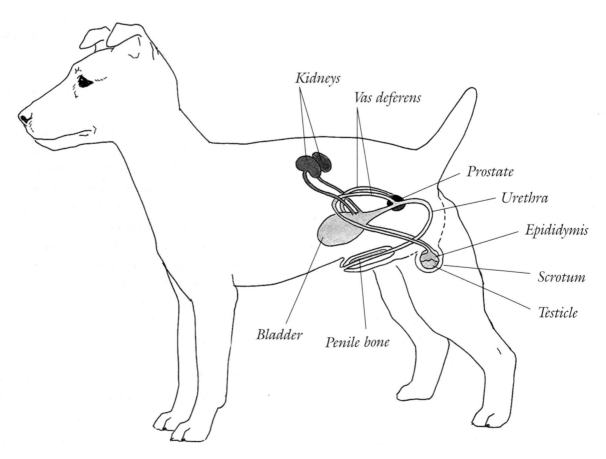

Kidneys

Vas deferens

Prostate

Urethra

Epididymis

Scrotum

Testicle

Bladder

Penile bone

growth due to demands of pregnancy but some hereditary diseases (see Chapter 10) may not be apparent at this early age. Breeding after 12 months allows time for health screening tests on a bitch to make sure she is fit to produce puppies.

CORRECT FEEDING ROUTINES

Deciding when a puppy should eat is far less important than what foods he should eat, but mealtimes should be arranged to suit the dog owner's timetable. The place where the puppy is fed should be thought about as well. It should be away from the main stream of people walking through the house. Cooking, and the food smells of kitchen dishes, may stimulate a puppy's appetite, so a quiet room or area just off the kitchen would be ideal. Preferably, if there is an exit door adjacent to the feeding area, the puppy can be encouraged to go outside once the food has all been consumed and defecation takes place out of doors.

If there are too many distractions, the puppy may become nervous; the shy feeder stops eating after the first few mouthfuls and runs away before the stomach has been filled. A puppy may feel he will be trodden on if there are too many people walking past his food bowl. The presence of a large cat, or an older dog perhaps fed only once a day, may make the puppy insecure and break off from eating before his hunger is fully satisfied.

The opposite reaction is for an older puppy to start protecting his feeding place. The puppy that guards his food and shows aggression when someone comes too close should be corrected. Any such tendency should be attended to early on, an alternative feeding place found and then various household members asked to offer the food to the dog, who is then left undisturbed during feeding. A puppy should never feel rushed or threatened while eating; it is one of the most primitive survival instincts to feed and make sure no others steal the food supply.

When a puppy wakes at 6 or 7 am or even earlier, an early start with such a young animal should be allowed for! The older puppy can be allowed to wait longer, as he will sleep if he is not hungry. After toilet training, be ready to feed the tiny puppy who has lasted 12 hours without a morsel of food in his stomach! Prepare the bowl of food, allow a drink of fresh water, then out in the garden for a scamper round and, hopefully, bladder-emptying occurs out of doors. Play will be followed by sleep.

By 12 noon the puppy wakes again and is hungry. Try distracting him or her for half an hour, copying the hunting instincts before food is available. If out-of-doors games are possible immediately on waking, then the toilet training problem is easier for the very young. Prepare the next meal. The same routine in the afternoon but more daytime play and less sleep time is advised.

Feed the young puppy again at 5 pm with the milky meal, then play, toilet and sleep before the final meal of the day at 7 pm. Supervising the puppy's day should be planned; the actual times for feeding should be arranged to suit the owner's routine, but try to stick to the same times once the routine is agreed. It is important to be able to leave the puppy through parts of the day but, once a time schedule is established, stick to it, as late rising on the weekend will lead to more messes to clean up and a hungry puppy crying for breakfast!

PUPPY DIARRHOEA

One of the most frequent reasons for the owner of the puppy needing dietary advice

A pup with diarrhoea must not be allowed to become dehydrated; small sips of boiled water must be encouraged.

is when the pup is sick, and often diarrhoea follows as a way of removing toxic waste. Overload of the stomach's digestive juices, or the eating of stale food with toxins in it, may result in the puppy throwing back his recently eaten meal. This is not an illness in itself and often, if solid food is withheld for 12 hours and sips of boiled water from a saucer are allowed every two hours, the condition will correct itself without medication. Light foods such as scrambled egg or shredded chicken (without any skin) can be offered as the first solid food.

Sometimes diarrhoea persists and this can be more stubborn to put right. The same diet, control of fluids for 12 hours, then fat-free, easily digested food, given as several small meals throughout the day, will be needed. Boiled rice flavoured with a meat cube or fat-free stock can be given to provide more bulk. Toasted bread with the crust well burnt is smooth and the black

charcoal helps to absorb gases etc. in the intestine. If diarrhoea persists for more than 48 hours, consult your vet.

Infections such as campylobacter, salmonella etc. may need antibiotic treatment. If the fluid loss from the puppy's body is excessive, then fluid therapy either by mouth or by an intravenous drip is called for. If a puppy should be unfortunate enough to become infected with parvovirus, urgent treatment is needed in the first 12 hours of the illness. Most puppies should be protected against parvo either from their mother or after successful vaccine protection.

THE IMPORTANCE OF VACCINATIONS

There are five major diseases that the pup can be protected from by two injections. Protection against rabies has also been permitted on a voluntary basis since 2000 in the UK; previously the vaccine could only be obtained by government authorisation if the dog was due to leave the country and live abroad.

The most sensitive development period of the puppy is between five and 14 weeks of age. The modern approach to protecting the puppy is to have the vaccination completed as young as possible so that the puppy goes out earlier than before. For over 25 years, the Guide Dogs for the Blind Association have practised early socialisation of puppies by giving the pups a first vaccine at six weeks and exposing puppies to sights and sounds outside the protected home from seven weeks and beyond. These puppies had two or three further vaccinations to provide long-lasting immunity.

A routine of vaccinating the newly-acquired puppy at eight and 10 weeks of age, using one of the effective new

1) **Canine distemper** was the first killer of puppies to be controlled by an effective vaccine. Only those persons dealing with stray dogs in city areas now see distemper, since the use of vaccine on over 90 per cent of the puppy population has almost removed the viral disease as a threat to the pet dog. Older breeders may remember puppies that developed green eye discharges, cough, diarrhoea and then progressed, after four or six weeks, to fits or paralysis. Recovered dogs were left with the permanent twitch of the head muscles known as chorea.

2) **Canine parvovirus** emerged as a new disease in the late 1970s and caused the death of many puppies from severe diarrhoea and shock. Effective vaccine has almost removed this threat but parvo may appear from time to time, fortunately in a milder form, so that with prompt recognition and treatment puppies are less likely to die than before.

3) **Adenovirus**, known also as hepatitis, is included in a puppy's protection by vaccination. It is now of lesser importance than the first two diseases but has in the past been responsible for death after a short illness of internal bleeding and liver failure.

4) **Para-influenza** is another viral infection included in the vaccination programme. It is one of the viruses that contributes to 'kennel cough' or infectious bronchitis. Where there is a kennel cough-infected dog severely ill, with a high temperature and an unusually persistent cough, this virus is suspected and can be shown to be present by taking blood samples during a kennel cough outbreak.

5) **Leptospirosis**, unlike the previous four diseases, is caused by a bacterial infection. Protection has to be given by two doses of killed vaccine and it is especially important to keep up the 12-monthly booster

Early vaccination is essential for assistance (service) dogs for whom young puppy socialisation is particularly important.

vaccines, seems a good compromise. There is the risk of the tiny puppy catching parvovirus, or even distemper, before he is fully protected, although the need for early socialisation of the individual pet puppy is not as urgent as for an organisation like the GDBA, which is sending out over 1,000 puppies a year from a breeding centre. However, it gives you confidence about taking your own puppy out of the house soon after 10 weeks when so many other puppies have been brought up this way in order to produce intelligent and well-adjusted guide dogs.

163

Vaccination protects your pup when he ventures forth into the big, wide world.

A more frequent worming programme may be advisable if you have children in the family.

injections when ensuring protection against this potentially fatal disease. Leptospiral jaundice is the most common disease seen in dogs that walk in the country; gundogs and town dogs living near canals or other rat-infested areas are especially susceptible unless vaccinated.

6) **Rabies protection** with a single dose of vaccine has been commonplace in many countries but the use of this vaccine on a widespread basis is new in the UK. Annual boosters are required and the level of protection can be checked by a blood test four weeks after the injection has been given. The vaccination is essential in the UK if dogs are leaving the British Isles with the intention of them returning without undergoing quarantine.

7) **Kennel cough** protection by the use of a Bordetella vaccine, given as nose drops, is recommended where there is the risk of infection to the dog. A combined Bordetella and para-influenza vaccine to use nasally is also available now. Traditionally, the infectious bronchitis was caught while dogs mixed with others in boarding kennels

but now it is almost as likely that the dog will catch the cough in a public park, or any other place where dogs come within a three-foot coughing distance of each other. The use of this nose-drop vaccine will have to be repeated every three or six months to keep up a strong level of immunity.

8) **Lyme disease** vaccine can be given at eight weeks, with a second dose at 13 to 15 weeks as advised by the vet. It is not used in the UK.

9) **Coronavirus** as a non-fatal diarrhoea of puppies can be protected against. The vaccine in the USA can be used if a pup is vaccinated against all possible infections. It is currently not available to use in the UK.

WORMING

The control of internal parasites is important. The various worms that affect the puppy are dealt with in Chapter 10. A routine worming of the puppy every three weeks up to four months is advised to stop roundworms developing. Worming at six months and then at 12 months is probably all that is then necessary. Where there are young children in the household, who may be inclined to suck their fingers after handling the pet dog, worming the pup from four months onwards at six-week intervals would be a wise precaution. A tapeworm dose is usually advised, combined with the roundworm dose, at six months.

SOCIALISATION AND STIMULATION

The smaller breeds will exercise themselves by running around the house but it is considered good for the socialisation of all breeds that they should be taken out of the home and made to walk on the lead where they can experience new sounds and sensations. As the puppy grows, agility exercises are good for the growing puppy and can give them a reason to work and play harder. Play is a stimulating process and it also helps to develop the muscles and stimulates mental development too.

NEUTERING FOR HEALTH

Neutering is accepted as a way of keeping pets in urban areas in order to cause the least inconvenience to both the dog owners and their neighbours.

It is not essential that every pet is neutered – and the entire female or male dog may be the one with the most 'character' in its behaviour. The opposite view is that the female will be on heat for six weeks in every year and many will show behaviour changes with a false pregnancy after the heat. Not every bitch develops milk at six to eight weeks from the end of her season but, when this does occur, coupled with maternal behaviour, the bitch may have to spend one-fifth of her life subjected to the various hormone changes.

I strongly believe in neutering bitches after their first season unless the intention is to breed puppies. The increased risk of mammary tumours, or cancer, in the older bitch that has been allowed to have these hormonal surges affecting her body twice a year is well known. Pyometra, as an infection of the uterus affecting the middle-aged or older bitch after she has completed her season, is again another avoidable disease if spaying is done much earlier in life.

CASTRATION

Neutering the male dog is a fairly simple operation. Both testes should be outside the abdominal cavity and are quite easily found and removed with a single incision. There is a reason why castration should wait until the puppy matures enough to be seen to lift his hind leg to 'mark' a place as he passes urine from the bladder. This indicates that the male puppy has acquired a male behaviour pattern and then, even if he is neutered, he will retain much of his masculine dog characteristics throughout adulthood. The main disadvantage is decreased activity after castration due to a lack of 'drive' in free exercise. A weight increase may be anticipated and this is why it is essential to weigh the recently castrated dog and use this as a reference weight for the rest of his life.

The only time a castration operation may be a problem is if one of the testes is hidden inside the abdominal cavity; this is known as the cryptorchid dog. Sometimes the term monorchid is used as only a single testis can be felt in the scrotum. But, invariably, there is a hidden testis that may be found anywhere between the kidney and the external inguinal canal. It is advised that both testes should be removed, as an abdominal testis may lead to 'feminisation' later in life due to abnormal hormone output and neoplasia of the retained organ. Castration between six and 10 months is usual, although it can be done much later.

RETAINED (UNDESCENDED) TESTICLE

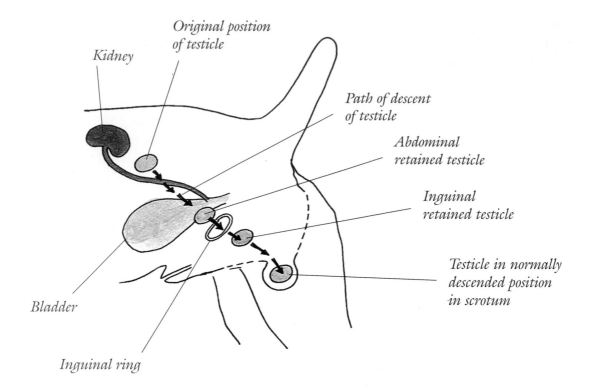

Kidney

Original position of testicle

Path of descent of testicle

Abdominal retained testicle

Inguinal retained testicle

Testicle in normally descended position in scrotum

Bladder

Inguinal ring

VASECTOMY

Occasional requests to vets are made for a dog to be sterilised but not by removing the testes. The mistaken idea is that the dog can be allowed to mate bitches without the risk of pregnancy, but there is no loss of masculine behaviour and the weight increase associated with castration is not a problem. This is rather a selfish attitude, as bitches are more than likely to be pestered by the vasectomised dog that has had experience of previous matings. Except in very exceptional circumstances, the request for a dog vasectomy is likely to be refused.

SPAYING

Do you want to breed a litter of puppies with your bitch? If the answer is yes, then do not spay. In all other circumstances, spaying is recommended. The age to spay a bitch will vary depending on circumstances. Where there is high-density housing, or the bitch pup has been supplied by a rescue organisation (often the foundling puppy was the result of an unplanned pregnancy), then it is permissible to spay between four and six months so that there is no risk of the first heat developing, with the unwelcome attention of free-roaming male dogs coming around. In all other circumstances, spaying at a slightly older age, three or more weeks after the end of the first season, is preferred.

The largest UK organisation breeding and training dogs has followed this routine and I must have spayed over 4,000 guide dog bitches at this age in the last 41 years. The false pregnancy period of about eight to 11 weeks from the end of each season is best avoided, as sometimes removing the ovaries brings on a flow of milk, so the bitch's mammary glands after spaying become uncomfortably distended. With the year-old bitch this milk can be stopped but, occasionally, in the slightly older bitch, the milk persists and the healing of the midline wound may be delayed.

The downside of having a bitch spayed is a more placid character, and some softening or similar change in the coat, but the most troublesome complication of all is a leaking bladder known as 'urinary incontinence'. Some breeds seem more likely to show incontinence after spaying, and this has been linked to the shape of the pelvis and the bladder being drawn up into a horizontal position inside the bony pelvic canal, which allows leakage to occur more readily. There are some surgical measures that make incontinence less of a problem. Medical treatments available are those using replacement therapy with an oestrogen hormone, or those using medication to constrict the bladder outlet more tightly.

Sexual maturity, and whether to neuter, may worry the owner of the newly-acquired puppy. Dogs and bitches are not difficult to control but they should be kept well apart at times of reproductive activity. Discuss the probability that neutering is for the good of your puppy with your vet at the time of vaccination and rely on the advice given by someone who knows the breed and the circumstances of the adult dog's lifestyle.

FEMALE REPRODUCTIVE SYSTEM

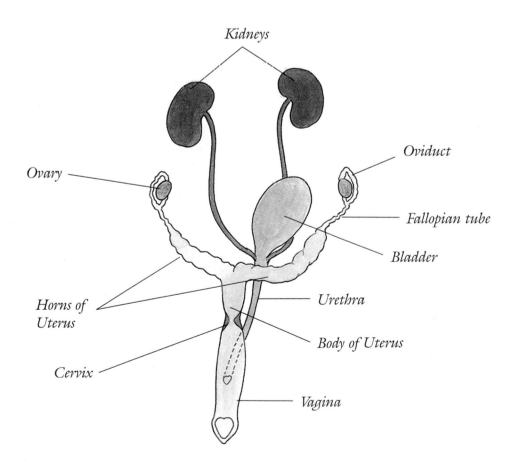

Kidneys

Ovary

Oviduct

Fallopian tube

Bladder

Horns of Uterus

Urethra

Body of Uterus

Cervix

Vagina

Spaying a bitch is considerably more intricate than castrating a male.

7 *LOOKING GOOD*

When I started grooming dogs there were two pets' parlours within about a 20-mile radius of where I lived. There was also a lady named Olive, trimming 'Poodles only' from her home, to whom I am indebted because she allowed me to help her bath Poodles and, consequently, to learn to clip them. When I left school I constantly pestered the two parlours for a job. Eventually, I am pleased to say, I managed to convince the owners of one of them that I was just what they needed. There I learned how to trim any breed of dog with a coat and to make crossbreeds look cute, taking into account their age, their health and their owner's ability to sustain a grooming regime.

Today, the situation is very different. There are many groomers, which is the modern-day word for those who trim dogs professionally, and there are dog lovers who wish to become groomers once they get the feel of grooming their own dog. But, regardless of whether you decide to clip or strip your own dog's coat, or to take him to a professional for his required hairdo, regular brushing and care of your dog's coat is an absolute necessity, no matter what the breed.

THE BENEFITS OF GROOMING
For the average pet owner of one of the numerous breeds that require specific

The relationship between a pup and his dam is reinforced through licking and grooming.

attention to their coats, a visit to a professional groomer will be necessary at regular intervals. However, the basics of brushing are all that is required for the average young pup and this is easily dealt with by his owner. Caring for the coat of your puppy, whatever the breed, will provide a wonderful interaction between you that is both therapeutic and bonding.

Consider a breed's grooming needs when buying a puppy. The Bull Terrier is a low-maintenance breed.

In the nest, the puppy is constantly licked by his mother, the dam. This practice provides many benefits. Not only does it stimulate the puppy's digestive system to function properly, it also bonds the pup to his mother, keeps him clean and teaches him some basic manners. The pup is in no position to argue and, in fact, puppies adore this process of being cared for. Dogs, after all, are very gregarious animals.

As the puppy grows, the breeder begins the weaning process (usually from three weeks, depending on the size of the litter and the dam's milk supply) together with the daily care of checking over each pup and stimulating his system by brushing the coat, thereby continuing his training merely by association.

When you purchase your puppy it becomes your responsibility to assume grooming. Whether the pup has a long coat like the stunning Afghan Hound and the Old English Sheepdog, a thick coat like the Rough Collie, Alaskan Malamute and Samoyed, the slick coat which adorns the beautiful English Setter and the Golden Retriever, the non-shedding wool of the Poodle, or the short, moulting coat of breeds which include the Dalmatian, the Labrador Retriever and the Boxer, time and attention to grooming, and the daily or weekly interaction between you and your puppy, will benefit you both life-long.

When regular attention is paid to grooming, early detection of problems in the puppy, such as runny eyes, bad breath, skin disorders and allergies, is possible and they can be nipped in the bud. One flea sighted means that many are present, and recognition of the first signs of allergy to parasites will not only save the dog from considerable discomfort and pain but it will save you a great deal of money.

Those who do not bother with grooming their dogs are missing out on one part of the really close association that takes place between a pup and his owner. Brushing the dog relieves stress both in dogs and in humans. It is thought by many to ward off heart attacks and to help stroke victims; certainly it stimulates pleasure and relaxation.

ROUTINE CARE

A dog's coat is genetically inherited, but is also affected by the way in which you treat your dog. What you feed him, the way he is kept, his housing and bedding and exercise, all have a bearing on the appearance of the coat. Your dog can look good with just a little effort and a lot of consideration about his individual needs.

When considering feeding, it is always advisable to listen to your breeder's advice. Assuming you have purchased a puppy from a caring and experienced breeder whose dogs you were impressed with, it goes without saying that they will have tried and tested different forms of feeding to establish good coats, especially if they show their dogs. Feeding the dog will be dealt with on a larger scale elsewhere in this book but, when talking skin and coat care, I think it is essential to point out that needs can differ, and not all dogs, even within a particular breed, will suit the same diet. However, if a natural diet is fed, then there is far less likelihood of adverse reactions and remember, the coat of the dog is a shining example of what goes inside the dog.

My personal preference is to feed raw tripe, lamb, chicken and beef with organic vegetables and I use natural meal made from brown rice and chicken. My dogs also have raw meaty bones to chew on. I have found that with this diet additives are not generally required, but some dogs may benefit from evening primrose oil, especially when the coat is poor from a previous diet that leaves the coat looking far from good. However, you might like to use one of the brands of complete dog foods that are on the market.

Also, if your dog has worms, his coat will suffer. Your breeder must supply you with details of when your new puppy was wormed and you must continue with this worming process every six months.

HOUSING

Where do you intend to keep your dog? This will depend largely on what breed you have. A Poodle, or a Cavalier King Charles Spaniel, or a Cocker Spaniel, for instance, will certainly live in the house at all times and probably sleep as near to you as possible. A Bullmastiff, a Bernese Mountain Dog or a

A nutritious diet keeps the coat visibly healthy.

171

Newfoundland may live in a kennel but prefers to have company; an Alaskan Malamute may live outside. Personally, I wonder why anybody gets a dog as a family pet then bans him from the house, but that is another matter. The bedding and the housing you choose for your dog will have a bearing on his coat. A dog that constantly lies on concrete will wear the hair off his elbows and elsewhere. A dog lying on grass all the time may get bitten and will absorb the moisture from the ground which may irritate the skin. Scratching can destroy a beautiful coat overnight. Bedding should be constantly washed and floors kept clean, but remember, too strong a disinfectant can cause damage if absorbed via the dog's skin, or if he licks the floor.

EXERCISE

The many breeds of dog are so different in their requirement for exercise that this is a serious consideration when choosing your puppy. As regards the coat, a fit and healthy dog will be recognised in an instant by the gleam of his jacket. In order to produce excellence of appearance, the heart, lungs and general functions of the dog need to be in good working order, and fit dogs obviously perform better than overweight or undernourished dogs. The young bones of the heavy breeds cannot take the strain of too much exercise and this is best kept to a minimum in such dogs as the Bernese or the Great Dane, for instance, but moderate exercise will stimulate good health, which will show in the appearance of the coat.

WHEN TO START YOUR GROOMING REGIME

From day one, is the simple answer. For most breeds of dogs it is a simple task to put the puppy on a table and brush him.

Your pup needs to get used to the sensation of being touched all over.

A toy provides a useful distraction, and teaches the puppy to associate his early grooming sessions with an enjoyable experience.

Even in the heavier breeds, it is as well to put them on a table to begin with while carrying out routine brushing and combing, and checking ears, eyes and mouth, as well as ensuring that the anal area is clean and completely free of foreign matter or faeces, which it should be if the diet is correct and the pup is happy.

Choose a specific spot in a utility room or in the garage where it is warm enough or cool enough to be comfortable. Install a table large and stable enough so that the puppy does not feel insecure, and put it against a wall, or in a corner where it will be walled on two sides. It is essential to train the pup to stand still and be groomed for a few minutes. With very young puppies do not prolong this session until the pup objects through boredom, or the inability to concentrate for too long a period. Most puppies are pleased to have the attention of daily grooming and it only takes a little firmness of voice and hands to get them to respond. Dogs love interaction, and handling will be beneficial to growth and mentality. With only a minute or two a day spent on grooming, the dog will become accustomed to doing as he is told and will be more responsive to his owner and family.

One word of advice to the new puppy owner: do check that your new young pup has relieved himself before grooming commences – a pup that needs a pee will object and whine all the time you are trying to brush him.

I know some people who use their kitchen table to groom their dogs. One word of warning here – once you have introduced a dog to the table where he then gets attention, he will want to return to this spot as soon as you leave it, or use it as a place of rest. Poodles, I know from my own experience, love to sit on the kitchen table and look out of the window on a rainy day. My fault, not theirs. Small dogs like the Jack Russell, Chihuahua and Miniature Pinscher are great lovers of sitting high up to get a better view, if the ones I know are anything to go by.

EQUIPMENT

This will vary according to the breed of dog. Poodles and the Chow Chow, as well as the Whippet, Pomeranian, Old English Sheepdog or Cocker Spaniel, need brushes and combs to suit their differently textured coats. More attention will be paid to coat type later. For the first few weeks it is sufficient for you to buy the brush the breeder recommends for your particular breed and start brushing on a daily basis to begin with. This interaction will benefit the puppy and teach him to respond to you and to observe house rules and manners, as well as to relax him and make him feel secure, while you will learn more about the character you have chosen to live with for the coming years. With some breeds who do not need constant attention to their coat in order for it not to tangle or felt (mat), grooming may later become a weekly occupation rather than a daily one.

BRUSHES

There are many sorts of brushes and combs readily available from your local pet shop, veterinary surgery and even the supermarket store, as well as from garden centres.

- Slicker brush: This is a fine wire pin brush used for the unclipped hair of the Poodle and for coats which mat – Spaniels, Bichon Frisés, Old English Sheepdogs, Yorkshire Terriers, and for breeds with thick coats such as the Alaskan Malamute, the Chow Chow, the

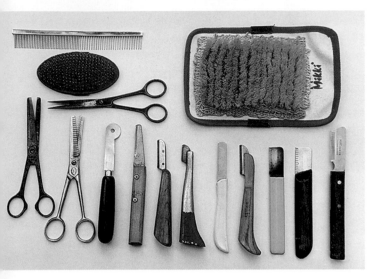 

The contents of your grooming kit will depend on your breed of dog. Left: equipment suitable for an Airedale Terrier. Right: basic equipment for a less intensive breed, such as the Labrador.

Pekingese and the Samoyed, as well as most terrier breeds such as the West Highland White and the Cairn Terrier, on parts that are not clipped or stripped.

- Bristle brush: This is a softer, oval-shaped brush which is used on shorthaired breeds like the Whippet, Dalmatian, Great Dane, Miniature Pinscher, Mastiff, etc.

- Pin brush: This brush varies in size and shape and can be used on many differently sized breeds of dog including the Collie and the English and Irish Setter, the Shih Tzu, the Maltese, the Miniature Schnauzer and the Newfoundland. It is used largely for breaking up coat to remove loose hair.

- Rubber brush: This is useful for removing dust and loose hair on the shorthaired breeds such as the German Shorthaired Pointer, Vizsla, Weimaraner, Bull Terrier, etc.

- Hound glove: This is ideal for brushing

short, smooth coats like the Beagle, Bloodhound, Greyhound, etc.

COMBS
These are an essential requirement and many different shapes and sizes are available – fine, medium, wide-tooth, with and without handle. Wide-tooth combs are best for longhaired coats and the wool of the Poodle.

- Mat combs: These are used to slice through thick mats without totally destroying the coat. They have heavy, sharp teeth and can be resharpened if required. Regular grooming of your dog will not require you to resort to this type of comb.

- Rake: This works on the same basis as the mat comb but has shorter teeth. It is a handy tool for keeping ears such as the Cocker Spaniel's from forming mats.

- Utility brush: This has a wooden handle and is perfect for getting through long hair like that of the Collie.

- Undercoat rake: This will loosen the coat and remove dead undercoat on breeds like the German Shepherd Dog.

HOW TO GROOM

Grooming is a word used in many parts of the world and it incorporates the clipping or stripping of the dog's coat. However, specialised or professional coat care is rarely undertaken by the average dog owner and certainly needs a specialised book of its own. For the pet owner, it is sufficient to understand the rudiments of basic brushing and, depending on the breed, combing and bathing.

Stand the puppy on the table, standing close to him, with a finger holding his collar to ensure, without doubt, that he does not fall or jump off the table and cause himself grave damage. Tell the puppy to "Stand". Commence brushing with your free hand, starting from the head and down the ears, working systematically down the body and legs and tail. Do this for a minute or two, then tell the pup to "Turn" as you turn the pup the opposite way round. Then again tell the pup to "Stand" and commence brushing this side, starting with the head as before. Stroke the coat firmly but gently and repeat the word "Stand" every now and then. If the pup stands still, even if only for a moment, say "Good boy" or "Good girl" while the pup is quiet and responding to your will. When you have finished brushing the coat, reward the pup with praise and a little piece of cheese or his favourite treat, then lift him down on to the floor. Brushing will, within a couple of days, become a nice affair, one the pup will look forward to.

Once the pup is accustomed to you handling him in this way, then progress to using a comb after brushing where the breed necessitates this, and gently turning

Hold the puppy securely while you gently brush and comb him.

over the flap of the ear, where applicable, and wiping it with cotton wool (cotton) or a cotton pad. This is more to get the pup used to the idea of having his ears touched, rather than him needing attention to his ears at this stage. While a puppy is teething I tend not to lift the flap of his mouth to check dentition more than once a week as the gums could be sore. Chewing on *raw* beef bones will help puppy teeth.

Bulldogs, and breeds such as the increasingly popular Chinese Shar-Pei with their many wrinkles, need special attention to keep the wrinkles dirt-free and dry, in order

Wrinkly breeds, such as the Bulldog, require particular skin care to keep their folds of skin clean, dry and infection-free.

A rubber mat will prevent slipping, especially in larger breeds.

to ward off irritation and infection. The skin must be parted and cleansed with warm water and then dried. A light dusting of baby powder or corn starch, applied by first putting it on some cotton wool or a cotton pad, may be necessary. This should be attended to weekly, as with all folds or wrinkles in the skin.

BATHING

All dogs benefit from a bath. Some breeders advocate that show coats, on terrier breeds for instance, are made too soft if the coat is washed clean. As far as a pet dog is concerned, I think it is up to the owner if they prefer a nice-smelling pet whose coat does not leave an odour or grease on the hands after stroking. Certainly, clean hair is easier to brush and comb than dirty, dusty hair. Bathing the dog is frequently left to the professional groomer. Many people book their pet dog into the local parlour for a bath, sometimes monthly, sometimes twice a year. If you intend to bath your own dog some thought must be given to this procedure, according to the dog's breed. Putting a St Bernard or a Newfoundland into a bath when he does not want to co-operate is no joke. It is best to get puppies used to brushing, being on a table, and having ablutions at an early age. They get used to the handling and are so much easier to deal with. Most dogs love a bath unless they have had a bad experience.

Before bathing it is a good idea to brush through the coat to remove any tangles, although with today's anti-tangle conditioners this is not as crucial as it used to be. However, bathing is made so much easier and quicker if the dog is properly groomed beforehand, and it makes the drying time far shorter.

Put a rubber mat in the bath to prevent the pup from slipping, then stand the pup

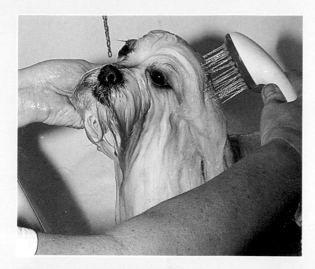

Wet the coat thoroughly.

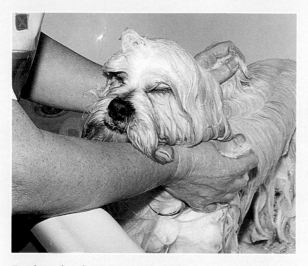

Lather the shampoo and rinse.

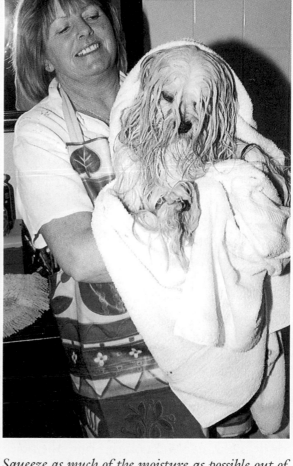

Squeeze as much of the moisture as possible out of the coat before blow-drying.

in the bath with a collar on, if this is necessary to keep control. Ensure the water from the spray is of the right, warm, temperature before wetting the coat. Be systematic. Start from the head and work downwards. Use the shower spray head direct on to the skull to prevent water being sprayed into the dog's face and eyes, holding the head slightly upwards to encourage the water to flow down the dog's neck rather than over his face. Wet the coat thoroughly before applying shampoo. Rub the shampoo in with your hands and massage well, adding water if necessary to ensure it works through the coat. Wash the entire dog before starting a rinse.

Again, be systematic when rinsing to ensure no parts are missed. Rinse out all shampoo thoroughly or you will have a very itchy dog on your hands, or one with white streaks or flakes of dandruffy-looking bits. Rinse well round and under the ears without spraying water into the ear canal. You can use your thumb to protect this area or put a little cotton wool (cotton) in the ear before you start bathing.

DRYING

Squeeze as much water out of the coat as you can, then wrap the dog in a large towel and remove him to the grooming table for drying. Use several towels if necessary to soak up as much moisture from the coat as possible. However, this does not necessarily apply to show coats like the Poodles, which need to be blown straight. Use a fast-drying blow dryer – the more coat you have, the better the dryer required. If you intend to bath a heavy-coated breed on a regular basis, you will save hours of time by purchasing a proper dog dryer on a stand. This enables you to have both hands free to hold the dog and groom while drying takes place. To obtain one of these wonderful machines that last a lifetime, visit a large dog show or get yourself a dog paper and you will see advertised all the different equipment available. A useful tip for owners of the short-coated moulting breeds like the Greyhound is to brush the dog's body thoroughly with a hound brush while he is wet in the bath; this removes a lot of the moult and you can rinse the hairs

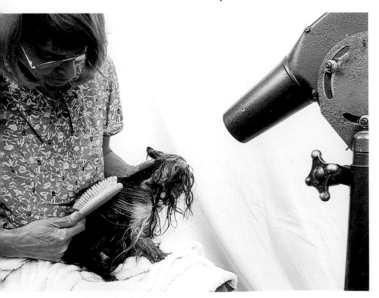

If you have a long-coated breed, such as a Yorkshire Terrier, a professional dryer may be a worthwhile investment.

away, rather than have them stick into your carpets and furniture.

SHAMPOOS

There are many shampoos on the market especially designed to deal with individual coats. Some shampoos are very drying and some smell better than others. A mild shampoo is all that is required for the average pup. Puppies with fleas should be sprayed with a preparation obtained from the vet which is less harmful to the skin and coat than many of the flea shampoos on the market, many of which do not work in any case.

CONDITIONERS

With some long coats, and coats that are going through a tangling stage at the time of changing from fluffy puppy coat to maturity, it is sometimes a good idea to use a conditioning cream after bathing. These vary from a spray which is left in the coat, to ones that are massaged in and rinsed out. Choice will depend on what suits your breed of dog and why the individual animal has a problem coat. Often it is as well to add a teaspoonful of baby oil to the made-up conditioner if the skin is dry. Baby oil can also be used to rub directly into dry skin.

CLEANING EARS

Most ears are trouble-free, but some collect dust and debris, and some accumulate hair which blocks the canal. Dogs can get ear mites from rabbits and cats, whether they have flapped or pointed ears. For the normal ear, a wipe round the top part of the canal is all that is required. To remove dead hair, or where brown wax has formed, use one of the preparations available, such as Thornit powder, as directed. If hair must be removed from the ear, only take very small strands at a time, holding the flap back over the head to protect the inner ear.

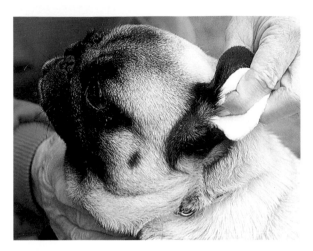

Ears should be cleaned regularly to prevent the build-up of wax and dirt.

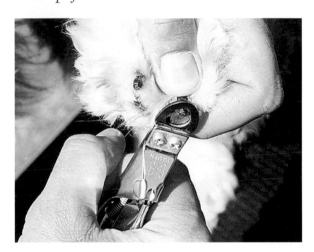

Nail-clipping should take place after bathing when the nails are softer.

Some prefer to file the nail with a 'grinder'.

Applying a dusting of powder to the ear will help loosen the hair and make it easier to remove. Do not go exploring down the dog's ear; you may cause pain and further trouble. Ear problems are best left to the experts. However, with care and correct feeding most ear trouble can be avoided. Dust around the outer canal with a suitable ear powder at the first sign of brown wax and continue to use as instructed on the information sheet provided with this product to keep mites at bay.

NAIL-CLIPPING

Dogs that have regular road exercise should wear their nails down naturally. If you need to shorten the sharp ends of the pup's nails you can use a large, rough file, holding the nail with your thumb and rasping the file upwards, or you can cut across the nail with dog nail-clippers. It is relatively easy to purchase a pair of nail-clippers with a guard to prevent too much nail being taken off at a time. All dogs have a quick inside their nails which will bleed dreadfully if cut and cause them a great deal of pain. So do take care. Sit or stand the pup on the table, hold the paw in one hand firmly, but being careful not to squeeze the foot, and snip off the very end of each nail. It is a good idea to do this after the dog has been bathed as the nail is softer and easier to clip.

DIFFERENT COAT TYPES

Without a doubt there is a tremendous difference in the coat types typical for each breed. Certainly you should take this into serious consideration before taking on the breed of dog you like the look of. Can you cope with the hair? Will you need professional help? Can you afford the outlay of regular trips to the grooming parlour? Are you, or one of your family, asthmatic or allergic to moulting dog hair? These are

The Poodle's non-shedding coat is a bonus – but it does require regular clipping.

The Akita's thick coat requires regular brushing and combing.

just a few questions that need to be considered before deciding on the right breed for your family. Here we will look at some of the most popular dogs and their coat type.

Puppies of all breeds have a softer coat than the one they will have on gaining maturity. Poodles, for instance, have a soft, fluffy, wool coat that is easy to care for until they are about seven months of age when the coat thickens. Then it will mat or 'felt' solid against the skin unless it is properly groomed. The advantage of the Poodle coat is that it does not moult and does not cause allergies. But, before considering this breed, it is essential to realise that the Poodle will need care and attention to grooming more, perhaps, than any other breed of dog. Most Poodle own-

ers adore the different coat of this breed and relish the fact that their dog looks stunning after a shampoo and trim, and that there are no dog hairs about the house.

The **Afghan Hound**, as a complete extreme in example, has a thick, silky, fine-textured coat which is not clipped or trimmed but which requires extensive brushing.

The **Airedale Terrier's** coat tends to vary from coarse to soft and cotton-like. It has a tendency to matting and requires brushing, combing thoroughly and regular hand-stripping.

AKITA
A slicker brush is required for this thick coat and, with regular brushing and

combing with a wide-tooth comb, little else will be required between the usual twice-a-year casting of coat. Constant combing at this time should quickly clear dead hair ready for the new coat to grow through, and a good bath at casting time will help loosen the unwanted hair.

ALASKAN MALAMUTE

This has a thick, coarse guard coat, which is dense, in an oily, woolly undercoat which is generally medium in length along the sides of the body and increasing in volume around the shoulders and neck, breeches and plume.

BOSTON TERRIER

The coat is short, smooth, bright and of a fine texture, easy to maintain. Bath as required and remove unwanted hairs in the bath with a hound glove.

BRITTANY SPANIEL

Spray coat conditioner enhances this breed. Brush through with a moulting comb to remove the dead undercoat of this dense, flat or wavy, but never curly, coat which is not as fine in texture as some other Spaniel breeds.

BEAGLE

This short, dense and waterproof coat needs little maintenance but the dogs enjoy the interaction of brushing and bathing.

BICHON FRISÉ

This pretty breed has a pure white coat of fine, silky texture with soft corkscrew curls. It has a lot of coat around its face which will need regular attention and cleaning to keep it free from food and debris. Attention to grooming is essential. Brush with a slicker, and comb with a

The Bichon Frisé's coat is particularly profuse around the face and head.

wide-tooth comb. Bath regularly, or take to a professional for frequent expert care.

BULL TERRIER

This breed has a coat which is short, flat, even and harsh, and easy to maintain.

BORDER TERRIER

Although natural-looking and not requiring clipping or cutting, this breed does need to be hand-stripped twice a year to keep the dog looking smart and to remove layers of dead hair that may cause irritation. The puppy coat stands in a frizz which is easily removed with thumb and finger, stripping individual hairs. Some owners painstakingly endure this operation; for others a simple trip to the doggy hairdresser for an expert to deal with it is far more acceptable. When resorting to a stripping knife, use one with a serrated edge rather than one which

The Border Terrier's coat looks natural – but it needs to be hand-stripped.

incorporates a blade. Your dog's breeder will show you how to do this.

Many terriers, including the Fox, the Cairn, the West Highland White, etc., will benefit from this same treatment and care of their coats.

CHOW CHOW

These dogs, which have fluffy coats in puppyhood, will mature to owning an abundant, dense, straight, stand-off coat which is more harsh in texture, with a soft and woolly undercoat. Use a slicker brush to deal with the entire coat, layering the coat to allow you to get right down to the skin to remove mats and prevent bunching-up of the coat. These dogs look magnificent after a good bath but rinsing shampoo

carefully from the coat is essential and is a lengthy task.

COCKER SPANIEL

The English and American Cocker Spaniel vary considerably in coat length and style of trimming. The coat texture on the American Cocker should be silky and flat, or slightly wavy, permitting reasonably easy care. Often in the grooming parlour we see thick, matted hair which needs considerable effort to groom. These coats need to be brushed with a slicker on a regular, even daily, basis to keep them looking good and tangle-free. Use a steel comb after brushing. When bathing, an anti-tangle conditioner may need to be applied. The body will need stripping with a knife. Pet dogs are often clipped with electric clippers to shape the coat into place. High-maintenance.

The English Cocker has less hair and is easier to keep in this regard. Although regular attention and expert stripping is essential, the pet owner can keep on top of the coat if the pup is introduced to brushing and combing at an early age and this is continued throughout the dog's life. This coat should not be too profuse but, once clipped with electric clippers, it will grow more curly and thicker. Use a soft brush on the head and body, and a pin or slicker on the leg feathering and ears. A fine-tooth comb will remove many unwanted loose bodycoat hairs. Young puppies are easy to deal with but, as the coat matures, a lot more attention is required to prevent extensive matting, as with the American Cocker. It is cruel to neglect the grooming of these dogs. To keep their Cocker Spaniels looking good, many breeders bath them once a week. Certainly, pets of this breed will benefit from regular attention to their coats. Most Cockers will need to be

Cocker Spaniel puppies are easy to care for, but the workload increases when the coat is fully grown.

professionally stripped four times a year, or more. Owners can remove many unwanted hairs by holding the hair away from the body and using finger and thumb to pull away loose hair. This is an on-going and often lengthy task.

ENGLISH SPRINGER

These dogs, and the Field Spaniels, look stunning when their coats are properly maintained and they take less maintenance than the Cocker as the hair is closer and straighter, with only moderate feathering on the ears, forelegs, underline and hindquarters. A weekly grooming is sufficient for the adult dog. Use a medium-tooth comb all over and a stripping knife for the body. Excess hair is periodically trimmed from the feet and the inside of the ears. Normally this routine care can be easily managed by the owner.

ENGLISH SETTER

The slightly wavy, long and silky coat of this

breed, with the feathering on breeches and forelegs and lower body, enhances the appearance of this friendly and quiet-natured dog. The entire coat needs brushing with a pin or slicker brush, and a certain amount of stripping or clipping of the neck and body is often undertaken to enhance the general outline. Clipping with electric trimmers on the body will ruin the coat and promote thick, curly hair.

IRISH SETTER

These elegant dogs have smooth hair on the head and a long and dense coat which is well feathered on the front and hind legs and on the tail. It is fairly easy to brush, using a pin brush for the long hair to keep the feathers free of twigs, etc.

The elegant Irish Setter has extensive feathering.

The Miniature Pinscher's coat is straight and lustrous. Photo courtesy: Saxonya Miniature Pinschers.

MINIATURE PINSCHER

This sturdy and structurally well-balanced dog is smooth-coated with hard, short hair which is straight and lustrous. Brushing with a bristle brush or hound glove will enhance the richness. The same treatment would apply to the coat of the Dobermann Pinscher.

MINIATURE SCHNAUZER

These are extremely smart little dogs with a hard and wiry coat which is short on the body, and clean on the neck, shoulder, ears and skull. The legs are covered with plenty of hard hair and a good undercoat is essential. To keep this breed looking as good as it should, expert help is required in the art of hand-stripping the coat. Often groomers of less experience, or less incentive, clip these dogs; it is certainly quicker. However, it is a pity to ruin a good coat and the owner of this breed should seek a qualified hand-stripper wherever possible. Once the coat has been clipped with electric trimmers it is normally

The Miniature Schnauzer before stripping.

The smart-looking appearance after professional grooming.

ruined for hand-stripping. The maintenance in between professional trims is easy, with only brushing with a slicker or pin brush being required, plus the odd bath. The same would apply for this breed's big brothers, the Standard and Giant Schnauzer.

PUG
This smart little jolly dog that often gets called a baby Boxer has a fine, smooth, soft coat that is short and glossy. It is low-maintenance, but it does benefit from regular brushing with a bristle brush and grooming mitt. A bath enhances the coat, leaving it looking good.

POMERANIAN
This includes the German Spitz right through to the Keeshond. They have magnificent coats which are dense with an abundance of ruff, feathers on legs and breeches that are well plumed. There are two coats, an undercoat and an overcoat, which will require thorough grooming with a slicker or pin brush, as with the Samoyed and most Spitz breeds.

A grooming mitt helps to keep the Pug looking in tip-top condition.

SHIH TZU
Here we have a breed with a long, dense coat which is not curly and has a good undercoat. It needs brushing and combing with a slicker and a wide-tooth comb frequently, and the hair on the head should be pulled back from the eyes and secured

The Shih Tzu needs regular brushing and combing.

with a rubber band. Many pet owners find they cannot be doing with the adult coat once it has grown long after the adorable fluff stage of puppyhood and resort to using a professional for regular grooming and bathing, or to having the dog's coat trimmed back to give the appearance it had in puppyhood. The same thing generally appears to happen to the similar Lhasa Apso.

STAFFORDSHIRE BULL TERRIER
Smooth, short and close to the skin, this coat should gleam after being brushed with a bristle brush or hound glove. Low-maintenance but the dog loves the attention of grooming.

POODLE
Toy, Miniature or Standard all have a wool coat that does not moult and is relatively easy to bath, brush and comb and keep untangled when long hair is regularly brushed with a slicker and combed with a wide-tooth comb. Part the hair to get down to the skin to remove any dead hairs. This breed must be clipped and scissored and for this the average owner will have to find a suitable, and kind, experienced professional groomer. Not all groomers are well trained in the art of trimming a Poodle. The puppy's face, feet and tail are clipped by the breeder as a rule, from the age of five to six weeks. They are bathed and blow-dried before leaving for their new homes. From then on, for the rest of the dog's life, the Poodle must be trimmed regularly every four to six weeks. The advantage is having no hairs in the house, and no dog allergies for those that are sensitive. You are also taking on a tremendous friend.

YORKSHIRE TERRIER
This long-coated Toy terrier has a coat which hangs quite straight and evenly down each side of its body, with a parting extending from the nose to the end of the

The Poodle's coat can be clipped into a number of different styles. Pictured: Continental Lion Trim.

The glorious Yorkie coat is very hard to maintain at full length.

tail. Glossy like silk, and of a fine texture, the entire coat can be brushed with a slicker and combed through with a wide-tooth comb. These terriers often have coats that are a bit cotton-like and mat easily. Yorkshire Terriers are frequent visitors to the grooming parlour, and some owners like the hair cut short as they find the length too much to cope with. As with many breeds, people often prefer the puppy look to the adult.

THE CORDED COAT

Way back in 1886, a popular dog in the show ring was Champion Achilles. He was a Poodle measuring 21 inches at the shoulder and had cords of coat that were 23 inches in length. Corded dogs, which include breeds like the Hungarian Puli, the Komondor and the Poodle, have coats that are allowed to grow and are never combed out, but which are continually rolled and twisted between the fingers with oil or Vaseline to cause longer and ever longer

dreadlocks with the appearance of cords or tassels. The type of coat that cords consists of a longer, coarse outercoat and a softer undercoat. The hair tends to cling together like tassels which, when corded, are strong and heavy and felty to the touch. If neglected, this coat will form into large matted plaits which could attract foreign bodies which invade it and find a good habitat. I read somewhere about it being a superhuman task to bath such a dog, and I can believe it. Personally, I am not in favour of cording coats because I cannot see that the dog is comfortable at all. The ownership of such a dog would require total devotion to the coat, I imagine.

CHOOSING YOUR GROOMER

It has to be said that most pet owners take their dogs to the grooming parlour or to one of the professional groomers who trim at their home. Some owners have groomers come to their own homes as they do not have transport. All these outlets can only be good for the wellbeing of the dog, provided, that is, that the groomer is chosen with care. Without doubt the majority of professional groomers are people who are devoted to dogs and will take every care of your pet. However, there are some groomers that go it alone too soon. They go on a three-week course to learn the art of clipping and then believe they are ready to trim any dog. They are not.

Considerable experience is required to deal with the numerous range of coats as well as, even more importantly, the varying temperaments of the numerous breeds of dog.

Some breeds are far more tolerant than others, but all breeds benefit from being handled from a young age. Often problems

The groomer needs to know and understand dogs, as well as being skilled at his or her work.

occur because the owner does not think about taking their pup for professional grooming until he is over one year old, or until the time comes when they can no longer cope with the mats and tangles that have formed in the coat, thus making the dog's first experience of being professionally trimmed less enjoyable than it should be. The Poodle will already have had his face and feet clipped at eight weeks old, and had a bath and blow-dry, before he leaves any reputable breeder. The grooming is recommended to continue thereafter every four to six weeks.

Terriers have a completely different attitude to Poodles, and the different breeds of terrier, from Lakeland, Airedale, Fox, Tibetan and West Highland White, vary in nature, and need handling according to their previous experience, rearing and temperament. How do you choose the right person to trust with your most precious pup? I heard a horrific story from a lady with a Miniature Poodle who took her dog to a groomer. She said the lady groomer threw her dog over the back fence and he landed on his side. This was in her full view, so what happened when she was out of sight?

Probably a good indication that your groomer is kind and thoughtful is if the dog likes going to be groomed. The only thing wrong with this theory is that dogs that dearly love their owners and are, perhaps, a little spoilt, do not like to be parted from them so they will object when the groomer tries to take them away.

EXPERIENCE REQUIRED

Perhaps the first question you should ask a groomer is not how long they have been trimming, but how long have they been closely involved with dogs. I have lived with dogs all my life. When I was 14 years

An experienced professional groomer will instil confidence in your dog.

and started trimming Poodles, we had several dogs in the house and were always looking after somebody else's. These varied from a beautiful Golden Retriever to a sloppy and heavy-to-move Pyrenean, a protective but lovable German Shepherd, a Whippet and a Dalmatian, and then the Poodle. Also, I attended dog training classes from a very early age. Not all groomers can be this lucky, but at least two to three years in a kennel or grooming parlour would prove a great asset in learning about breeds of dogs and their different characters and, consequently, their different needs when being handled. All dogs, of course, respond to kindness, but some need

a firmer hand than others, or a sterner voice. Dogs that appear to want to snap have to be analysed, to distinguish between fear and bad temper.

I used to trim a Westie called William for a friend. Then the family moved away and the owner took William to a groomer, whom he bit three times. I could not believe this at first, until I remembered that William was very arthritic and I always trimmed him with this in mind. He never once attempted to snap at me. So maybe you should ask the groomer if they have ever been bitten, and how often. I am always wary, for instance, when I talk to groomers at a seminar and they say "I hate doing Poodles, they are nasty, snappy things". If they cannot get on with the tolerant Poodle, well!

However, we must not assume this is the norm. Most groomers do care and are passionately devoted to their job and grow to love the dogs they trim on a regular basis with some depth.

BUSINESS DIVERSITY
There is an incredible difference in the way groomers perform, or run a business. Some parlours or grooming outlets are adjacent to kennels, some are shops in the high street. Groomers trim dogs in garden sheds and garages or in a purpose-built room at home. Some may suit your dog, others may not. Perhaps your dog, and you, might prefer a one-to-one basis where your dog is the only one being dealt with at the time and so gets individual treatment. Parlours may be like your busy hairdressers, and do a certain amount to a dog and then pass him to another person for washing, etc. The individual temperament of your dog will make him react according to how he feels. Some dogs thoroughly enjoy the hustle and bustle of a busy salon, others find it intimidating and snap or shiver with fright. Some people use cage dryers which some dogs hate, others use hooks to tie dogs to, while some of us prefer to train the dog from puppyhood to sit or stand on a table to be groomed without any restraint other than the voice.

Visit the place where you think you may take your dog to be professionally groomed. Look at the equipment – lots of gadgets does not necessarily mean an impressive service. Ask to stay and watch the trimming of your dog. No groomer with confidence in their own ability will object to this request. It has to be said that some dogs play up a bit to begin with if

their owners are present. But if the owner ignores the dog and just sits quietly watching, the dog will soon settle.

The cost of having a dog professionally groomed does vary according to the breed. For example, American Cockers take longer than English Cockers as a rule. Other considerations are whether the dog is hand-clipped or stripped – hand-stripping takes far longer; whether the dog is having a bath, whether or not his coat is full of tangles or has a few or none at all. Then there is the matter of what trim he is in – all cut off, lamb, dutch, lion etc.

It has to be said that if you choose to own a coated breed of dog such as a terrier, Afghan, Old English Sheepdog or a Poodle you will have to take him periodically to a professional groomer for a haircut. Hopefully you will have considered carefully before purchasing your puppy and you understand this. The only other alternative, of course, is to learn to do this yourself.

DO-IT-YOURSELF
This is not a suitable option for all. There are some pet owners who have lessons from their dog's breeder and learn the art of clipping their own Poodle to a reasonable standard, or of taking care of their terrier's coat, but this is not as easy a task as you may think. However, if you have the determination and the application, it is wonderful to be able to trim your own dog. There are self-help books on trimming, but, from speaking to people over the years, they say they only find these understandable once they can actually trim. Far better to get your friendly breeder to help you. Buy from a breeder that is willing to help you care for your puppy.

There are courses to teach grooming but these are expensive and you may feel the

The Old English Sheepdog is one of the hardest breeds to keep in top-class condition.

A sensible option for the pet owner is to have the dog clipped.

expense outweighs the benefits. Clipping a Poodle, for instance, may prove too messy for some. Also coarse hair, such as some terrier hair, gets everywhere and so a suitable place is required for the ablutions. I know a lady who clips her dog in her bathroom and then spends days removing snips of hair. Likewise, a friend of mine baths her German Shepherd in her own bath and has oodles of hairs to deal with to prevent the drain blocking. Lots of Poodle owners bath their dogs, but, as this breed does not moult, there is relatively no hair. However,

clipping or trimming the Poodle is another matter; the hair blows everywhere and sticks to walls and ceilings. But do not be disillusioned if you want to have a go.

Choose a convenient place to do it and get expert help to set you on your way, then read a grooming manual or the trimming section of your breed book to learn the technique. Whichever path you choose to tread, the first consideration is the welfare of your chosen breed. There is nothing like having a dog for a friend. Look after him or her, you owe them that, and they deserve it.

8 ADOLESCENT AGONIES

Despite all your efforts, sometimes problems occur in training. There is nothing worse than owning a dog that controls what you do rather than the other way round! We have all met that type of dog, or an owner of one complaining "I can't leave the dog because he wrecks the house if left for more than ten minutes"; "I sneak out after dark to walk the dog so we don't meet any other dogs because he is so aggressive"; or "My friends don't come to the house any more because the dog jumps all over them and I cannot stop him", and "My husband is the only one who can walk the dog now because the dog pulls so much".

RECOGNISING PROBLEMS

At some point in your dog's learning some aspects can go wrong. Even the best trained dog will go through phases of apparent deafness or defiance. Stages of physical development will affect your dog's behaviour. A bitch's first season can be a time when unusual behaviour shows. The maturing male dog will frequently flex his adolescent muscles and try his owner out. He is developing in strength and attitude and, because this happens gradually, it often goes unnoticed by the owner until it has become a more serious problem.

Dogs are opportunists and, given the chance, they will take full advantage of the

A puppy will not grow into good behaviour – unless he is trained.

sympathetic handler or an owner just having a bad day.

A mistake often made by first-time dog owners is the expectation that, as a puppy matures, he will stop behaving badly. In

Some behaviour is breed-specific. Border Collies (above) have a tendency to chase moving objects. Digging (below) is common in terrier breeds.

reality, bad behaviour becomes an established pattern and, as it develops, it becomes increasingly difficult to change.

UNDERSTANDING YOUR DOG'S NEEDS

Your dog cannot teach himself. He is dependent on you to care for, love and train him. Shaping good behaviour takes time and effort. Bad habits are quickly established and, all too often, the dog is blamed for an undesirable behaviour that you have not controlled early enough or have unintentionally praised the dog for. Your dog will be happier if you make your desires clear and establish house rules from day one. Touch, voice and eye contact are essential means of communication between you and your dog. Your dog's behaviour will develop acceptably if, when you use them, you remember how much influence, positive and negative, that these communications have. Your dog perceives these communications as forms of praise.

- Training your dog should be an enjoyable experience for you and your dog.
- Learn to read your dog's facial expressions and body postures. This will help you to interpret his attitude or intentions in different situations.
- Reward good behaviour and there is a good chance it will be repeated.
- Ignore unacceptable behaviour and it is likely to decrease.
- It is not necessary to shout or bully to achieve good results.
- 'Think dog' and do not attribute human reasoning or feelings to your dog.

It is important to be consistent with your dog. All members of the household should be encouraged to adopt the same attitude

TONES OF VOICE

Effective use of voice, and accurate timing of commands and praise, will help your dog learn quickly.

Listen to your own voice. Does it sound cheerful and genuine? Practise getting the tone right. Women find the deeper, stern voice of disapproval difficult to achieve. Men, on the other hand, find the lighter, more encouraging tone needed for praise more difficult or embarrassing.

An important rule of dog training is to try *not* to be self-conscious. Inhibited body language, or a subdued tone of voice, will block communication and understanding. Learn as much as you can about the natural instincts of your chosen breed to avoid problems developing into unacceptable behaviour. For example, the herding breeds such as the Border Collie and German Shepherd will often chase traffic or other moving objects. Gundog breeds, such as Labradors and Golden Retrievers, enjoy using their sense of smell to flush out game and rabbits; this can lead to poor recall. The digging and ratting tendencies of the terrier breeds, such as the Jack Russell, may give a keen gardener nightmares.

Your dog must be taught right from wrong from day one. Discipline should be in the form of:-

- Disapproval – using a firm low tone of voice.
- Distraction – diverting your dog's attention.
- Control – attaching the collar, lead or long line.
- Indifference – deny your dog attention while he is displaying unacceptable behaviour.

Error-free learning is the key to success. For example, if your dog is standing in the

Error-free learning is the key to success.

and approach. Decide beforehand on the standard of behaviour you wish to achieve from your dog and what you will, and will not, allow.

Everyone has their own rules but, usually, unacceptable behaviour includes: jumping up, mouthing/biting, excessive barking, stealing or letting your dog climb on furniture. A dog that is allowed to take control will behave like a spoilt child. He will demand to be the centre of attention at all times and will soon become a nuisance.

middle of your flower bed, he does not know that this is wrong. The error is that you assume the dog understands he is not allowed on the flower beds. Your dog's understanding of the situation is that he is being disciplined for whatever he is doing at the moment you started to shout. He was probably sniffing! That is what you have controlled. Ask your dog to do something he can do, such as "COME". If, after coming to you, he immediately turns to step on the flower bed again then, at that point, you can say "NO". He has been caught in the act of going somewhere he shouldn't. So, when your dog is doing something wrong, avoid looking at the whole picture. It is like pressing the shutter on a camera; your discipline applies to the moment that you react.

TRAINING EQUIPMENT

LEAD Treat yourself to a good-quality lead, made of leather or strong nylon web-

The lead is your means of control.

bing. Avoid chain leads, as they are very uncomfortable to hold, especially if your dog pulls. The lead should be at least 4 ft long and wide enough to sit comfortably in the palm of your hand.

LONG LINE Anything from 6 ft to 15 ft long. Lightweight nylon that is washable (a piece of light rope would also be suitable). Do not use an extending lead enclosed in a plastic handle. Your dog needs to be able to trail the line without it getting caught up or causing damage.

The lead is an important item of your dog's training equipment. Owners often experience control problems because they have stopped using the lead too soon. Few people think of using the lead to control an indoor problem.

Whenever you are introducing a puppy or an adult dog to a new procedure, or you are re-educating to eradicate a problem, always attach the dog to a lead or long line, for indoor or outdoor training sessions. The lead is not only invaluable to you to apply control but it will enable you to teach your dog that interaction with you is essential, not optional.

It is also important to understand how your dog perceives the lead and the restrictions it imposes. The dog does not perceive the lead as a colourful fashion accessory but as an extension of your arm; the lead is a part of you, not part of the dog!

For a sensitive dog lacking in confidence, the lead can be an invaluable prop. Feeling your presence, and constant direction provided by light leash contact, can boost the confidence of even the most shy dogs.

For the confident, self-assured dog, incorrect use of the lead can give the wrong signals and further encourage bad behaviour. Think of the lead as an extension of

An outing is spoiled if your dog pulls on the lead.

your arm; when the lead is tight, the signal to the dog is the same as touching him, which is a form of praise.

A common scenario is the dog that jumps up at visitors. The owner holds on to his collar to control him, but it does not work; the dog continues to leap around boisterously. Touching the collar is encouraging the dog to continue to perform in this way.

A second scenario is the dog that pulls all the way to the park. He is being rewarded twice; the tight lead is saying "Good boy" for pulling and then he is given his freedom.

PULLING

Question: My dog pulls. He is small but very strong, how can I stop him?

A dog that pulls is controlling the situation in two ways. The speed and tension, which

you find so uncomfortable, enables your dog to get to his desired destination as quickly as possible. The dog is also dictating the route to the park, probably pulling from right to left across the pavement, choosing where he wants to sniff or cock his leg and who or what he wants to greet. Going for a walk is probably an unpleasant experience for the owner, who dreads having to take the dog out, and walks are, therefore, regularly postponed!

The aim for most pet owners is to have a dog that walks beside them without pulling. This can be taught by combining the correct use of the lead and use of voice. The desired position is with your dog's shoulder by your leg. Letting the dog walk too far ahead of you puts him, not you, in charge of the walk!

CORRECT USE OF THE LEAD/LONG LINE

The most important aspect to learn is that the lead must be slack. There must be no tension on the lead at all, otherwise you are giving mixed signals. The voice is commanding "Steady" or "Heel" and a tight lead in a lot of situations is telling the dog "Good boy". There is quite a knack to achieving a slack lead once a dog has learned to pull. Look carefully at what you are doing.

- The command "Steady" must be said in a calm, slow way – "STEA - DY".
- Avoid pulling backwards on the lead. If it is already taut, this only creates a tug-of-war situation.
- Avoid shortening the lead, holding the dog in position beside you. Again, you will only develop a tug-of-war scenario of who can pull the hardest – and usually it is the dog!

The lead must always be slack; a short, tight lead encourages a tug-of-war scenario.

- Ensure you have a good-quality, wide collar fitted to your dog. If the collar is thin, the dog tends to hang his head heavily over the top of it.
- Ensure that the collar is tightened up a hole or two before going for a walk. This will avoid the collar sitting low on the dog's shoulders, which is the strongest part of his body; this would also encourage him to pull (like a horse in a harness).

The lead action can be tricky to perfect, so persevere. If the dog is pulling, a quick forward movement, going with the dog, and then a flick backwards, should immediately release the tension. The dog, initially, will start to pull again so you have to be as persistent as he is to achieve the desired response.

Your vocal command must be simultaneous with the tug on the lead. Take a few steps backwards and praise the dog when he is back in position beside you. Continue to walk forward only if the lead remains slack.

Lure the dog with a tasty treat or a favourite toy into the correct position beside you. Use the "HEEL" or "CLOSE" command when you have achieved a few paces, then reward him. Give the treat on the move while the dog is still in the correct position, or break off and have a game of tug-of-war with your dog. Both of these methods teach your dog to pay attention to you and that it is fun to stay beside you.

Using the lead correctly can now help you to solve many of the common problems pet owners experience.

JUMPING UP

Question: My dog constantly jumps up at me or at visitors when they first arrive.

Avoid touching the dog to push him off, or holding on to his collar. Remember, dogs like touch. A harsh push may appear unpleasant to us, but to the dog it is the contact he craves. Greetings have become a great rough-and-tumble type of game. Avoid making eye contact with your dog. Too much eye contact will either make your dog challenge any control command or the dog can feel encouraged to jump up again.

Next time you return to your dog after he has been left for some time, walk into the room with your arms folded, look at the ceiling and do not speak to him. By denying him the three pleasures in life, touch, eye contact and vocal praise, he will

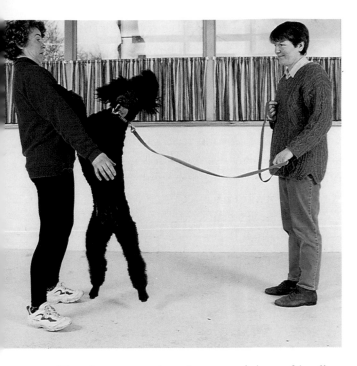

Your dog may see jumping up as being a friendly way to greet someone, but it can be unnerving for the visitor and should not be tolerated.

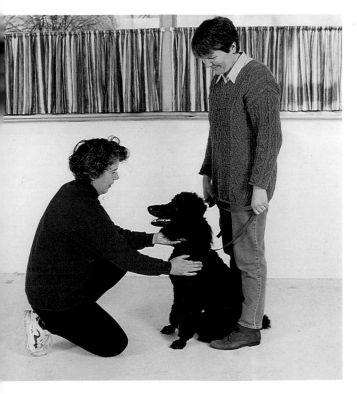

Teach your dog to sit politely and to wait patiently until he is greeted.

jump at you a few times and, because you are no longer playing the game, he will either back off or sit. This action should be rewarded by then giving the dog all three responses. If he starts to jump again, immediately return to ignoring him. It usually takes three or four attempts for the dog to learn the new procedure.

Do not wait for your dog to jump up at you. Counter-command him to sit as he approaches, then praise him for doing so. The praise is important but can often encourage your dog to jump again, so be quick and, as he starts to take off, stop praising him and command him to sit as you stand up straight and avoid the eye contact. This may have to be repeated two or three times, then he will realise he will get eye contact and praise for sitting.

Attach a long line to the dog. When you answer the door, allow the dog to go forward on the slack line to greet the visitor. As soon as the dog attempts to jump up, take a step backwards and flick the line and say "Sit", then praise and allow the dog to be praised by the visitor for doing so. Repeat the action should the dog attempt to jump up again. Your dog will quickly learn that he is allowed to go forward and greet people, but on your terms. The visitor should stop giving touch, eye contact and praise immediately the dog starts to misbehave.

Encourage visitors to ignore the dog completely for a few minutes and greet you first instead! Most visitors find this extremely hard to do, but, if you are persistent and prepared to nag them for a while, it is very effective.

Many of the gundog breeds can be encouraged to carry a favourite toy to control a boisterous greeting. These breeds enjoy parading around with a toy in their mouth, so encourage this behaviour when

When your dog responds by sitting to greet visitors make sure he is rewarded.

everyone sitting at the table to ignore the dog. Do not look, touch to push him off, or speak to him. This is one time the children can put their elbows on the table! This will encourage the children not to touch the dog. The dog will probably try you all out by jumping and pushing on your lap but, if you completely ignore the unacceptable behaviour, he will give in and walk away to find something else to do. As soon as your dog picks up a toy, or lies down, praise him. This inevitably will encourage the dog back to the table, so get everyone to go into 'ignore' mode again and remember to praise the dog for moving away. If the dog does not get a response from you there becomes no point in trying. This will teach your dog to amuse himself or to settle when you are all sitting up to the table.

It is important to remember never to feed the dog from the table. If you have

people arrive. Keep a toy by the front door for this purpose only. Give the dog the toy before opening the door and praise the dog repeatedly for walking around holding the toy. Stop praising the dog the moment he drops it. Stimulate the dog's interest in the toy with an excited voice and praise for picking up and carrying the toy. The dog will only need to be encouraged to carry it for a few minutes, as his interest in new arrivals will soon fade. Replace the toy in its place by the door once the situation has calmed and the dog has settled.

Question: How do we stop our dog jumping up? He pesters us and the children while we are sitting at the table eating our meals.

A similar approach to the problem of jumping up at visitors is required. Get

A begging dog should be ignored, however persistent he is.

Food left unattended, and within your dog's reach, is just asking to be eaten.

leftovers that you want to give to him, put them in his bowl and give them at his feeding time. This will discourage him from begging and hanging around the table, just in case he might be slipped a tasty morsel.

POOR RECALL

Question: Why does my dog ignore me, or return slowly, when I ask him to come at the end of a walk?

There are several reasons why most dogs will not return to their owners enthusiastically. It is usually the bad habits of the owner that cause the breakdown in the "Come" response.

Common handler mistakes:

- Your dog has to want to return to you because you are always friendly, fun and

you always remember to praise and/or reward him. This, unfortunately, is not always so. We usually start to shout at the dog for not returning quickly because we should have been collecting the children from school ten minutes ago. Or the dog has acknowledged your call but gives you that look that says "in a minute". What has actually happened is that he has heard the stern sharp voice and has taken one look at your annoyed body language and, rightly so, has decided to give you a wide berth.

- Remember to use the word "Come". All too often, a handler calls the dog by his name, but does not tell the dog what to do. For instance, they will say "Ben, Ben, Ben". If you were calling a person in this way, they would eventually say "What?". It is the same principle for the dog. So, get into the

Poor recall is a common, and infuriating, problem.

Go back to basics: position your dog a short distance away from you, (left).
When he comes, give lots of praise (right).

habit of calling the dog's name followed by the command "Come". Keep the tone of your voice light and interesting.

- Practise the "Come" response throughout the walk, so your dog never anticipates when he is going to be put back on the lead. Keep the lead hidden until you have got hold of the dog, then produce it.

- Always reward your dog for coming back to you, even if you have not called him. Touch him, give him a treat, then send him off again. Try and get into the habit of touching him before you present him with a tasty morsel or before having a game and then give him permission to go off again.

- Never tell your dog off for a slow response to the "Come" command, however long you have waited. Vocally praise when your dog returns – though you may be gritting your teeth!

- A dog that will not come in from the garden is unlikely to "Come" to you in the park where the distractions are greater. Ensure that you teach your dog that coming to you is not optional. Have some treats ready, make sure your dog knows you have them. Put your dog on a long line within the house. Hold on to the line, then back away asking your dog to "Come" in a cheerful tone. As the dog approaches you, touch him first, while offering the treat, then praise and release him. Only give the line a sharp tug if the dog chooses to ignore you. Praise as soon as he realises you are in control and starts to re-approach you. Avoid bending forward towards your dog as he will then stop just out of reach. Stand up straight and encourage the dog to come right up to you using the treat as a lure.

- Avoid asking the dog to sit at this stage of learning to come. Otherwise you will be rewarding the dog for sitting, not for coming.

TRAINING THE RECALL

Increase the distance gradually and practise the recall in a variety of settings.

SEXUAL PROBLEMS

Question: My puppy can be rather embarrassing, as he will grab a cushion or a piece of his bedding and proceed to mount it enthusiastically, especially when we have visitors. How can we stop him?

As with most undesirable behaviours, the more you make of it the worse it will become. Your dog has learned that his behaviour gets a reaction and, therefore, attention from you. Puppies and adolescent dogs often get sexually aroused after they have eaten, with a sudden boost of energy or when excited, (e.g. when visitors arrive) and start to perform. Try to anticipate the behaviour, as it often occurs at a regular time of day. Try to distract his attention. Provide the dog with a hide chew or a smoked sterilised bone to chew, praising him for doing so. Give a chew or bone only at this time. Remember to take the chew away; do not leave it with him once he has settled, put it away for the next occasion. If he has access to chews and bones all the time, he will lose interest and they will no longer be as desirable.

If your dog does not calm down even after you have provided him with something else to do, you must take further action. Clip on his lead or long line and make him lie down beside you and again give him a chew. Alternatively, attach the line or lead and allow him to trail the lead around the house. Often just being on the lead is enough to calm your dog. It also provides you with the opportunity to control the situation in a calm, relaxed manner. As soon as the dog begins his unwanted behaviour, pick up the end of the long line and ask the dog to do something you know he can do and reward him for it. For instance, tell him to "Sit". Remove the lead once your dog has remained settled for a while. Do not leave the dog unattended while the lead is attached.

Controlling sexual behaviour in your dog must be achieved in a calm manner. Pushing him off and shouting at him will

The behaviour of some adolescent males can cause their owners many blushes.

only encourage the dog to become over-excited and more assertive. If you have young children and find the problem difficult to control, castration can be an option with this type of dog. Results from this take time to show. It is not an instant cure and it must, therefore, be combined with handler control to be effective. Your vet will advise you accordingly.

DOG AGGRESSION

Question: My dog has attended dog training classes regularly since he was a puppy, with no problems. He has suddenly become very wary of other dogs. His hackles rise and he looks like he is about to pick a fight. What can I do to control this behaviour?

When a friendly, well-socialised dog becomes worried in this situation it usually indicates that he has been frightened by another dog's attitude. Your dog now reacts to other dogs by pretending he is bigger and braver than he really is, just in case! Raising the hackles is not only an assertive act, it can also be an apprehensive reaction. The handler can sometimes, in this situation, make the apprehensive dog's behaviour worse.

If your dog is reacting unacceptably towards another dog, do not reassure by stroking or picking him up. This action is perceived by your dog as praise for the way he is behaving. Ignore the behaviour and walk away and then call your dog to follow you. You may need to re-establish the "Come" command for this purpose.

Do not shout or interfere by pulling your dog away from the situation. Most dogs will sort out their differences quickly, without aggression, if you do not get involved.

If you meet another dog when your dog is on the lead, then allow the dogs to greet

Distract your amorous adolescent's attention by giving him a bone to chew.

each other. It is important to keep your dog's lead slack at this point. A tight lead indicates to your dog that you are worried and it restricts your dog's freedom. Praise your dog when he greets another dog in a friendly manner. Once they have said 'hello', call your dog by his name and command "Come". Reward your dog with an irresistible treat once he has walked away and acknowledged you.

Try to protect your dog from obviously aggressive dogs. Avoid confrontation – cross the road or change your route in the park if you become aware of problem dogs. At training classes, avoid getting stuck in a corner and keep clear of dogs that you know are a problem.

If your dog has behaved aggressively towards another dog, fit a Halti-style head collar, or even a muzzle, to your dog. You now know he cannot do any damage to

Young puppies, introduced in a calm, controlled environment, can quickly become firm friends and lively playmates.

another dog and your attitude will change. If you are relaxed in the company of other dogs, he will be. A positive approach will instantly affect your dog's attitude. It is essential that your dog only meets friendly dogs while wearing a muzzle because has no way of protecting himself from an aggressive dog, so you must do it for him.

Dog aggression is a complicated problem. It is a combination of temperament and the attitude of dog and handler, added to the situations that arise, and also of learned behaviour. It can also be breed-specific. If you have a problem, I would recommend that you should seek professional help sooner rather than later.

AGGRESSIVE TENDENCIES IN THE CAR

Question: I take my dog out regularly in the car. He hops in the back quite happily but, once the car is moving, if we pass another dog, or a person, he goes crazy, barking and throwing himself at the window. What can we do to stop him?

Your dog is protecting the car which he sees as his territory. Your dog has to learn that you disapprove of such behaviour and you can control him even when he sits in the back of your car.

A noisy dog can be distracting for the driver and is, therefore, dangerous. Avoid shouting, it only makes the problem worse; remember. you should ignore undesirable behaviour. Attach your dog to a long line and thread it through to the front of the car. Initially this training exercise will require two people, the driver and a handler to control the dog.

The handler should sit in the back seat to start with, to be as close as possible to the dog without actually looking at him. Quick reactions are essential. As soon as the dog starts to bark, yank the lead and command the dog to "Sit"; repeat quickly if necessary. Your dog should react immediately, as he is now aware that you are able to insist that he interacts with you.

Praise your dog for quiet, settled behaviour. Once you have achieved a few successful journeys, the handler should move to the front seat and repeat the same procedure when necessary. Take the dog out for a local drive on your own but keep the lead or line attached, draped over your shoulder, to use if required. Remember to praise good behaviour, especially when you pass another dog and your dog remains quiet! However if the problem re-surfaces, you must use another handler, as you cannot concentrate on driving and your dog at the same time.

Some dogs benefit from the security that a dog cage or crate provides. The large amount of space provided in the back of some estate cars can promote unsettled behaviour. Introduce the dog to the cage outside the car. If you feed the dog in the

cage a few times, he will soon associate the cage with a pleasant experience. Put the cage in the back of the car and feed your dog in the cage for a few more days. Once the dog is happy to hop into the cage, it is time to take him for a short ride around the block. Cover the cage with a sheet or blanket so the dog cannot see out of the windows; this provides your dog with a shaded, secure den. Ensure there is good ventilation. Only praise your dog for settled, quiet behaviour.

NOISY BEHAVIOUR IN THE CAR

Question: I take my dog to the local park by car. He knows the route very well and starts to bark and whine well before we get there. The noise is unbelievable, and he is driving me round the bend!

Freedom is one of the most desirable factors in your dog's life! Your dog has learned that barking and whining is rewarded. You cannot get the tailgate open quickly enough, because it stops the noise. Once more your dog has achieved his objective! He has trained you well. He has also learned that you cannot do anything about it. This type of dog often has control of the back door. Barking gets you to let him in and out of the house every time he asks – which can be more frequently than necessary. Ignore your dog's demands and he will soon realise you are no longer available to answer his every beck and call.

Teaching your dog to be quiet on a known route takes time. To break the pattern of behaviour, he needs to be taken on the known route and not be allowed out at the end. Freedom is a strong reward and your dog has been conditioned, inadvertently, by you, to think that noise is rewarded. In future, only quiet behaviour is

Canine passengers should be quiet and under control at all times.

rewarded. For a lot of dogs, the long line training procedure, talked about in the previous paragraph, is sufficient to control the barking. Some dogs require a more subtle approach. This type of dog is probably vocal at other times and a general approach of not rewarding noisy behaviour is required.

Drive to the park and sit there but do not get out. Drive home again. If your dog is noisy on the journey home, leave him in the car until he is quiet. Take the dog out on journeys to the supermarket and on shopping trips where he is left in the car. However, you *must* ensure that he is not left unattended in the car on a hot day. And he must learn that not all car journeys are for his benefit.

Once he is travelling on journeys to the park quietly, each stage of getting your dog out of the car has to also be achieved in silence.

- The handler getting out of the car.
- Opening the tailgate.
- Attaching the lead.
- Walking to the point where you let the dog off.

If the dog is noisy at any point, you must take him back a stage. No progress must be made if the dog utters a sound. It is a lengthy procedure to teach, but well worth the effort. A dog barking incessantly in the car is very stressful and can affect your driving and concentration. Clicker training is also very effective for this problem.

RETRIEVE PROBLEMS

Question: My dog loves playing with his ball. I take it to the park to throw it for him but he will not bring it back. How can I get him to give it to me?

This common problem has to be looked at from the dog's point of view. He thinks you have an obsession with the ball, as all you want to do is take it away from him. The link that is missing is the understanding by your dog that it is fun to bring the ball back. He gets praised for doing so and, when you take the toy away, it does not mean it is the end of the game! Retrieve is a complicated procedure, with several actions that have to be taught separately and then put together. Practise these exercises at home first, before attempting it in the park.

EXERCISE ONE Sit on the floor, throw the ball, or toy, which is attached to a long piece of lightweight rope. This will enable you to prevent the dog running off with the toy and controlling the game. Allow your dog to run out to "FETCH" the toy. As he picks it up command him to "HOLD" it and let him parade around with it. Slowly reel your dog in, like a fish on a line. Avoid grabbing at your dog as he parades past. Ask him in a excited tone "What have you got?" Do not touch the toy at this stage. Touch and praise your dog for coming extremely close to you, allow him to move away and then re-approach. Rub his back, his chest – anywhere but his head! Get your dog confident that you are only going to touch him, not the toy. If he drops the toy, throw it again. When the dog is beside you, or even on your lap, offer a treat with one hand then, as he spits the toy out into your other hand, say "GIVE". Repeat the exercise frequently. Once your dog is returning to you confidently and quickly, practise the procedure sitting on a chair. Then progress to standing up.

EXERCISE TWO Your dog should learn that playing tug-of-war with you is fun. Put

TEACHING THE RETRIEVE

1. *Put your dog in a Sit, and throw the ball which is attached to a rope.*

2. *When your dog picks up the toy in his mouth, tell him to "Hold".*

3. *Slowly reel him in.*

4. *Give a treat and say "Give", and he should be happy to relinquish the toy.*

5. *Immediately throw the ball again for your dog to fetch.*

a command word to the action of your dog taking hold of the toy by saying "HOLD". Praise your dog for tugging on the toy: "GOOD BOY TO TUG". With your right hand on the toy, stop tugging and talking to your dog, and offer a treat with your left hand. As the dog spits the toy out, say "GIVE". If the toy is dropped on the floor, pick up the toy before giving the treat. Offer the toy to your dog with the "HOLD" command and repeat the exercise.

Exercises One and Two can now be linked. Sit on the floor, throw the toy, tell your dog to "FETCH". As he picks it up, say "HOLD" and praise the dog for returning, with lots of touches and stroking of the body first, then take hold of the toy and have a game of "TUG". Ask the dog to "GIVE", reward with a treat and immediately throw the toy again. Teaching your dog to "HOLD" on command prevents your dog snatching at the toy and biting your hand by mistake. Teaching your dog to "GIVE" on command enables you to use the command in other situations, for example if the dog has stolen an item that is not his.

DESTRUCTIVE BEHAVIOUR

Question: My dog gets very agitated when we leave him for any length of time. He barks and whines and, often when we get back, there is some damage done. Why will he not settle?

Is your dog bored? Are you leaving him for long periods regularly? A lot of dogs are expected to keep their own company for long periods of the day and, understandably, look for further amusement. Dogs are pack animals and enjoy companionship. Dog owners who work all day and experience destructive behaviour should consider employing a dog walker. Some owners expect their dogs to sleep all night for

Boredom is often at the root of destructive behaviour.

A tough, safe chew will help to keep your adolescent occupied if he needs to be left for short periods.

seven to eight hours, then sleep all day for the same length of time, and are then amazed when their dog chews something valuable. You would not leave a child unattended for long periods, so why expect it of a dog?

Introduce your dog gradually to being alone. Leave him for short periods to start with. On your return, do not be tempted to make a huge fuss of him. This only reaffirms his need for you. Leave the dog with something to do by providing activity toys such as a stuffed Kong, a Buster cube or a Nyla Bone.

Avoid taking your dog for a free run and then leaving him as soon as you have brought him home. Free-running your dog has the effect of revving him up, not tiring him out. Give him a short free run, then a short training session, either in the park or at home. Encouraging your dog to concentrate on some training exercises will make him mentally tired and he will be ready to

settle and sleep on his return home.

If your dog is destructive when you leave him, look at the sort of items he is chewing; often it is something you have recently touched. If you provide your dog with an item of old clothing, (a tee-shirt or sweatshirt is ideal since it is an item that smells of you), it will provide your dog with the security that he is looking for. Only give your dog the piece of clothing when you leave him. On your return, take it away, as he now has the real thing.

Avoid sending your dog to his bed as a form of punishment. An unpleasant association can lead to the dog not wanting to use his bed at all. Your dog must enjoy going on his bed, which is step one to settled behaviour. Some dogs can become hyperactive and need to be taught to settle. An indoor kennel or crate can be very useful for this purpose. It provides a secure, quiet, dark resting place, especially if you cover it with a blanket or sheet.

The Ultimate Puppy

9 THE PERFECT COMPANION

As your puppy approaches maturity, training can be fine-tuned, and more challenging targets can be set. The more you can teach your puppy, the better, as being busy and stimulated will keep him out of mischief. Above all, this is the time to have fun with your puppy, and to look forward to the years of companionship that lie ahead.

GAMES TO PLAY

WATCH ME
This exercise is very simple and is the most positive way in which to teach your puppy to focus on you when you most need it, instructing him to ignore distractions in the street, such as cats, bicycles, pushchairs and other dogs, or when you are in a training class.

To encourage positive eye contact, hold a treat or a toy in your hand and ask the puppy to sit in front of you. Your hand, containing the reward, should be held up in front of you, high enough for your puppy to be looking directly into your eyes. While he is sitting still and looking at you, you can say "Watch me", or something similar. If your puppy jumps up, be patient, wait until he sits and start again. You can reward, intermittently, with tidbits, and gradually increase the time between giving them. If using a toy, give, or throw, the toy

The Watch Me command diverts your dog's attention away from distractions, and focuses it on you.

as a reward at the end of the exercise – much more fun than food treats for certain breeds of dog.

GIVE A PAW

With your puppy in a sitting position, hide a tidbit in your hand and hold it in front of him, at about his chest height. He will investigate your hand with his nose but do not give him the treat just yet. Keep your hand still and watch his paws for any movement in the right direction. Your puppy may bring his paw straight up and touch your hand. If this happens, instantly release the reward – do not use any command yet.

Repeat the exercise, being very patient, and he will soon touch your hand again. Once your puppy has understood what he has to do to get the reward, you can say "Paw", "Shake", or "Gimme five" as you release the food.

Some puppies are slower at using their paws than others, so you will have to watch your puppy carefully, for any movement at all in any direction, and reward it. This is called shaping. Shaping is rewarding, a step at a time, each correct response towards your desired goal, which in this case is getting your puppy to lift his paw higher and higher until he touches, or targets, your hand – jackpot! This way you are breaking down the exercise into smaller pieces at which your puppy, and you, will find it easier to succeed. This method of training also teaches your puppy to 'think' and keeps his brain active. 'Give a paw' is useful if you want to teach your puppy to shut doors, for instance, or for Flyball.

CATCH A TOY

This game comes naturally to many breeds of dog and they do it instinctively. Others need to be taught how to catch a toy. Use a soft toy to start with to avoid hurting your puppy, as this will be very off-putting. Make sure the toy is big enough so as not to be swallowed accidentally. You can then

Giving a paw is a fun, simple trick that can be developed for a multitude of purposes.

progress to an appropriately-sized ball, one that is not too small.

Start with your puppy sitting, and you standing or kneeling in front of him. Throw the toy toward, and slightly above him. If the toy is not caught by your puppy straight away, it will fly over his head, or land at his feet. Pick it up, wiggle it about to gain his interest, and try again. He should soon get the idea.

Your puppy will need to catch a ball in the sport of Flyball. You might also like to teach your puppy to chase and catch a Frisbee – a good way of giving your puppy more exercise.

TUG-OF-WAR

Many dogs and owners like to play tug-of-war, but you will need to teach your puppy to release the tug toy as soon as he is asked to "Leave", "Drop", or if you say "Thank you". By doing this you will ensure that your puppy does not get overexcited, or aggressive and out of control. It is not a good idea to let very young children play tug-of-war with your puppy either, as the game can, suddenly, turn into 'tug-on-arms-and-clothing' instead of the toy.

With your puppy tugging on an appropriate toy, keep the toy still and offer your puppy a treat, which has to be something tasty. As the puppy lets go of the toy to take the food, say your chosen word, for example "Thank you", give him the reward, and play again, repeating the 'release' exercise.

Ensure the game is not getting uncontrollable and your puppy too excited, or he will not want to let go of the toy. Once your puppy has learned the words "Thank you", for example, you can practise when he is a bit more excited. You are aiming, eventually, to get an instant response to your command, and this will be invaluable

A game of Frisbee is a great way to exercise your puppy.

Tug rules should be set and followed to ensure the game does not get out of hand.

when your puppy has picked up something he should not have. When you have finished your play session, take the tug toy and put it away.

Remember that when your puppy is playing 'shake and kill' tug-of-war, and chase and retrieve games, he is using all his natural, predatory instincts, so being in control of these games will help you be in control if your puppy decides that he would like to try to chase sheep, cyclists, or rabbits.

HUNT THE TREAT

This game uses your puppy's natural hunting instincts, using both sight and smell. This is a fun way of keeping your puppy's interest on a walk, and a great way of exercising both his body and brain in the house and garden too.

You will need to restrain your puppy – someone else can hold him – while you hide the toy or the treat, but let him see in which direction it went. You could start by

throwing the object into fairly short grass, or behind the sofa. Immediately let your puppy run after it, and say something like "Seek" or "Find".

Once your puppy has found the toy, or eaten the tidbit, call him to you, start again, and throw the treat in a different direction. If it is a toy that you are using, encourage him to bring it to you, but do not snatch at it in order to take it away from him, or this will spoil his retrieve when you come to teach it, as he will run away with the toy instead of giving it to you.

Once your puppy has got the idea that he needs to search for the object, you can get him to hunt 'blind' for it. This means having him look for something which he has not seen you throw. Make it very easy for him to start with, or he will lose confidence in the game, and you. Make sure that he is successful every time. If he cannot find the treat, always have another one to

The gundog breeds particularly love hunting out treats and hidden objects.

drop for him, in case. This is very important if you wish to train your puppy for Working Trials or gundog work.

RETRIEVE

Retrieve, or fetch, games are great fun for you and your puppy. Retrieving comes naturally to many puppies. They instinctively chase a toy when it is thrown, and bring it back – not necessarily letting it go though! Some puppies need more encouragement to retrieve, with a few never showing any interest at all.

Do not chase your puppy when he has something in his mouth, be it a ball or your chequebook, if you want him to learn to retrieve properly. Otherwise, when you throw a toy for him, he will just run about with it in his mouth waiting for you to run after him. If he does have something which he should not have, distract him with a toy, or tidbit, and he will drop it and lose interest in it. Do not make too big a deal out of it or he may learn that this behaviour is the best way to get your attention and 'get you going'.

Teach your puppy that "Hold" or "Fetch" means to have something in his mouth. You can say "Hold" or "Fetch" every time he picks up a toy, and give him lots of praise but do not try to take the toy away from him too soon. You can gently stroke his body and then, after waiting a while, take hold of the toy and give him his release command, such as "Thank you". Do not tug on the toy or he will tug back. Show your puppy a tidbit, or another toy, and give it to him as a reward for letting go. He will soon learn that "Hold" means to pick something up and give it to you. This Hold and Thank You game is the basis for retrieve.

Once your puppy has understood the game, you can progress to throwing the toy

Whether it is a dumb-bell (above) or a newspaper (below), many dogs relish retrieving items for their owners.

away from you, not too far at first, making sure that he can see it, and saying "Hold". Squat down close to the ground and, when your puppy has taken hold of the toy, encourage him to bring it back to you, gently praising him as he comes. Do not worry if he circles you or runs around with the toy. Be patient and keep your cool. Praise, as before, when he finally comes back to you, and gently take the toy, asking him to release it. Reward your puppy and throw the toy again. Do not overtire your puppy with this game and always leave him wanting more.

Once your puppy is enthusiastically running after a toy and bringing it back to you, you can hold on to his collar for a second after throwing the retrieve article out, to restrain him and ask him to "Wait". Do not let him chase the toy until he is sitting or standing still, and then ask him to "Hold" or "Fetch" as usual. You will then be able to increase, gradually, second by second, the amount of time he has to wait until you send him for it. This teaches your puppy good 'chase' control and patience.

When he is reliable, and you are not having to hold on to his collar, you can progress to throwing his toy out a short distance and picking it up yourself occasionally! This teaches steadiness in your puppy and that not everything that is thrown is necessarily for him to go out and get – important in gundog work, Obedience, Working Trials etc.

If your puppy starts showing reluctance to retrieve after denying him a retrieve, stop, and try this exercise again at a later date, or you will confuse him and put him off retrieving altogether. As with any exercise, always work at your puppy's pace, not yours.

HIDE AND SEEK

This is best taught with two people present, one to restrain your puppy and one to hide behind furniture, doors, trees and bushes. Once the person to be found is out of sight, he or she can call or whistle to attract your puppy's attention, and the person holding your puppy can run with him, giving him lots of encouragement to "Find". Reward with a tidbit, or a toy, when he is successful.

Playing hide and seek on a walk teaches your puppy to keep an eye on you, as he never knows when you might 'disappear'. It can improve the recall too, in that, if you whistle or call your puppy, and he does not come instantly, keep quiet, hide (keeping one eye on him in case he thinks he is lost and panics), and let him find you. He should come to you a bit quicker next time you call in case he should lose you again!

DOWN AT A DISTANCE

Once your puppy has learned to lie down when he is close by you, you can progress to teaching him to Down when he is further away from you. This is an important exercise, as some dogs only take notice of their owners while they are near to them. As soon as they are past a certain distance away from their owners, they take not one blind bit of notice of them at all. Your puppy should learn to pay attention to you wherever you are, whether he is on his lead next to you, or 100 metres away.

Have your puppy sit in front of you, ask him to "Wait", and take a step backwards. Show him a tidbit and ask him to "Down" or whatever word you use. When he lies down, reward him instantly. You may have to use a hand signal at this stage as well, but do not bring your hand down to the ground as he may move forwards to investigate it. If your puppy has learned the words "Down", "Lie" or "Flat" properly, this should not really be necessary, and the hand signal should be phased out quickly, as your puppy will not always be looking towards you, for

The basic Down exercise must be mastered before attempting the more challenging Distant Down or Hit-the-Deck commands.

example if he is running after something or towards a road, and this could save his life.

Gradually increase the distance between you and your puppy and always return to praise and reward him when he gets it right. Remember to finish on a 'high note', while your puppy is still enjoying it, and, maybe, end with a game of tug or fetch – whatever your puppy enjoys best.

Some puppies learn this exercise very quickly. Others take a little longer to learn

what you want them to do, so be patient. This exercise has to be learned with your puppy sitting still before he can be expected to Down on the move. Sit at a distance can be taught in this way too, from a Stand position.

QUICK DOWN OR HIT-THE-DECK
When your puppy understands the word "Down", or your alternative, you can teach him to drop to the ground more quickly, so

improving his Down response.

With a toy or a tidbit in your hand, play with the puppy, keeping the toy at his eye-level. When he is following the toy excitedly, drop it to the floor, but do not let go, and say, "Down". As he lies down, release the toy or tidbit as his reward and play again. This quick Down response can then be shaped, by rewarding only the fastest efforts. Great fun!

DROP ON RECALL

Once your puppy has learned to Down at a distance, you can teach him to Down as he is running towards you.

Leave your puppy in the Sit position, ask him to "Wait", back away from him, and ask him to "Down" on the spot (this will give him an idea of what is coming next). Return to him and reward him. Ask him to "Sit" and "Wait" again, back away for a few paces, and encourage him to you. As soon as he takes a step forward ask him to "Down". If he does it, return and reward him with food or a thrown toy. This can then be practised with you going further and further away and aiming to 'drop' him halfway to you.

This exercise can also be trained in the opposite manner, with you calling the puppy to you and asking him to "Down" as he reaches you. You can then ask him to "Down" earlier and earlier, until he is, again, 'dropping' about halfway to you, or wherever you wish him to. Be careful not to overtrain this exercise as it can slow down your puppy's recall. It is a good idea to practise the recall before and after this exercise.

SENDAWAY

This exercise is to teach your puppy to lie down as he is running in the opposite direction from you. Have something as a

Once mastered, the sendaway can be used to stop chasing behaviour.

marker that you can teach your puppy to run to, such as a mat (carpet sample), or a plastic cone – the choice is yours. You could also use three pots or cones etc., in a triangle shape, or four in a square, and teach your puppy to lie down in the centre.

Start with your puppy sitting by your side, and ask him to "Stay". Move away from your puppy in a straight line, and not too far to start with, and put your marker on the ground (or pretend to put a tidbit in the middle of the square or triangle). Return to your puppy and, with a sweep of your arm, encourage your dog to run to the marker. At the same time say something like "Away", or "Get on", and run with him. When you both reach the marker say "Down". When your puppy does lie down give him lots of praise. Then, pick up the marker and go back to the starting position.

Repeat this exercise until your puppy understands what to do, then try sending him to the marker without your running with him. Once he has grasped this exercise thoroughly, you can increase the distance at which you place the marker. Eventually, you will be able to send your puppy out, without the marker, with him running in a straight line away from you, until you ask him to stop ("Down").

This exercise can then be trained to teach your puppy to stop while chasing a moving object, be it a cat, a toy, bicycle, car, jogger, rabbit or squirrel.

CANINE SPORTS
Advanced training for your dog is not only fun. It will also result in you having a puppy that is not a nuisance to other dogs, and to people, both in and out of the home, and who is a reliable, trustworthy member of society. There are plenty of canine sports available. Here are details of the most popular ones, but do contact your local training clubs, your breed club or your national kennel club if you would like more information.

BREED-SPECIFIC SPORTS
Lively, energetic breeds need plenty of activity to keep them physically and mentally healthy. If you have chosen such a breed – a working sheepdog, a Collie or a gundog, for example – you will need to channel your dog's natural instincts into relevant games and activities.

Collies, and Collie-type dogs, may start to herd children and 'nip' if they are not given something to occupy their minds. These dogs are particularly enthusiastic about Agility, Obedience and Flyball. Many love to chase and catch a ball or Frisbee, and are happy to do so all day long, if allowed!

Most dogs thrive on the mental stimulation offered by advanced training.

AGILITY

All breeds can take part in Agility – a sport enjoyed equally by dogs and owners.

Most gundog breeds love to use their sense of smell to the full. They like to play the 'search' and 'retrieve' type of games, and, if this instinctive behaviour is not utilised, they will be off, hunting by themselves.

You may be able to find a training class that will help you to teach your puppy to 'stop' and 'recall' to a whistle, and to 'retrieve'. Even if you are not going to use your puppy as a working gundog later on, this type of training is highly enjoyable. Some dog trainers run classes for pet gundogs.

AGILITY

This is a great, fun activity that can be participated in as soon as your puppy is old enough – usually at about 12 months of age. Puppies, especially of the larger breeds, should not be jumping obstacles intensively until then.

There is no reason why you cannot have basic control beforehand, such as going through a child's tunnel, or walking through a tyre held on the ground, stepping over an obstacle, or going over tiny 'bunny hop' jumps.

As well as jumping, Agility involves teaching your puppy to weave in and out of poles, to walk over high 'dog walks', climbing A-frames, etc. If you decide to have a go at Agility competitions, there are classes for smaller dogs as well.

Agility training will help with you and your puppy's relationship because you will be working as a team, and it will improve his obedience too.

To teach your puppy to go through a child's play tunnel, have someone restrain him at one end and then entice him to you, through the tunnel, with a toy or a treat as a reward. He may be reluctant at first. Do not push or force him through the tunnel as this will be very off-putting. Be patient.

Once he is enjoying the game, you can introduce the command cue, for example saying "Through" or "Tunnel" as he is running through it.

Use the same method to teach your puppy the basics of jumping on command. As your puppy treads or 'bunny hops' over a low obstacle, you can say your chosen word, such as "Over" and then reward him. Never encourage your puppy to jump too high while he is young and still growing quickly as this can put unnecessary strain on his joints.

As the first stage towards getting your puppy used to walking over a high 'dog walk', you can put planks of wood on the ground for him to walk along. Then he will progress to that high 'dog walk' – a narrow walkway which dogs have to negotiate, travelling upwards, then along it, and then downwards, with contact points at each end which their paws have to touch. This type of exercise will develop your puppy's confidence and learning potential if it is done at an early age.

Agility competitions are extremely popular, often with hundreds of dogs entered in each class. Many different breeds – and many mongrels and crossbreeds – participate, but the working sheepdogs and the Collie excel.

FLYBALL

This is a very fast game, in which dogs negotiate several jumps before pressing a lever on a box which ejects a ball for them to catch. The dogs then return, over the jumps, to their handlers. Dogs and handlers usually compete as a team.

To participate in Flyball you will not only need to teach your puppy to catch a toy or a ball, to 'Give a paw' and to 'Target' with his paw, he will also need to jump and retrieve as well.

FLYBALL

Flyball: a sport which tests a dog's speed, accuracy, and agility.

To teach your puppy to 'Target' an object, hold a book, or a piece of cardboard in front of him and teach him to touch that article with his paw, instead of your hand, as in 'Give a paw'. Reward him just for trying at first and then, when he gets it right, start to 'shape' the behaviour. You can then introduce the word "Touch" for instance. You can teach your puppy to shut doors this way!

COMPETITION OBEDIENCE

In this canine sport, dogs are taught to do close heelwork (on- and off-lead), formal retrieves, to find their handler's scent on a cloth (from a selection passed out at random), sendaways, recalls, and Stays – often, in the higher classes, with the handler going out of sight of the dogs. Not all dogs are suited to this kind of training,

but a lot do enjoy it, especially if it is kept on a fun basis and the dogs look upon it as a big game.

WORKING TRIALS AND TRACKING

In Working Trials, dogs learn to master many different disciplines, such as Obedience and Agility. They use their sense of smell to the full to search for, and track down, hidden/missing objects.

To teach your puppy to 'track' a scent to a toy or treat, walk, without him, over a piece of undisturbed land. Use short distances at first and 'plant' a favourite toy or tasty morsel of food at the end of the trail. Turn and follow the same route back again. Encourage your puppy to follow your scent along the track you have made, using his keen sense of smell, until he finds the reward at the end. Once your puppy

Obedience is a challenging but rewarding sport.

Give a positive command when setting your dog up to track a scent.

understands the game, you can lay longer and longer 'tracks' and include changes of direction.

BACK RETRIEVE

To teach your puppy to go back and retrieve an object or a toy that you have dropped, either deliberately or accidentally, walk with him. Let him see you drop a toy, walk on a little further and then ask him to "Sit". Stand in front of your puppy so that you are facing the toy and he has his back to it, and ask him then to go "Back" or "Back fetch". Praise and reward him when he brings it to you. Gradually increase the distance that you send him for the toy. Once he understands the exercise properly, you can drop the toy without him seeing it. This makes it a much more interesting game. This exercise is taught to working gundogs to enable the handler to send his dog further out towards the retrieve article, be it a gundog dummy, which is a canvas training aid, or dead or wounded game.

Tracking is a natural skill. As your dog becomes proficient you can increase the length of the trail and introduce changes of direction.

10 *HEALTH CARE*

The young puppy should have a good healthy coat, and an occasional scratch with a back leg is not unexpected. Any patchy coat, areas of hair loss, scaly skin and persistent scratching may be due to a parasitic skin disease. The most frequently encountered insect living in the coat of the puppy is the flea. There are many other parasites that may be found on the skin, ranging from the clearly visible tick to the *Cheyletiella* mite, which is only recognised as 'walking dandruff'. A black-coated puppy can have white skin scales visible on the coat surface and some of these may be seen to move if closely observed in a bright light. Itchy skins, and white eggs or 'nits' stuck to the hairs, will suggest one of several types of body lice as a cause.

Then there are the burrowing mites that invade the hair follicles and the skin thickness: *Demodex* and *Sarcoptes* are the most frequently encountered mites of dogs. A further possibility is mites living in the outer ear canal; the *Otodectes* surface mite can cause intense ear irritation and a cat in the family is often the source of infection. Another possibility of a parasite, fortunately rare, is ringworm as a mycosis or skin fungus infection.

If fleas and lice come with your puppy, it is comforting to know they greatly prefer the taste of dog blood and skin to the human equivalent, so do not think all these parasites will nibble or bite people. The flea, when hungry, will bite humans but the bites will only be recognised later by an intense itching, minutes or hours after the flea has bitten the person. The same can be said of *Cheyletiella* as it is often the human's itchy skin that first draws the dog owner's attention to this parasite living on the dog's coat.

FLEAS

In recent years the flea has benefited from a warmer climate in the UK and an increase in the domestic cat population. In England, hedgehogs are often found in gardens used by puppies for exercise and they can bring in their own type of flea parasite to bite the puppy. Foxes may also carry fleas and, by entering gardens, may deposit parasites. Puppies will then nose out any smelly stuff and roll in it.

Cats seem to tolerate a few fleas living on their body and the remains of flea-feeding activities may only be recognised as black 'crumbs', or a gritty substance, lying close to the cat's skin. In the dog, the flea is more likely to cause intense irritation after it has punctured the skin and sucked some of the blood. This is recognised by a patch of thin undercoat, a few broken hairs and some brown scales on the skin surface. Even a young puppy will, with his teeth,

A young pup can become anaemic through heavy flea infestation.

lick and groom the itchy area around the flea bite; there may be short broken hairs as well as signs of hair loss.

Another clue may be the dampness of the hair where the dog has excessively groomed by licking, and coated the hair with his own saliva in an attempt to catch the flea. The person inspecting the dog's skin should part the hairs to see down to the skin level then look for live, brown-coloured fleas running through the coat or, possibly, find black flecks that are the flea dirt or excreta. A very bright light helps to find fleas and often the heat of the lamp makes the fleas more active and easier to see when they move across the skin.

A further tip is, if the black flea crumbs are found, brush them on to a white surface such as clean paper: if moistened, the black crumbs become reddish-brown on the white background. The flea dirt still contains some dried blood, which accounts for the colour change on moistening. A fine-toothed comb, similar to a human louse 'nit' comb, can be used to look for fleas in the coat but most puppies are too wriggly to allow for the patient comb-through necessary to find one flea.

ANAEMIA

A young puppy with a heavy flea infestation may become anaemic due to the amount of blood lost through these suck-ing insects. The female fleas feed for longer than the male flea as they need an extra food supply to lay many eggs. Systemic flea preparations such as the monthly tablets are more likely to kill off the female fleas. The male fleas usually only need a short feed. After one bite they then leave the dog's skin to wait elsewhere. A spray with a quick-kill component may be the best way of ridding the body of both sorts of fleas. A further risk to the puppy is that some fleas contain the tapeworm intermediate stage so, if licked and swallowed, the puppy has a tapeworm too – see later about tapeworms.

FLEA ALLERGY

Allergy to flea bites and irritants in the flea saliva can produce long-lasting itching and scratching, even when all the fleas have apparently been removed from the dog. Fleas are one of the commonest causes of long-lasting skin disease in adults. A further problem is that, as each female flea lays at least 100 eggs, all these eggs fall off the dog or cat. The eggs hatch on the ground or in carpets in two to 10 days, depending on temperature. The eggs are oval in shape, a pearly-white colour about 0.5mm long, so are barely visible to the human eye.

Your vet will recommend the appropriate flea control treatment.

Once the eggs hatch, the larvae live away from the dog host. They are creamy yellow, 2 to 5 mm long, and very rarely seen. A period of 21 to 53 days is the average time for a flea egg to grow and become an adult flea. Flea control involves removal of flea larvae from the environment, as well as the 'on the dog' treatment for fleas. Any flea larvae can lie dormant for up to a year if no host is present that an adult flea could feed from. In a cold and dry house area, the larva, or pupa as it next becomes, can lie in wait until an animal or human passes through so that a flea can emerge and jump towards and then on to the host. A human footfall from across an empty room will attract many fleas to a person when a house has been left unoccupied for months.

TREATMENTS

There are numerous preparations now available for flea control and the most appropriate product to use can be recommended by the veterinary surgeon or nurse. Some products should not be used until the puppy is three months old. The young puppy can be sprayed with liquid Fipronil from two days of age, and this is the only safe method for the tiniest puppy that comes with fleas, but the 'spot-on' concentrate should not be used until the puppy is 12 weeks old. Bathing with a mild puppy shampoo will not necessarily kill all the fleas but they will then show up in the wet coat or may be washed off in the rinse water. Live fleas need squashing with a fingernail or similar, since their hard-shelled, flattened bodies withstand normal thumb pressure on a hard surface. Drowning eventually kills fleas but they swim for some time and will still be able to hop away if allowed to dry out!

One of the easiest flea treatments is a concentrated solution used as a 'spot' of liquid applied directly to the skin halfway down the neck. The place of application is important, as the puppy should not be able to lick it. Although safe, as I have said, Fiprinol as a 'spot-on' should not be used on the puppy under 12 weeks of age. The 'spot-on' concentrate containing Imidacloprid can be applied from 10 weeks of age. Selamectin can be used on puppies aged 10 weeks or more; it is unique in also controlling roundworms internally. Repeat treatments with 'spot-on' products are needed monthly in the flea season.

Aerosol sprays of insecticides can also be used from 12 weeks of age but repeated applications may be necessary and some animals become fearful of the hissing sound that many sprays make. Flea collars placed around the dog's neck are treated with chemicals against fleas. Collars are often less effective, as the fleas prefer the rump area to feed rather than the neck area of the dog where the collar rubs the dry skin. A further method of control is the flea growth regulator Lufenuron that stops the pupa developing into an adult flea. A puppy can be dosed with this as young as two months, as soon as he is taking solid food; any fleas on the treated animal leaving eggs in the house will not be able to reinfect the pup. The tablet has to be given every month. There is the risk with this method that other dogs or cats may drop flea eggs around the house that are not inhibited from turning into adult biting fleas.

TREATING THE HOME
A necessary part of flea control, once a dog has come into the home carrying a flea, is to treat the floors, carpets and furnishings used by that dog. Any surface may have flea eggs dropped there; on hatching into larvae they can spin a sticky cocoon and any bits of fluff and dirt stick to them as a source of food and protection. There are a number of environmental sprays to kill larvae on the market and they can last for between three and 12 months. The use of a vacuum cleaner is beneficial in removing flea debris but the cleaner needs emptying in an outdoor bin to stop an adult flea developing from the pupa left in the bag. Furniture should be moved and carpet edges treated, as larvae migrate into the depth of the fabric and away from light, so deep-pile carpets can be a special problem.

Some dog owners prefer to use naturally occurring products; of those available against fleas, pyrethrum from poppies is probably the most effective. Pyrethroid, manufactured to mimic the natural pyrethrum, is an effective flea killer and can be purchased in dusting powders. Generally speaking, powders do not get deep enough into the coat of longer-haired dogs to be fully effective. Baths containing pyrethroids are the most effective way to apply the product. Garlic in the food has been praised by some breeders as a way of keeping their dogs entirely free of fleas. Other essential oils such as lavender used on the coat have some repellent action. In former times, dogs were kennelled on shredded pine wood used as bedding and fleas were unknown. Unfortunately 'wood wool' has gone out of fashion as a bedding material, since much timber wood is treated with potent chemicals before processing. Cedar or eucalyptus wood shavings can sometimes be used for the same purpose. Eucalyptus oil and penny-royal can be poisonous to a puppy if licked off the coat and should not be used.

LICE
As surface-feeding parasites these may be found on the occasional puppy especially if

Puppies raised on farms can be more prone to lice.

he has a farm or rural birthplace. The eggs of lice stick to the hair and are difficult to kill off. These eggs or 'nits' can be seen as tiny white objects glued to the puppy's hair, the ear fringes being a good place to look at first. The only way to rid a puppy of lice is by washing with an insecticidal shampoo. Clipping the ear fringes and paying attention to the area at the front of the elbows can also help to remove lice. It is necessary to know that there are two sorts of lice affecting dogs: the surface feeders that bite are probably easier to remove and the burrowing type that suck are the more difficult to eliminate. The sucking lice can cause anaemia from blood loss but the effect of lice usually first noticed is an intense skin irritation.

TICKS

Much bigger than the last two parasites described, so that the owner of a puppy having a tick is more likely to think it is a wart growing on the animal's head or body than an insect sucking blood. Sometimes multiple tick infestations occur and many pinhead-size ticks will be found at various places on the body.

The tick is an eight-legged insect that attaches itself by very strong 'teeth' or mouthparts to the puppy's skin and then proceeds to suck blood. As the tick feeds, its reddish-brown body becomes more bloated and slate-grey as it fills with blood. Eventually the tick drops off as a fully-fed adult. The female tick then deposits thousands of eggs on the ground that hatch and turn into larvae, awaiting the arrival of another animal to feed from. Ticks found on the body should be removed as soon as possible, before they have sucked too much blood and before they are ready to lay their many eggs on the ground. In the UK, the most common ticks are those that come from sheep and those that come from hedgehogs; they are different in size and colour and they can be identified at a veterinary clinic if you capture them in a bottle.

As well as causing anaemia, the tick can be a vector or carrier of serious life-threatening disease. Lyme disease is a major problem in some areas of the United States and occurs from time to time in the UK. Enquire of your vet if it is a problem in the area where your puppy will live. There is a Lyme disease vaccine too.

Ticks can be carriers of life-threatening diseases.

There are other tick fevers that are a problem in many countries. In the USA, Rocky Mountain Spotted Fever was a problem for many years. It is necessary to inspect the puppy every day during his grooming period if there are ticks about. This is especially the case in spring and summer. Small ticks should be looked for and the ears, the neck and under the forelegs should be closely searched for ticks. Ticks may also carry the blood parasite Babesia which, in southern areas worldwide, can cause sudden collapse and death. The parasite destroys the blood cells, so red urine or haematuria may be the first sign of babesiosis.

TREATMENT

Ticks should never be plucked off as this will leave the hard mouthparts firmly embedded and the puppy will develop a hard nodule and a non-healing wound around the embedded part. Use tweezers or a plastic 'tick hook' to get close to the head and gently pull with a slow twisting movement until the tick lets go. This procedure is made easier if the tick is first coated with olive oil or a mineral oil to block its breathing tubes;

even better is to use an oily ear mite preparation that contains an acaracide. It may be wise to give an antibiotic soon after the tick has been removed to avoid any blood poisoning.

MANGE MITES

These are less frequent, as better hygiene and feeding help to promote resistance to chronic mange disease. Sarcoptic mange is spread by direct contact, so the puppy may arrive with intense scratching due to a parasite brought from his mother, or another dog sleeping with the pups in close contact with them. Mange mites are often associated with stray or uncared for dogs. Foxes and other animals may also be responsible for spreading mites, so the pup's breeder should not be blamed. The second most common mange is demodectic mange. This parasite, *Demodex,* seems to live in the skin without causing too much harm but, if disease or poor nutrition lowers the puppy's immunity, the mange mite becomes a problem.

The puppy with sarcoptic mange will be very itchy. The ear tips and the face are affected, later large areas of the legs or the flanks become hairless, scaly and red. The vet should be consulted about any severe scratching; tests such as skin scrapings for microscopic examination may be needed and even then the mites may not be found on the first visit. Bathing, with suitable mange preparations as advised, will clear the skin but repeat treatments may be required to prevent reinfection. The product selamectin used as a 'spot-on' monthly is also effective against Sarcoptic mange.

Demodectic mange is more seen in short-coated breeds such as Bull Terriers and Dobermanns. The parasite lives in the depth of the hair follicle and is more difficult to find, so bald patches and hair loss may be the first sign that this sort of mange is present. There may be little scratching or itching and no recent contact with another dog. The parasite becomes embedded in the skin at, or just after, birth and may lie dormant until some stress effect makes it become active.

There is a growing tendency not to use potent chemicals to try to kill off this parasite but instead to improve the dog's immunity and only treat any secondary bacterial infections. It has been noticed that some bitches, after they have come on heat for the first time, will develop areas of baldness on or about the head, as hormone levels influence skin resistance. *Demodex* can be found in scrapings or hair pluckings from these areas, since the oestrogen of the first heat makes the parasite active. Both sorts of mange need veterinary advice, and experience will decide as to which medication and for how long the treatment needs to be given.

Ear mites are a special problem. The parasite *Otodectes* is usually caught from a cat. Close contact with the cat is not necessary as a cat while shaking its head may propel pieces of wax containing mites that fly through the air and can arrive on the pup's coat. One or two mites in the ear produce redness and intense irritation. If the puppy then scratches the ear with his hind toe nails, scratch marks will be found in the ear and bacteria will then infect this warm, red, moist ear area, with severe consequences. Daily treatment for a week using an acaracide will be necessary to get rid of ear mites. Cats in contact must also be treated to reduce the risk of reinfection.

Short-coated breeds, such as the Bull Terrier, seem more susceptible to demodectic mange.

OTHER SKIN PARASITES

The most common one found in puppies with white scurf or dandruff on their coats is *Cheyletiella* (pronounced key-let-e-ella). The puppy may not be itchy at first but, if the hand is brushed against the lie of the hair on the back, more scurf comes off. Under the microscope, the eight-legged parasite that causes 'walking dandruff' is quite easy to see. Hair is not lost from the puppy but the parasite may walk on to humans and small, raised, itchy, red spots appear on the arms or all over the body. The parasite is quite easily killed with shampoos or Fipronil spray. On humans, the parasite feeds but does not live long, so bathing or showering is sufficient to wash these mites away.

Ringworm is a much talked about parasite as it causes hair loss and humans can be infected too. Caused by a fungus (not a worm), the infection is spread by dead hair and scales or from direct contact with another animal. Cats should be considered as a possible source of the fungal infection. Scaly, very itchy spots are the first indications of ringworm, and bare, hairless areas may be a later sign. Any round spots with a pink 'ring' around them are not necessarily ringworm and may be a bacterial Staphylcoccus toxin response in young dogs. Veterinary diagnosis is obviously of importance and there are good specific treatments for ringworm available as baths and tablets by mouth. Ultraviolet light is used as one test for ringworm hairs, in the form of a Wood's lamp. The vet will decide which treatments are most appropriate. There will also be a warning that ringworm is contagious to people handling the pet and good hygiene is necessary.

The harvest mite, *Trombicula*, is now rare in the UK but it was often seen in the autumn after dogs had walked through stubble – the remains of a corn crop after the longest part of the plant had been removed at harvesting. Affected dogs had very itchy feet, orangey-brown mites could be found between the toes and it was quite easy to wash them away with an anti-parasitic shampoo.

Cats are sometimes responsible for transmitting ringworm to dogs.

Children should be taught to wash their hands after contact with puppies.

INTERNAL PARASITES

The roundworm is probably the most frequent internal parasite problem. As well as irritation in the intestines, it can cause lung and eye damage and a tangle of worms in the intestine will cause an obstruction and the death of a pup. Any eggs passed into the environment may also affect humans.

Tapeworms can be acquired young but cause less disastrous effects. Parasites such as Giardia can also cause severe diarrhoea and debility. Hookworms in some countries cause anaemia and severe illness but are still uncommon in the UK. Whipworms, tracheal worms, bladderworms and heartworms all may be found in puppies if samples are examined. The heartworm, spread by mosquito bites, may cause severe illness and death in countries outside the UK. Veterinary advice on the risk is important and regular medication may be needed for prevention.

ROUNDWORMS

The two sorts of roundworm, *Toxocara* and *Toxacaris,* are similar enough to deal with together. New-born puppies may carry worms acquired before birth from the mother's body. Toxocara larvae in a bitch pass into puppies after six weeks of the pregnancy. Puppies with a heavy worm infestation will be subject to diarrhoea and grow more slowly, but have an abnormally hungry look when food is put down as if the pup will never be satisfied. Obviously, the worms get the first choice of foods entering the intestine and the pup's body only gets the leavings. Pups may vomit for various reasons but, sometimes, a white-coloured worm will appear in the vomit, and the abdomen is unnaturally distended even long after a meal has been eaten. The coat may be poor and lacking in shine. Hiccups are not necessarily a sign of worms; all young things that have difficulty in controlling their breathing may be subject to such hiccups.

TREATMENT

Worm eggs are passed out of the puppy on

to the ground where eggs will remain for up to a year as a source of infection to others. Preventive treatment, by early worming of puppies and repeating this dosing on a regular basis, is vital to stop the worms in the puppy getting to a size where more eggs will be laid. There are many safe wormers that can be obtained from veterinary suppliers, including a safe, antibiotic-type wormer, selamectin, used as a spot of liquid on the back of the neck once a month.

Liquid wormers can be given to puppies every two weeks from 14 days old, so the puppy purchased at six or seven weeks should not have a problem. The new keeper of the puppy should aim to give a reliable wormer every three weeks between 9 weeks and four months of age. After that, worm the pup at six months and at 12 months. At this age it may then be advisable to use a combined roundworm and tapeworm tablet.

Worming the pregnant bitch from the 42nd day of her pregnancy until a few days after whelping aims at producing a worm-free puppy to sell later. Young children handling puppies should be told not to suck their fingers after touching any unwormed puppies and they should be made to wash their hands before eating any food. The prompt removal of dog faeces from the ground, and the use of designated toilet areas for dogs away from children's play areas, are advised.

About one in ten adult dogs carry a few roundworms, so a regular worming routine for dogs throughout life, with a combined roundworm and tapeworm dose, is recommended.

TAPEWORMS

Tapeworms are more likely to be a problem in the puppy over six months of age than in the very young pup. The main source of infection to a puppy with the *Dipylidium* tapeworm is from the flea or the biting louse. An infection could develop within weeks of the young puppy swallowing a flea on his coat, as the flea is the tapeworm's intermediate host. If the tapeworm segments, looking like flattened grains of rice, are seen on freshly voided faeces, or stuck on to tail hairs, treatment of a puppy is urgently required.

Routine worming at six months with an effective tapeworm tablet is always advised. Some of the worming products can be given at any time of day on an empty stomach, while others specify that the tablets be given in the morning with a small breakfast meal, then the rest of the food given five hours later. Usually, no signs of the worms are seen after dosing, as they are dissolved away, once killed, as part of the puppy's digestive process. It is also necessary to remember that there is a more deadly tapeworm, *Echinococcus*, that is a danger to dogs and humans but is only found where dogs have access to dead sheep in certain areas of the countryside. There are other tapeworms that have the rabbit as an intermediate host, or infected raw beef, sheep or pig meat were at one time carrying cysts of tapeworms.

HOOKWORMS

The tail of this worm is like a curly whiplash, which allows the worm to burrow into the wall of the large intestine to feed. As eggs are not produced every day by the worm, it may be necessary to take faeces samples for several days before the characteristic thick-walled eggs are seen under the microscope. Blood-stained diarrhoea leading to an anaemic, thin dog are the signs to watch out for. The eggs remain in the soil for a year or more, so a

dog that eats grass or buries bones in soil infected by previous exposure to dogs, is the one most likely to have these worms. Many wormers used have the ability to kill hookworms.

HEARTWORMS

These worms live in the bloodstream and there they block the upper heart chambers and blood supply to the lungs. The oxygen carried by the circulation to the rest of the body is restricted and a puppy may collapse and die. An adult dog with heartworms produces millions of little worms in its blood which can be sucked in by a biting mosquito, then later be transferred to the next animal bitten by the mosquito. Only certain climatic conditions suit these mosquitoes and the UK is still considered free of heartworms. Early diagnosis and treatment should be given, as it is very effective if given early enough, but always consult your vet.

LUNGWORMS

Strictly speaking, there are no such worms that can infect puppies. However, it is best to be aware that in southern parts of England some puppies may get special worms in the artery supplying the lungs, causing shortness of breath and coughing. A snail carries this worm, the intermediate stage of *Aelurostrongylus*. Care should be taken with puppies in already infected areas when snails are about! There is also a worm that lives in the base of the windpipe just before it enters the lungs. *Oslerus osleri*, named after the eminent Canadian Doctor Osler, will be looked for in persistently coughing young dogs. A ten-day course of the wormer Fenbendazole is very effective as a treatment for this type of worm that, fortunately, is rare.

GIARDIASIS

This can be a cause of severe diarrhoea most likely to be found in kennelled dogs. Although it is not caused by a worm but by an amoeba-like parasite, the protozoa is common in wild animals and thrives in wet areas. Camping trips, where the dog drinks from water even when it looks clear, may bring the parasite back into an urban area. If you and your puppy both feel ill after such a trip, then have samples examined for this nasty parasite. Treatment with Fenbendazole wormer is again very effective.

FIRST AID FOR COMMON ACCIDENTS AND INJURIES

Much of the treatment learned for human first aid can equally well be applied to the puppy. For any puppy showing sudden collapse, the A B C routine should be applied.

A Pull out the tongue, check the mouth for any obstruction swallowed and provide a clear AIRWAY.

B The loss of blood should be controlled if there is visible bleeding. Pressure with a pad of cotton wool (cotton) or a damp tissue will reduce the blood flow from a wound. Feet cut with glass will bleed profusely as the pup runs around, so try to keep him still as well as bandaging to stop BLEEDING.

C Cold follows shock, so wrap the young dog in a coat or a blanket to retain his body heat. Common sense tells you that if the dog has collapsed on a hot day then cooling by a flow of water from a hosepipe is equally valuable. Moistening the lips with water is often beneficial, but drinking may have to be restricted until the vet has examined the dog. C is also for 'circulation', especially in human first aid routines. There is not a lot of benefit in mouth to mouth respiration and cardiac massage in these types of animal collapses, so think more about avoiding COLD.

There is an increasing tendency to do less in the form of first aid and it is often better to transport the puppy to the vet's surgery, where more specific treatment can be given. It is best to ask someone else to phone in advance that a puppy is on its way to the veterinary centre, and any information on how the injury occurred will allow the emergency team to prepare for the puppy's needs. This advice applies to broken legs as much as accidental poisonings.

Pups are particularly accident-prone, so be prepared for unexpected emergencies.

BROKEN BONES

If the leg is at an unusual angle and swings like a pendulum when the puppy is lifted up, it is likely the bone is broken. Splinting should not be attempted. Carry the dog by his head, neck and body and allow him to lie down on a soft surface so that he can be transported to the treatment centre. An exception to this method of carrying is if there has been a back or neck injury with a fracture risk: in this situation, slide the dog on to a board, or a puppy can go into a large basket, as long as he can stretch out at full length.

BLOAT

Bloat of the stomach is another emergency; it causes distension of the left side of the abdomen. This is an urgent situation, which can get suddenly worse if the stomach twists, and then the condition known as gastric torsion causes distress and collapse. This emergency needs the dog transported to a veterinary centre where facilities are ready for an immediate operation on the stomach. Fortunately, the younger puppy with a bloated stomach seems to be able to get rid of the 'wind' and torsions are only seen in dogs over nine months. A silicone-based indigestion mixture for human use can be given as a first-aid measure and this will help to disperse excess stomach gas. Try lifting the front legs up and massaging the stomach area if a puppy looks distended.

WOUNDS

Accidental injuries may also need first aid. Wounds from sharp objects, or the teeth of other dogs, can be treated by warm bathing. A mild antiseptic added to the water helps to clean away soiled areas. If the puppy is used to being handled, clip the hair well away from the edges of any wound as this allows wound drainage and cleaner healing. A teaspoonful of common salt in half a pint of warm (first boiled) water makes a very safe and effective wound application. Depending on the depth of the injury or the length of a tear, antibiotics and, possibly, stitching may be necessary at the vet's surgery to provide proper treatment.

DIARRHOEA AND SICKNESS

These symptoms, often the result of overeating, can be treated as a first-aid condition. Prolonged sickness or diarrhoea, say lasting more than 12 to 24 hours, may need urgent veterinary attention. Fluid losses dehydrate a puppy quickly and professional treatment is then needed. In simple cases, take away solid food for 24 hours. If sickness is not violent, allow about a tablespoonful of water every two hours, more for a large breed. An electrolyte replacement solution is best, but the homemade remedy of half a teaspoonful of salt and, if available, half a teaspoonful of bicarbonate of soda in a litre of water can be tried; give in small amounts at a time. Egg white and water is another remedy using available household supplies. In case of severe sickness, offering ice cubes in a saucer allows the puppy to lick very small quantities of iced water at a time. The first foods fed after 12 or 24 hours should be simple, smooth substances such as scrambled eggs, boiled rice flavoured with meat extract or lean, shedded chicken meat.

PUPPY DISEASES AND INHERITED DISORDERS

When you obtain your puppy, whether it be from a reputable breeder, a friend down the road or from a puppy rescue centre, you will want to know about some of the things that might be wrong or how he

There are a number of conditions that are inherited.

could become ill. The majority of puppies are very healthy, although the occasional 'tummy upset' can happen after different foods etc. are eaten. This can be dealt with by diet restriction alone as described above.

There are some severe infections that, at one time, killed puppies but, if you have been following the proper vaccination routine, the risk of severe disease should be minimal.

Another group of conditions are those that come from the parents: these may be present from birth (congenital) or, more likely when inherited through the genes (genetic), the condition may not appear until the puppy grows or, in some cases, not until middle age. Studies on the canine genome are now bearing fruit and it is already possible to have blood samples taken from puppies and their parents to see how diseases are inherited. To date, 495 canine genetic diseases are recognised and further studies on inheritance will help dog

breeders, as only in 180 is the mode of inheritance known. Two-thirds are due to recessive genes, so it will be difficult to totally eradicate most hereditary disorders.

The diseases and disorders listed may be very rare but you should know what the words mean. Other veterinary books will give more detailed descriptions of the condition if you are unlucky enough to have an affected puppy. Some inherited disorders are found in certain breeds more than others, and these breeds are listed at the end of each condition, though this does not mean that it is only these breeds that can be affected.

Those breeds of greatest popularity are those, too, most frequently seen by vets. They appear most often in the lists but this in no way means that all puppies of a breed will be expected to develop such defects. The lists are based on my own veterinary experience of puppy problems in the last 50 years or so.

AIRWAY OBSTRUCTION
Any restriction in the nose, throat or in the air passage to the lungs may cause wheezing, snoring or even collapse, with a blue-coloured tongue. Tracheal collapse affects the windpipe due to weak or incomplete cartilage support.
Bulldog, Mastiff (nose), Pug, Yorkshire Terrier.

ALOPECIA
Symmetrical hair loss may result from skin infections and self-injury, but baldness in a pattern, or hair loss in matching places on either side of the body, will probably be due to an inherited condition.
Belgian Shepherd Dog, Boxer, Staffordshire Bull Terrier, Dachshund, Dobermann Pinscher, Great Dane, Labrador Retriever, Whippet.

Anaemia is a condition to which some Irish Setters are prone.

Atopy in a Labrador, showing the skin prick sensitivity test site.

ANAEMIA
Immune-mediated disorders of the red blood cells may prevent oxygen being carried to the muscles and other organs, seen as weakness, tiredness on exercise and pale gums, etc.
Irish Setter.

AORTIC STENOSIS
A heart disease mainly studied in Sweden, congenital defect. Boxer.

ATOPY
An inherited tendency to produce allergic signs, usually seen as a skin disease, watery eyes and digestive disorders.
Belgian Shepherd Dog, Boston Terrier, German Shepherd Dog, Irish Setter, Labrador Retriever, Mastiff, Miniature Schnauzer, Shih Tzu, West Highland White Terrier.

BONE TUMOURS
see OSTEOSARCOMA

CARDIOMYOPATHY
An inherited heart weakness producing an enlarged heart and collapse on exercise.
Boxer (USA), Dobermann Pinscher, Great Dane, Wolfhound.

CATARACT
An opaque lens in the eye is seen as a grey eye with a dilated pupil and little or no vision. May be seen at birth but many cataracts develop later in life, and some are inherited defects.
American Cocker Spaniel, Belgian Shepherd Dog (all varieties), Boston Terrier, Cavalier King Charles Spaniel, Chesapeake Bay Retriever, German Shepherd Dog, Golden Retriever, Jack Russell, Large Munsterlander, Miniature Schnauzer, Norwegian Buhund, Old English Sheepdog, Staffordshire Bull Terrier, Standard Poodle, Siberian Husky, Welsh Springer Spaniel, West Highland White Terrier.

CDRM
A disease where the nerves of the spine degenerate so, eventually, the toes of the hind legs drag and the hindquarters sway from side to side, not usually seen until middle or old age. May also affect the brain cells.
German Shepherd Dog.

CEREBELLUM DISEASE
Disorder of the hind brain affecting walking and balance. Puppies may have an unusual way of walking soon after birth. Progressive 'abiotrophy' type in Bernese Mountain Dog, Irish Setter.

CERVICAL SPONDYLOPATHY
Narrowing of the spinal canal of the neck bones can cause neck pain, loss of balance and collapse from pressure on the nerves.
Dobermann Pinscher (wobblers), Great Dane (develops when young).

CERVICAL VERTEBRAL STENOSIS
Similar to cervical spondylopathy where the spinal canal in the neck is too narrow.
Basset Hound.

CHONDRO DYSPLASIA
Abnormal growth of the cartilage leads to limb shortening as seen normally in Dachshunds. Some other breeds develop like this as a disease state and are undersized.
Alaskan Malamute, Basset Hound, Miniature Poodle, Norwegian Elkhound.

CLAD
Canine leukocyte adhesion disease is only found in Irish Setters and was one of the first diseases for which a DNA blood test could be used to identify the recessive gene.
Irish Setter.

CLEFT PALATE
Found soon after birth when the pup fails to grow or, when sucking, the milk comes back down the nose as part of the roof of mouth is missing.
Boston Terrier, Bulldog, Cocker Spaniel.

COLITIS (Histiocytic)
Persistent mucoid diarrhoea that responds poorly to treatment with antibiotics and normal diarrhoea treatments.
Boxer.

COLLIE EYE ANOMALY (CEA)
An inherited condition that is present at birth; in the worst form of the defect the eye bleeds and the sight is lost. Lesser forms cause pits or coloboma in the back of the eye and loss of vision.
Border Collie, Collie Rough, Collie Smooth, Shetland Sheepdog and many other non-Collie breeds such as Australian Shepherd Dog.

The Shetland Sheepdog, in common with other collie-type breeds, is susceptible to Collie Eye Anomaly.

COLOBOMA OF THE EYE
A weakness in the eye structure that is only seen as holes or pits when the vet uses an ophthalmoscope to examine the eye.
Beagle, Shetland Sheepdog.

CORKSCREW TAIL
Short, twisted, tail deformity. See also 'screw tail' below.
Mastiff.

CORNEAL LIPIDOSIS
White patches may be recognised in the front of the eye often associated in breeds with too much fat in the diet, possibly hereditary.
Cavalier King Charles Spaniel.

CPRA
An inherited condition of central progressive retinal atrophy may be confused with a similar condition seen due to a dietary deficiency at birth.
Border Collie, Cocker Spaniel, Collie Rough, Collie Smooth, English Springer Spaniel, Golden Retriever, Labrador Retriever, German Shepherd Dog, Shetland Sheepdog, Welsh Cardigan Corgi.

CRANIO-MANDIBULAR OSTEOPATHY
A condition of the growing puppy where the jaw bone thickens excessively and other parts of the skull swell up.
Boxer, Cairn Terrier, Pyrenean, West Highland White Terrier.

CRUCIATE LIGAMENT INJURY
The ligaments supporting the stifle or knee joint are arranged inside the joint in a cross-like structure. Some large breeds are more likely to strain or tear their anterior cruciate ligament.
Bernese Mountain Dog, Bullmastiff, Chow

Large breeds, such as the Bullmastiff, may sustain cruciate ligament injuries.

Chow, Golden Retriever, Labrador Retriever, Newfoundland, Rottweiler, Bull Terrier, St Bernard.

CRYPTORCHIDISM
The testes of the male start their development near the kidneys but just before, or shortly after, birth, each testis should come outside the abdomen to lie in the scrotum. Some strains in breeds are more likely to have only one of the testes in the scrotum – the testis is 'hidden'. Sometimes called monorchid if only one can be found outside.
Cocker Spaniel, Chihuahua, Labrador Retriever.

DEAFNESS
Autosomal recessive inheritance. The loss of hearing is not always easy to identify in a puppy.
Akita, Australian Cattle Dog, Border Collie, Bulldog, Bull Terrier, Dalmatian, Dachshund, Great Dane, Merle colour gene in Collies, Great Dane, Shetland Sheepdog, Piebald colour gene in Dalmatian, Bull Terrier, English Setter.

DEMODEX SKIN DISEASE
Some breeds have a greater tendency to show the signs of disease with this parasite; it causes one type of mange in the dog.
Bull Terrier, Bulldog, Dobermann Pinscher, German Shepherd Dog.

DERMOID SINUS
An inward turning of the skin at the centre of the back, producing an oozing 'hole'.
Rhodesian Ridgeback.

DISTICHIASIS
A double row of eyelashes that produces a wet eyelid with irritation.
American Cocker Spaniel, Bulldog, Cocker Spaniel, Dachshund, Flat Coated Retriever, Poodle.

DYSTOCIA
Difficult birth, often due to a narrow pelvis or an overlarge puppy head, that may genetically pass to the bitch puppy used for future breeding
Boston Terrier, Bulldog, Bull Terrier.

ECTOPIC CILIA
Eyelashes that grow at an unusual angle so they rub the eye surface, causing a watery eye condition.
Flat Coated Retriever, Pekingese and other breeds.

ECTROPION
An outward turning of the eyelids causing a red eye rim.
Basset Hound, Beagle, Bulldog, Bullmastiff, Cocker Spaniel, Mastiff, Newfoundland, St Bernard.

ELBOW DYSPLASIA
General term for any developmental disease of the elbow: see also osteochondrosis, ununited anconeal process (UAP).
Basset Hound, English Mastiff, Great Dane, Newfoundland, Rottweiler, Labrador Retriever, Bernese Mountain Dog, German Shepherd Dog (UAP), Golden Retriever, Irish Wolfhound.

ENTROPION
An inward turning of the eyelids causing a painful eye and watery discharge.
Akita, Basset Hound, Bernese Mountain Dog, Bulldog, Bullmastiff, Chow Chow, Cocker Spaniel, Flat Coated Retriever, Great Dane, Golden Retriever, Labrador Retriever, Newfoundland, Old English Sheepdog, Rottweiler, St Bernard, Vizsla.

EPI (Pancreatic Insufficiency)
A deficiency of digestive enzymes from the pancreas that causes a greasy diarrhoea and weight loss.
German Shepherd Dog.

EPILEPSY
Seizures due to abnormal brain activity, varies from mild fits to severe convulsions.
Beagle, Belgian Shepherd Dog, Bernese Mountain Dog, Border Collie, Brittany Spaniel, Cavalier King Charles Spaniel, Cocker Spaniel, Dalmatian, German Shepherd Dog, German Shorthaired Pointer, Golden Retriever, Irish Setter, Jack Russell, Labrador Retriever, Poodle,

Epilepsy can occur in many breeds, including the Poodle.

The Siberian Husky is generally a healthy dog, but some instances of glaucoma have been reported in the breed.

Rough Collie, Vizsla.

EPIPHORA
A watery eye condition. Seen in Shih Tzu and other breeds that may have entropion, distichiasis etc. or a blocked tear duct.

FALLING or Butterfly Catching Disease
Strange behaviour, where the dog looks up in the sky then may collapse, a now-rare brain abnormality.
Cavalier King Charles Spaniel.

FOOTPAD HYPERKERATOSIS
Hard, scaly pads due to excess keratin production.
Irish Terrier.

FURUNCULOSIS
Infection with Staphylococcus deeply under the skin so that little oozing tunnels break out on the skin surface.

Bulldog, German Shepherd Dog.

GASTRIC TYMPANY
Accumulation of gas in the stomach causing uncomfortable distension and the risk of torsion. May cause sudden death.
Chow Chow, Irish Setter, German Shepherd Dog, Great Dane.

GLAUCOMA
Fluid distension of the eyeball.
American Cocker Spaniel, Basset Hound, Beagle, Cocker Spaniel, Flat Coated Retriever, Siberian Husky, Welsh Springer Spaniel, Welsh Terrier, Vizsla.

GLUTEN MALABSORPTION SYNDROME
Intolerance of the protein found in wheat products.
Golden Retriever, Irish Setter, Labrador.

HAEMANGIOSARCOMA
A tumour of blood vessels, especially in the spleen, where there may be a digestive upset and sometimes sudden collapse and death when the tumour bleeds internally. German Shepherd Dog.

HAEMOPHILIA
Disease where the blood fails to clot properly, may be seen as bleeding gums, swollen joints or sudden death. Alaskan Malamute, Cairn Terrier (Haemophilia A & B in the USA), German Shepherd Dog (Haemophilia A), St Bernard (Haemophilia B and Factor IX).

HAIR LIP
The lips fail to join together before birth, leading to a puppy with a deformed face. Boston Terrier.

HEART MITRAL VALVE DISEASE
Leaking of the heart valves causes a 'murmur'. Noise often not found until four to five years of age but disease then can lead to premature death.

Cavalier King Charles Spaniel, Dachshund (later onset from 8 to 12 years).

HEART MURMUR CONGENITAL
Leaking of the heart valves causes a 'murmur'. Noise heard at birth. Border Terrier, Boxer.

HEREDITARY CATARACT
An opaque lens in the eye, may be seen at 10 days when the eyes of the puppy open or sometimes later in life (see also CATARACT). Early onset breeds are Boston Terrier, Cavalier King Charles Spaniel, German Shepherd Dog, American Cocker Spaniel, Golden Retriever, Miniature Schnauzer, Old English Sheepdog, Staffordshire Bull Terrier, Standard Poodle, Welsh Springer Spaniel.

HEREDITARY LUPUS
An auto-immune disease. German Shorthaired Pointer.

HIP DYSPLASIA
Malformation of the ball and socket joint

Hip dysplasia features in many breeds, including the Golden Retriever.

The Newfoundland is one of the breeds that can suffer from immune mediated arthropathy, an auto-immune disease.

of the hips producing restricted movement of the hindquarters and eventual arthritis.
Akita, Alaskan Malamute, Belgian Shepherd Dog, Bernese Mountain Dog, Border Collie, Boxer, Bullmastiff, Chow Chow, Cocker Spaniel, Dalmatian, Dobermann Pinscher, English Springer Spaniel, Flat Coated Retriever, Irish Setter, German Shepherd Dog, German Shorthaired Pointer, Golden Retriever, Great Dane, Labrador Retriever, Mastiff, Old English Sheepdog, Rhodesian Ridgeback, Rottweiler, Samoyed, Siberian Husky, Vizsla, Weimaraner.

HISTIOCYTOSIS – SYSTEMIC
Tumour of the body that can spread internally and cause early death.
Bernese Mountain Dog.

HYDROCEPHALUS
Fluid retained in the skull; puppy may be dull with a large head at a young age. May later develop fits.
Boston Terrier, Bulldog, Bullmastiff, Chihuahua, Maltese Terrier, Pekingese, Poodle (miniature), Pomeranian, Yorkshire Terrier.

IMMUNE MEDIATED ARTHROPATHY
Auto-immune disease affecting one or several joints at a young age.
Akita, Bernese Mountain Dog, Boxer, German Shorthaired Pointer, Newfoundland, Weimaraner.

INGUINAL HERNIA
Any weakness in the abdominal wall may cause a bulge; this type of hernia at first mainly consists of fat through the inguinal canal.
Cairn Terrier, Cocker Spaniel and many other breeds.

Like many small breeds, the Yorkshire Terrier is prone to Legge-Perthe's Disease.

INTERDIGITAL CYSTS
Small swellings between the toes containing fluid, often difficult to treat with antibiotics etc.
Bulldog, Bull Terrier, Dachshund.

INTERVERTEBRAL DISC DISEASE
Any tendency to weakness in the structure of the discs between the bony vertebrae may cause a protrusion, with back pain or even sudden paralysis.
Beagle, Cocker Spaniel, Dachshund, Pembroke Welsh Corgi.

KERATITIS
Inflammation of the cornea or 'window' of the eye. Appears as a bluish haze or black pigment is deposited.
Boxer, Pekingese (Pigmentary type).

KERATO CONJUNCTIVITIS
SICCA (KCS)
A dry eye surface due to a failure to produce enough tears. Any breed may be affected after disease, medication etc.
Bichon Frisé.

LEGGE-PERTHE'S DISEASE
A flattening of the head of the femur so that the hip joint does not bend smoothly, seen at five months and leads to arthritis.
Bichon Frisé, Yorkshire Terrier, many other small breeds.

LENS LUXATION
A weakness in the support holding the lens in the eye may lead to sudden blindness as the lens dislocates.
Border Collie, Jack Russell.

LEUCODYSTROPHY
Recessive genes cause a 'storage' disease, shown as a dog with inco-ordination, blindness, fits and leg paralysis.
Cairn Terrier (USA only), Basset Hound, Beagle, Dalmatian,

Pomeranian, Poodle, West Highland White Terrier.

LIVER PORTO-SYSTEMIC SHUNT
A development failure of the blood supply through the liver, found in the younger puppy.
Labrador Retriever, Staffordshire Bull Terrier.

MALABSORPTION
Digestive problem where food passes through the small intestine without all the nutrients being absorbed, seen as a thin puppy with constant diarrhoea.
German Shepherd Dog.

MAST CELL TUMOURS
Small skin tumours that grow rapidly in puppies; some may be malignant so should be examined and treated by vet.
Staffordshire Bull Terrier.

MEGAOESOPHAGUS
Disorder with an enlarged oesophagus tube to the stomach (the gullet) seen as regurgitation of undigested food.
German Shepherd Dog, Great Dane.

MICRO OPHTHALMOS
An underdeveloped eye size so the lids are not fully stretched and the eyeball is deeply situated in the skull.
Rough Collie, Shetland Sheepdog.

MOTORNEURONE DISEASE
Specific disease with wasting of the back muscles, first seen in late puppyhood.
Brittany Spaniel.

MYOPATHY
Muscle disease, may show pain after extreme exercise.
Labrador Retriever.

Mast Cell Tumours sometimes occur in Staffordshire Bull Terrier pups.

Some Chows suffer from myotonia, overdevelopment of muscles around the head, neck and forelegs.

MYOTONIA
Disease where the muscles overdevelop, especially head, neck and forelegs, giving a 'bunny hop' type of movement.
Cavalier King Charles Spaniel, Chow Chow, Staffordshire Bull Terrier.

NEPHROPATHY (FAMILIAL)
Kidney disease often present from birth but signs may not be seen for several months.
Alaskan Malamute (Kidney dysplasia), Boxer, Cocker Spaniel.

ONCHODESIS
Shedding of very brittle toe nails, a form of auto-immune disease.
German Shepherd Dog.

OSTEOCHONDRITIS (OD)
Disease of growing puppies where the elbow or shoulder joint cartilage becomes so thick that great slices fall off and cause severe lameness.
Boxer, German Shepherd Dog, Golden Retriever.

OSTEOCHONDROSIS
General term for the disorder of the growth of cartilage of individual bones, may be seen in the older puppy as stiffness of elbows, shoulders or the hocks of back legs.
Bernese Mountain Dog, Bullmastiff, Mastiff, Newfoundland, Old English Sheepdog, Rhodesian Ridgeback, Rottweiler, St Bernard, Weimaraner.

OSTEO-CHONDRODYSPLASIA OF CARPUS
A specific disease of the joints of the foreleg that represent the wrist joint of a human.
Basset Hound, Border Collie.

OSTEOSARCOMA
Tumour of bone, may affect any breed but is most common in the largest breeds.
Great Dane, Rottweiler, St Bernard.

PANNUS (Keratitis)
Cloudiness in the corner of the eye that leads to blindness if untreated.
Border Collie, German Shepherd Dog.

PATELLA LUXATION
Instability of the stifle (knee) joint due to a weak attachment of the kneecap or as the result of an injury.
Bichon Frisé, Cavalier King Charles Spaniel, Chihuahua, Chow Chow, Flat

Patella luxation can occur in many breeds, including the Pug.

Persistent pupillary membrane is an eye disorder that can occur in the Pembroke Welsh Corgi.

Coated Retriever, Jack Russell, Miniature Pinscher, Staffordshire Bull Terrier, Labrador Retriever, Maltese Terrier, Pekingese, Poodle, Pomeranian, Pug, Yorkshire Terrier.

PEMPHIGUS
An auto-immune skin disease with small blisters etc.
Shetland Sheepdog.

PERSISTENT PUPILLARY MEMBRANE
Shreds of tissue remain inside the eye so that a strand may be seen attached to the lens or the inside of the cornea.
Basenji, Bullmastiff, Pembroke Welsh Corgi, Siberian Husky, Cocker Spaniel, West Highland White Terrier.

PHPV VITREOUS EYE DISEASE
Development fault, with a strand of tissue running from the back of the eye to the retina, causing partial blindness.
Dobermann Pinscher, Staffordshire Bull Terrier.

PITUITARY DWARFISM
Stunted growth of the very young puppy, becomes obvious as early as three or four weeks.
German Shepherd Dog.

PRA (GENERALISED)
Disease of the retina inside the eye that leads to partial or complete blindness. It is not manifested until four years or later, so it is necessary to test the older dog every year, especially retriever-type dogs.

American Cocker Spaniel, Australian Cattle Dog, Border Collie, Border Terrier (in USA), Cairn Terrier, Cocker Spaniel, Collie (Rough), Dachshund (Min. Long Hair), Elkhound, English Springer Spaniel, Irish Setter, Irish Wolfhound, Golden Retriever, Labrador Retriever, Lhasa Apso, Miniature Schnauzer, Newfoundland, Poodle, Portuguese Water Spaniel, Retriever (Chesapeake Bay), Tibetan Spaniel, Tibetan Terrier, Welsh Corgi (Cardigan).

PROGRESSIVE AXONOPATHY
Nerve disorder that causes hind leg weakness and collapse.
Boxer.

PROLAPSE OF THIRD EYELID
The small eyelid in the corner of the eye may swell and turn over, causing a red, cherry-like lump between the lids.
Bulldog, Beagle.

PYODERMA
Deep infection of the skin layers with a Staphylococcus, often due to lowered skin resistance.
Great Dane, Rottweiler.

RAGE SYNDROME
Mental instability with unprovoked attacks and aggressiveness.
Cocker Spaniel (solid colours), Golden Retriever (males).

RETINAL DYSPLASIA
Weakness in the attachment of the sensitive retina to the eyeball may lead to haemorrhage and blindness.
American Cocker Spaniel, Bedlington Terrier, Cavalier King Charles Spaniel, English Springer Spaniel, Golden Retriever, Labrador Retriever, Puli, Rottweiler, Sealyham Terrier.

RETINITIS
Inflammatory process of the sensitive retina of the eye with blindness.
Akita.

SCREW TAIL
Short, twisted tail deformity.
Bulldog, Bullmastiff.

SEBORRHOEA, PRIMARY
Skin disorder with excess greasiness but sometimes with dry, scaly skin.

Bulldog pup with Cherry Eye, caused by the prolapse of the third eyelid.

Retinal dysplasia can occur in the American Cocker Spaniel.

American Cocker Spaniel, Basset Hound, Dobermann Pinscher, English Springer Spaniel, West Highland White Terrier.

SHOULDER LUXATION
Loose attachment of the shoulder joint causing a peculiar gait.
Miniature Pinscher.

SKIN SEBACEOUS ADENITIS
Dry skin disease with hair loss on face, around eyes etc.
Akita, Samoyed, Vizsla.

TREMORS, IDIOPATHIC
Quivering of the muscles that may affect the head and neck, or sometimes the whole body shudders.
Beagle.

TRICHIASIS
Hairs on skin folds around the eye cause irritation.
Pekingese.

UNUNITED ANCONEAL PROCESS
Failure in the development of the bony structure of the elbow, the loose piece of bone may lead to a permanent arthritis and a stiff joint.
Basset Hound, German Shepherd Dog.

URATE UROLITHIASIS
Stones in the bladder usually specific to Dalmatians.

UROLITHIASIS
Includes anything from fine sand to pebble size 'stones' in the bladder and the urethra, formed from crystals in the urine.
Corgi, Dachshund, Terriers.

The Dachshund can be affected by Urolithiasis.

Urinary incontinence sometimes occurs in the Old English Sheepdog.

URINARY INCONTINENCE
Lack of bladder control, staining of coat from the urine dribbling out.
Dobermann Pinscher, Old English Sheepdog.

VON WILLEBRAND'S DISEASE
Failure of normal blood-clotting process, could lead to sudden death.
Basset Hound, Dobermann Pinscher, German Shepherd Dog, Pembroke Welsh Corgi, Rottweiler.

WHEAT GLUTEN SENSITIVITY/DIARRHOEA
Dietary intolerance or undue sensitivity to the protein in wheat.
Labrador Retriever, West Highland White Terrier.

The Dobermann is one of several breeds that can be affected by Von Willebrand's Disease.